IN SEARCH OF
DRACULA

Hie facht sich an gar ein grauſſem

lich erſchröckenliche Hyſtorien. von dem wilden wü=
trich Dracole weyde Wie er die leüt geſpiſt hat vnd
gepraten vñ mit den haüßtern yn einē keſſel geſotten

IN SEARCH OF
DRACULA
THE HISTORY OF DRACULA AND VAMPIRES

RAYMOND T. MCNALLY

and

RADU FLORESCU

HOUGHTON MIFFLIN COMPANY

Boston   New York

1994

The authors would like to thank Karen Potterton for typing the manuscript of this book; Cathy Krusberg for bibliographical assistance; Andrew Weisman and Arnold ter Schure for special photographs; Edward Gorey for his wondrously gory cover art; and Alan Andres, Lisa Sacks, and Robert Eighteen-Bisang for their editorial assistance.

The authors are also grateful for permission to reprint stills from the following movies:

Bram Stoker's Dracula. Copyright © 1992 Columbia Pictures Industries, Inc. All rights reserved. Courtesy of Columbia Pictures.

Dracula (starring Bela Lugosi). Copyright © by Universal City Studios, Inc. Courtesy of MCA Publishing Rights, a Division of MCA Inc.

Library of Congress Cataloging-in-Publication Data

McNally, Raymond T., date.
In search of Dracula : the history of Dracula and vampires /
Raymond T. McNally and Radu Florescu. —
[New updated and rev. ed.]
p.   cm.
Includes bibliographical references.
ISBN 0-395-65783-0 (pbk.)
1. Vlad III, Prince of Wallachia, 1430 or 31–1476 or 7.   2. Dracula,
Count (Fictitious character)   3. Vampires — Romania.
4. Wallachia — Kings and rulers — Biography.
I. Florescu, Radu.   II. Title.
DR240.5.V553M36   1994
809'.93351 — DC20   94-18233   CIP

Book design by Anne Chalmers

Printed in the United States of America

MP 10 9 8 7 6 5 4 3 2 1

Frontispiece: Page from a German pamphlet published in Strasbourg in 1500.

CONTENTS

· · · · · · · · · · · ·

PREFACE

· · · · · · · · · · · · · · · · · · ·

This is a new, updated, and revised edition of *In Search of Dracula*, a pioneering popular study of the historical Dracula which found readers throughout the world. Little did the coauthors realize at the time they embarked upon this project over a glass of plum brandy in Bucharest more than twenty-five years ago, that their work would result in the discovery of the authentic, bloodthirsty prototype for Bram Stoker's famous novel *Dracula*, one of the best-selling novels of all time. Our first book on this topic contributed to serious research on genuine vampire traditions in Transylvania, analyzed Stoker's novel, and appended a bibliography and filmography. The historical character the authors rediscovered was a fifteenth-century Romanian prince also known as Vlad the Impaler. This gave new historical dimensions to a subject that had been superficially treated, if at all, in the years following the publication of Stoker's novel. Although a few obscure articles had appeared on the subject, *In Search of Dracula*, with its broad international appeal, definitely contributed to the revival of interest in the subject.

Since publishing our "minor classic" we have continued to explore the subject of the historical Dracula and the many myths that surround his life and death. The extensive research was only possible over the course of many trips and through the examination of libraries and archives both in Eastern Europe and in the West. We have lectured extensively on our findings to college audiences, at international symposia, and on radio and TV. We also wrote articles and other books on the historical Dracula, including a definitive biography. Though well received as a scholarly endeavor and used as a textbook for college courses, readers and numerous fans appealed to us to incorporate our many new findings into a popular book addressed to the general public in the kind of language readily understood by the many readers who had used *In Search of Dracula* for their own Gothic studies. A new generation of readers could no longer find the original book in their local libraries. In fact, the book all but disappeared from circulation and had become a collector's item. It is by way of response to such pleas that we conceived this wholly revised work.

Among the many finds since our first book was written, perhaps the most significant was our discovery of the unpublished diaries and journals that Stoker wrote while he was composing his vampire masterpiece. This proved that far from being a work of pure fiction, Stoker relied on extensive research both on the historical Vlad and on the vampire lore of Transylvania, giving his plot a definite geographical and historical framework. Even the English background at Whitby or London and its vicinity relies heavily on Stoker's personal experiences. Among many interesting revelations in the author's notes, there is proof that the novel was set in the year 1893, making 1993 the centenary of the events in the novel. 1997 represents the centenary of the publication of the novel, which has not been out of print since it was first published in 1897. Thus *Dracula* achieves the benchmark for a work to be considered a classic — the hundred-year test of endurance. (A copy of the original manuscript of the novel *Dracula,* along with Stoker's corrections, was only discovered in 1984.)

Among the many new sources which have either amplified or in some cases altered some of our previous conclusions is the work of the poet-laureate Michel Beheim entitled *The Story of a Bloodthirsty Madman called Dracula of Wallachia.* Read to the Holy Roman Emperor Frederick III during the winter of 1463, the original manuscript, located at the Heidelberg University library, proved that the historical Dracula dipped his bread in the blood of his victims, which technically justified Stoker's use of the word "vampire." Research at the Vatican and other Italian archives helped revise some of our earlier conclusions which had been based largely on fifteenth-century German documents which had depicted the Romanian Prince as a mere sadistic psychopath. It revealed him as a true crusader, a subtle diplomat, and an extraordinary leader in battle — a fact that new Greek and Turkish material in the Topkapi archives of Istanbul confirmed.

Our chapter on Dracula's war against the Turks is based on this new material. We also embarked on further research on the mission of the Russian ambassador Fedor Kurytsin, who visited Dracula's wife and sons six years after Dracula's death. The Russian ambassador obtained fascinating information from eyewitnesses in Hungary, Transylvania, and Romania on Dracula's imprisonment in Hungary, his third reign, and his death. Kurytsin looked upon the Impaler as a kind of Machiavelli who used terror tactics to strengthen his rule over disloyal nobles and clergy. With the help of his report we were able to trace Dracula's Hungarian descendants, previously unknown. Field work at the site of Dracula's castle, which uncovered a more significant epic than at first apparent, was completed with the help of the Institute of Folklore in Bucharest. Yet an aura of mystery still haunts the place where he lies buried, and we collected new details concerning the enigma of Dracula's grave at Snagov Monastery in the marshes near Bucharest. We also travelled to Egrigoz in Asia Minor, and through Turkish sources gathered more accurate information on Dracula and Radu the Handsome's imprisonment, which was far less stringent than was suspected. The same was true of Dracula's lengthy years of imprisonment at Visegrad, Hungary, where we obtained the cooperation of local historians. With the help of Romanian scholars we were able to locate a hitherto unknown portrait of the Impaler at Stuttgart, and we found interesting new details on the Order of the Dragon in the Nuremberg archives.

In addition, this book reexamines the oral history of Dracula and vampire lore as well as recent research into the medical basis of rare diseases, such as porphyria, which affect "living vampires." Since the first publication of this book there has evolved a new vampire literary genre which relies more upon modern sensibilities than on the legend of Vlad. The finest examples of this latest incarnation are the popular works of Anne Rice. Thus, in a sense, the fifteenth-century Dracula myth and Stoker's nineteenth-century literary extension thereof have triggered yet a new dimension which strains connection with the original. The same can be said of the movies that have been produced during the past twenty-five years. They also followed an evolution of their own, from Frank Langella's famous New York–stage portrayal and George Hamilton's humorous *Love at First Bite* to extravaganzas like Coppola's *Bram Stoker's Dracula*. All the principal literary, film, and television interpretations deserve an assessment of their merits, and accordingly an updated filmography and a summary of lesser works is included in the appendix. And, finally, a guide to the principal locations in our extensive Dracula hunt is included for those readers who wish to follow in Dracula's — and our — footsteps.

IN SEARCH OF
DRACULA

···· CHAPTER 1 ····

INTRODUCING THE DRACULA
OF FICTION, HISTORY,
AND FOLKLORE

"Welcome to my house! Enter freely and of your own will!"
He made no motion of stepping to meet me, but stood like a
statue, as though his gesture of welcome had fixed him into
stone. The instant, however, that I had stepped over the threshold,
he moved impulsively forward, and holding out his hand grasped
mine with a strength which made me wince, an effect which was not less-
ened by the fact that it seemed as cold as ice — more like the hand of a
dead than a living man.

SO THE VAMPIRE DRACULA first appears in Bram Stoker's
novel. Published in 1897, *Dracula* is as popular now as when it was
written. Millions not only have read it but have seen it at the cinema.
Among the famous filmed versions are W. F. Murnau's *Nosferatu,* starring Max Schreck in 1922, Tod Browning's *Dracula* with Bela Lugosi
in 1931, Terence Fisher's *Horror of Dracula* featuring Christopher Lee
in 1958, John Badham's *Dracula* with Frank Langella in 1979, and
Francis Ford Coppola's *Bram Stoker's Dracula* with Gary Oldman as the
most recent cinematic count in 1992.

As for the book before you, the original idea is owed to one of the
coauthors. But let Raymond McNally speak for himself: "More than
thirty-five years ago, as a fan of Dracula horror films, I began to wonder whether there might be some historical basis for their vampire
hero. I reread Stoker's *Dracula* and noted that not only this novel but
almost all of the Dracula films are set in Transylvania. At first, like
many Americans, I assumed that this was some mythical place, in the
same imaginary region, perhaps, as Ruritania. I found out, however,

that Transylvania is a province, a historical region of western Romania bounded by the Carpathian Mountains, that had been independent for almost a thousand years but under Hungarian and Turkish influence. In Stoker's novel there are some fairly detailed descriptions of the towns of Klausenburgh (called Cluj in Romanian) and Bistritz (Bistrita in Romanian) and the Borgo Pass (Birgau) in the Carpathian Mountains. When I located the Borgo Pass marked clearly on a modern Romanian map, I had an intuition that if all that geographical data were genuine, why not Dracula himself? Most people had never asked this question, being generally thrown off by the vampire story line. Since vampires do not exist, Dracula — so goes the popular wisdom — must have been the product of a wild and wonderful imagination.

"Eventually I read an authentic late fifteenth-century Slavic manuscript in an archive in St. Petersburg which described the deeds of a Romanian prince named Dracula. After researching the little that was available about the historical Dracula in several languages, I consulted with my Boston College colleague, Professor Radu Florescu, who was in Romania at the time. With his encouragement and enthusiasm I

Woodcut frontispiece of Dracole Waida, *Nuremberg, c. 1488, a manuscript that begins "In the year of our Lord 1456 Dracula did many dreadful and curious things."*

took up the study of the Romanian language and in 1969 received an American government–sponsored fellowship to travel to the very homeland of Dracula to see what more I could discover about this mysterious man and his legend. There, underlying the local traditions, was an authentic human being fully as horrifying as the vampire of fiction and film — a fifteenth-century prince who had been the subject of many horror stories even during his own lifetime; a ruler whose cruelties were committed on such a massive scale that his evil reputation in the Western world reached beyond the grave to the firesides where generations of grandmothers warned little children: 'Be good or Dracula will get you!'

"Unlike myself, an American of Irish and Austrian ancestry who knew the fictional Dracula principally through late-night movies, my colleague Radu Florescu is a native Romanian who knew of a historical Dracula through the research of earlier Romanian scholars. But his ties with this history go deeper than that. As a boy he spent many hours on the banks of the Arges River, which bounded his family's country estate deep in the Wallachian plain, not too far distant from Castle Dracula. In addition, the Florescus can trace their line back to an aristocratic family of Dracula's time with marriage connections to Dracula's family."

It was autumn of 1969 when we tracked down Castle Dracula. The castle was by then abandoned, in ruins, and known to the peasants as the castle of Vlad Tepes, or Vlad the Impaler, a ruler notorious for mass impalement of his enemies. Vlad Tepes was in fact called Dracula in the fifteenth century, and we found that he even signed his name that way on documents, but this fact was not even known by the peasants of the castle region.

Using dozens of ancient chronicles, maps, and nineteenth- and twentieth-century philological and historical works, and drawing on folklore, we pieced together a dual history — an account not only of the real fifteenth-century Dracula, Vlad Tepes, who was born and raised in Transylvania and ruled in southern Romania, but also of the vampire who exists in the legends of these same regions. In addition, we studied how Bram Stoker, during the late nineteenth century, united these two traditions to create the most horrifying and famous vampire in fiction: Count Dracula.

What was known of this dual history before our research? In 1896 a Romanian scholar, Ioan Bogdan, noted that there existed various fifteenth-century German pamphlets which described the Romanian Prince Vlad Tepes as "Dracole." The Romanian historian Karadja published the texts, but neither made the connection between these references and Stoker, nor did Bogdan, as a philologist, concern himself extensively with the history and folklore. A few pertinent discoveries were later made by others. For instance, in 1922, the late eminent historian Constantin Giurescu discovered the foundation stone of the Church of Tirgsor, which indicated that Vlad Tepes as its founder and patron was a pious ruler. And in the 1930s, amateur archaeologist Dinu Rosetti and genealogist George Florescu opened the grave of Vlad Tepes at Snagov as part of a general excavation at the site. It was not until the 1960s that the scholar Grigore Nandris began to unravel the story. He studied the philological relationship between the names Dracole and Vlad Tepes and noted that for some unknown reason Bram Stoker had associated these names in his vampire story. The German Slavicist Julius Striedter compared Slavic manuscripts and German pamphlets about Dracula. The Soviet Slavicist Isaac Lurie analyzed Slavic documents in Russian archives. But it was Nandris's philological studies which prepared the groundwork for our investigation, and Harry Ludlam's biography of author Bram Stoker, curiously titled *The Biography of "Dracula": Bram Stoker* (1962), also proved invaluable.

What follows is a complex story involving seven separate research expeditions which resulted in four books: *In Search of Dracula* (1972), *Dracula: A Biography of Vlad the Impaler* (1973), *The Essential Dracula* (1979), and *Dracula, Prince of Many Faces* (1989). Some of the search resulted in the discovery of authentic Dracula documents and sites in the present territory of Romania, Bulgaria, Hungary, Turkey, the former Yugoslavia, Germany, the United Kingdom, Ireland, Italy, Switzerland, France, and even the United States. Study of both the mythical and the historical aspects of the story encountered difficulties. Countries previously dominated by Marxist ideology discouraged research on vampire beliefs as the authorities wished to portray peasants as "modern" and not superstitious.

Regarding Dracula, the historical personage, the official Communist Party historians portrayed him as a national hero and played down or rationalized his cruelties. None exhibited that hero-worshipping attitude more than the late dictator Nicolae Ceausescu who, according to some authorities, shared many character traits with Drac-

In 1976 Nicolae Ceausescu's Roma-
nia issued this portait of a rather
benign-looking Vlad on a commemor-
ative postage stamp. Ceausescu and
Communist Party historians endorsed
a revisionist version of the Dracula
story, portraying him as a national
hero and rationalizing his cruelties.

ula. Revolutionaries often caricatured him as a vampire with fangs. One incredible example of this admiration was the manner in which the five-hundred-year anniversary of Dracula's death was celebrated in 1976. Throughout Romania eulogies and panegyrics were ordered by Communist Party members; monographs, novels, works of art, a film — even a commemorative stamp was issued — to praise the Impaler. A short footnote — which to this day has not been fully elucidated — adds to the mystery of the Ceausescu-Dracula relationship. On December 22, 1989, the late dictator and his wife, surrounded by an irate crowd shouting for their death, finally realized that his reign was over. Ceausescu ordered his helicopter pilot to fly from the rooftop of the headquarters of the beleaguered Central Committee of the Communist Party in Bucharest to the palace he had built at Snagov, a short distance from where, according to tradition, Dracula lay buried. Even more mysterious were the motivations of the late dictator to try to move the capital city from Bucharest to Tirgoviste, Dracula's capital in the fifteenth century. In the last stage of the Ceausescu drama, Ceausescu ordered his pilot to leave Snagov, and then to land the helicopter on the highway leading to Tirgoviste. After highjacking two cars (one ran out of gas), Ceausescu ordered the driver toward Tirgo-viste, evidently seeking solace and support in Dracula's former capital. Finally, he was arrested by the army on the outskirts of the town and confined to barracks. Following a parody of a military trial, he and his wife were shot by soldiers not very far from Dracula's palace.

Was the real Dracula a vampire? Did the peasants of his time con-sider him associated with the forces of evil? What connection is there between the real prince and the vampire-count created by Bram Stoker? How did the name Dracula originate? What do Romanian peasants today believe about Vlad Tepes and vampires? And have we been dealing simply with history or are there mysteries here beyond the reach of historical research?

····CHAPTER 2····

BRAM STOKER
AND THE SEARCH FOR
CASTLE DRACULA

HIGH UP IN THE TRANSYLVANIAN ALPS we came to a halt. There, atop a black volcanic rock formation, bordering the Arges River and framed by a massive alpine snow-capped landscape, lay the twisted battlements of Castle Dracula, its remains barely distinguishable from the rock of the mountain itself, a sheer thousand-foot drop on all sides. This was hardly the grandiose, macabre mausoleum described by Bram Stoker, yet no matter how modest nor how tortured by time, it was a *historic* edifice, one challenging the historian to solve its mystery, to push back an unconquered frontier.

For our party of five, composed of two Americans and three Romanians, this was the end of a long trail. Our search for Castle Dracula had begun in a light vein at the University of Bucharest. It continued as an expedition marred by every possible frustration and by mysterious accidents.

This search began, as did so many other Dracula hunts, because of the extraordinary hold the Dracula vampire mystique still exercises upon popular imagination throughout the world. Unperturbed by the vampire myth, however, a handful of skeptics have always claimed that there was a factual basis for the Dracula story and that part of the setting indeed lay in Transylvania.

Bram Stoker, at the very beginning of his story, tells of his own painstaking efforts both to consult well-known Orientalists such as Arminius Vambery, professor at the University of Budapest and a frequent visitor to England, and to study the available literature concerning the frontier lands between the Christians and Turks. Even Stoker's mention of consulting maps of the area available at the British Museum library in London are intended to stress the historicity of the plot; he tells us they were not too reliable, but they proved to be far more accurate than he thought.

In Stoker's novel, the town of Bistrita, for instance, is accurately described and located, as are such small villages as Fundu and Veresti, places you will not find marked on any modern tourist map. The famed Borgo Pass leading from Transylvania to Moldavia, the northernmost province of Romania, really exists, and is beautifully described in Stoker's novel. The historic context, the century-old struggle between Romanians and Turks that was sparked in the fifteenth century, is authentic. The ethnic minorities of Transylvania — the Saxons, Romanians, Szekelys, and Hungarians — are known and are distinguished from each other by Stoker.

Dracula was in fact an authentic fifteenth-century Wallachian prince who was often described in the contemporary German, Byzantine, Slavonic, and Turkish documents and in popular horror stories as an awesome, cruel, and possibly demented ruler. He was known mostly for the amount of blood he indiscriminately spilled, not only the blood of the infidel Turks — which, by the standards of the time, would make him a hero — but that of Germans, Romanians, Hungarians, and other Christians. His ingenious mind devised all kinds of tortures, both physical and mental, and his favorite way of imposing death earned him the name "the Impaler."

In a rogues' gallery Dracula would assuredly compete for first prize with Cesare Borgia, Catherine de Médicis, and Jack the Ripper, owing not only to the quantity of his victims, but to the refinement of his cruelty. To his contemporaries, the story of his misdeeds was widely publicized — in certain instances by some of his intended victims. The Dracula story, in fact, was a "bestseller" throughout Europe four hundred years before Stoker wrote his version. Many of the German-originated, fifteenth-century accounts of the Dracula legend have been found in dusty archives of monasteries and libraries.

The names of Dracula and his father, Dracul, are of such importance to this story that they require a precise explanation. Both father and son had the given name Vlad. The names Dracul and Dracula and variations thereof in different languages (such as Dracole, Draculya, Dracol, Draculea, Draculios, Draculia, Tracol) are really nicknames. What's more, both nicknames had two meanings. Dracul

Coins minted by Vlad Dracul showing the sign of the Dragon, and the eagle of Wallachia on the reverse side.

meant "devil," as it still does in Romanian today; in addition it meant "dragon." In 1431, the Holy Roman Emperor Sigismund invested Vlad the father with the Order of the Dragon, a semimonastic, semimilitary organization dedicated to fighting the Turkish infidels. Dracul in the sense of dragon stems from this. It also seems probable that when the simple, superstitious peasants saw Vlad the father bearing the standard with the dragon symbol they interpreted it as a sign that he was in league with the devil.

As for the son, we now know that he had two nicknames: he was called Vlad Tepes (pronounced *tsep-pesh*), which means Vlad the Impaler, and he was also called Dracula, a diminutive meaning "son of the dragon" or "son of the devil." (A final point in this discussion of nomenclature: the association of the words "devil" and "dragon" in Romanian may be just one of the many reasons for the association of Dracula with vampirism in the eyes of his detractors.)

Other male Draculas, too, were known by evil epithets. Dracul's second son was Mihnea the Bad; another descendant was Mihnea II, the Apostate, and yet another indirect descendant was known as the Little Impaler. In an age of violence, all the Draculas lived violently, and with few exceptions died violently.

In his lifetime, Dracula had fame and notoriety throughout much of Europe, but rarely has such recognition of a public figure become so lost to posterity. Indeed, when Stoker mentioned Dracula in the late nineteenth century, few of his readers knew he was writing about a historical character. One obstacle to understanding arose from the fact that the Dracula stories circulated in diverse languages (German, Hungarian, Romanian, Slavic, Greek, Turkish) and in different worlds having little relation to each other. A chief difficulty, however, was the confusion caused by the name itself. Was it Dracula the son of the Devil, Dracula the son of the man invested with the Order of the Dragon, or simply Dracula the Impaler? Small wonder that the Byzantine scholar reading about Dracula's deeds of heroism against the Turks, the German reading of the atrocities of the Devil against his fellow Saxons, and the Romanian studying the Impaler's achievements, failed to attribute these actions to the same man. It is only of very recent date that Romanian historians themselves have pieced together some of the fragments of the formidable Dracula story.

If Stoker's Dracula story was essentially correct in points of history, if Dracula existed, why not a Castle Dracula? Since Transylvania was so minutely described by Stoker, what could be more logical than to begin the hunt in northeastern Transylvania, where the author set his plot on an isolated mountain peak, a few miles east of Bistrita on the road leading to the Borgo Pass.

Over the years, many persons had set out to find Castle Dracula in this general direction. They had traveled the way of Stoker's hero, Jonathan Harker, from Cluj to Bistrita and from Bistrita to the Borgo Pass. The travelers found countless superstitious peasants and were struck by the majestic beauty of this abandoned Carpathian frontier region separating Transylvania proper from Bukovina to the northeast and Moldavia to the east. But none had found the castle. Several expeditions ended on the same dismal note — not a trace of *any* castle.

Undeterred by past failures, we decided to undertake the venture and set forth on the Stoker trail, if for no other reason than to satisfy our curiosity. From the standpoint of scenery alone, it is easy to excuse Stoker for setting the story in the wrong part of Transylvania, thus leading the Dracula hunter some hundred miles or more astray. The anchor town of Bistrita, the departure point for any Dracula excursion, is a quaint medieval city, more German than Romanian in its character, with a mixed population of Romanians, Hungarians, and those mysterious Szekelys, whom Stoker erroneously took to be possible ancestors of Dracula. (Some historians claim just as formidable a pedigree of horror for the Szekelys, tracing them back to Attila's Huns.) From the crumbling walls of the old city, the most unsophisticated traveler can judge that at one time Bistrita must have been an impressive frontier point; from its oversized marketplace surrounded by the colorful baroque German-style homes of the well-to-do, one may safely conclude that the town was an important trading center, with goods plying north from Transylvania to Poland and Bohemia and east to Moldavia.

Beyond Bistrita, the road finally climbs to the Borgo Pass, along the Dorne depression, passing through several rustic mountain villages where life has not changed much in a thousand years. The peasants still wear their traditional garb — the fur cap or *caciula,* the embroidered shirt with motifs that vary from village to village, the sheepskin-lined vest or *cojoc* (lately sold as après-ski apparel in the elegant resorts of Europe), the roughly stitched pigskin shoes or *opinci.* These farm people are not without an artistic side. The women embroider; the men mold clay products with a technique kept secret, although the quality of the local clay certainly contributes to its success. The peasant house, made almost entirely of wood, delights one with the imaginative carvings of its *pridvor,* a kind of porch surrounding the house, and the decorative patterns of the main gate, giving the only access to the courtyard. Local folklore is rich: the *doinas,* a plaintive folksong the *strigaturi* or lyrical poetry, the *basme* or fairy tales, the ballads, and the *legende* or popular epics, all combine natural and supernatural elements. In the *doinas* there are frequent references to the wolves, which, traveling in packs at night in the midst of winter, were thought to do their worst to man and beast alike. In the *basme* the bat is often mentioned, and in Romania this creature is a messenger of bad luck. In the legends of old, one species of vampire is a supernatural being of demonic origin, fighting Fat-Frumos, the fairy prince who embodies moral power. The wolf-headed serpent is the motif used on the ancient standard of the Dacians, the ancestors of the Romanians.

Also interesting for our purposes are the historical ballads that speak of the ancient battleground among Romanians, Tartars, Turks, and Poles. These ballads commemorate countless heroes and villains, preserving by word of mouth a fascinating history — one quite as remarkable as the sagas of the Vikings.

Of late, the more wily peasants, impressed by the number of foreign tourists seeking Dracula's castle, have decided to play along with the search; and they do it well for the price of a few cigarettes and packs of chewing gum. Unwilling to disappoint the Dracula hunter, one imaginative peasant from the village of Prundul-Birgaului made numerous allusions to a castle that was *mai la munte,* a favorite Romanian expression of vagueness which means "a little farther up the mountain" (of course, when you reach one peak, as every alpinist knows, there is always another behind it). However, as historians have often found in regard to folklore, where there is smoke, there is fire. It so happened that the folklore references implying the existence of a castle near the Borgo Pass were quite correct. At Rodna, not far from the Borgo Pass, lie the remains of a small fortress. Only it was not the Castle Dracula that we were searching for, even though Dracula visited it during his lifetime, since he often traveled the solitary highway winding through the Romanian and Hungarian lands.

The historic route of the Borgo Pass was initially traveled by Romania's feudal leaders at the close of the fourteenth century, when they set forth from their haven in the Transylvanian plateau to found the principality of Moldavia. It goes through majestic country — Stoker's Mittlel Land "green and brown where grass and rock mingled, . . . an endless perspective of jagged rock and pointed crags."

Beyond the lower mountains, surrounding the Dorne depression, and rising to three thousand feet, lie the higher peaks, often snow-capped even during the summer. These are the mountains of Bukovina, a favorite alpinist playground which demands the skill and sometimes the equipment of the expert for tricky ascents of upwards of 6,500 feet. On the Moldavian side of the border, one reaches the watering spa of Vatra Dornei. Today this town is an important tourist center, not only because of the health-restoring springs, but because it gives approach to a dozen famed monasteries in Bukovina and Moldavia proper, representing extraordinary jewels of fifteenth-century Romanian artistry. The biblical scenes and history on the exterior walls of the monasteries, dating back to Dracula's time, are painted in shades of deep blue and purple, and they have survived virtually unscathed through some five hundred rigorous winters.

Castle Bistrita, located near the Borgo Pass, may also have served as a model for the castle in Stoker's novel. It was John Hunyadi who actually completed Castle Bistrita around 1449, four years before the fall of Constantinople. The *voevod* or warlord of Transylvania, foremost Balkan crusader, governor of Severin, hereditary duke of Timisoara, count of Bistrita, in charge of the Hungarian kingdom, John Hunyadi was in fact in control of the political destinies of what was left of the east and central European lands in their last and most desperate struggle with the Turks. He died in 1456 while defending Belgrade, the last great Christian bastion on the Danube, the year that

Dracula was enthroned as prince. Hunyadi was the father of Matthias Corvinus, the Hungarian king who kept Dracula imprisoned in his citadel on the Danube for twelve years, from 1462 to 1474. Relations between the Hunyadis and the Draculas were initially friendly, though never intimate.

During the years 1451 to 1456 Dracula may have stayed near Bistrita, a fortified town at that time, but few of the fortifications of Bistrita remain today. It is likely that Stoker heard the legends connecting Dracula to this region. The Saxon population of Bistrita, who disliked the Romanians and the Hungarians, doubtless heard of Dracula's atrocities against their brethren farther south in the towns of Brasov and Sibiu, where most of the horrors were committed and recorded. It is quite plausible that some Saxon refugee from southern Transylvania wrote a description of them. However, if there is a Bistrita document about Dracula, it is not known today. In any event, Bistrita Castle was attacked, ransacked, and totally destroyed by the German population of the city at the close of the fifteenth century as an apparent gesture of defiance against the Hunyadi family.

Hunedoara, castle of John Hunyadi.

Castle Bistrita was built on a small hill in the middle of the quaint twelfth-century German township surrounded by ditches and towers built by the various guilds for protection. The castle was later given to Dracula, who controlled it in recompense for his services to the Hunyadis at a crucial time of conflict with the local German merchants. Much of what was left of the original town was destroyed by the Turks during the Austro-Turkish wars of the seventeenth century, and in addition, as Stoker noted in *Dracula*, "Fifty years ago a series of great fires took place, which made terrible havoc on five separate occasions."

Castle Bistrita seems to have been a smaller version of Hunyadi's formidable castle of Hunedoara, one hundred miles to the southwest; a most impressive structure dating back to 1260 and today completely and beautifully restored. This is the castle of the Hunyadis where Dracula was greeted as an ally and friend in 1452, but as a foe in 1462. With its imposing donjon, smaller towers, massive walls, battlements, and drawbridge, it seems custom-made for a vampire film. But neither Bistrita nor Hunedoara convey the eerie atmosphere of the real Castle Dracula. Nonetheless, in the impressive Hall of Knights, with its lovely marble columns, once hung all the portraits of the "greats" of Dracula's time, including John Hunyadi and, undoubtedly, Dracula. A hostile hand, possibly that of a revengeful German, destroyed all these portraits. Fortunately, three paintings of Dracula and a number of woodcut portraits have survived the furies of the past.

In his novel, Stoker describes Dracula as "a tall old man, clean-shaven save for a long white moustache, and clad in black from head to foot, without a single speck of colour about him anywhere." The author depicts Dracula's mustache as heavy, his teeth as sharp and white, and his skin as sallow and pallid. In the portrait of Dracula that survives in the collection at Castle Ambras, the real Dracula is as startling and arresting in appearance as the figure created in words by Stoker, or the character created some years later by Max Schreck, in Murnau's 1922 classic horror film, *Nosferatu*.

CHAPTER 3

THE HISTORICAL DRACULA: TYRANT FROM TRANSYLVANIA

IN A BROAD SENSE, Stoker was quite correct in setting his Dracula story in Transylvania, even though he located his fictional castle to the northeast, miles away from the authentic one on the southern border. The real Dracula was born in 1431 in Transylvania, in the old German fortified town of Schassburg (Sighisoara in Romanian). One of the most enchanting Saxon burghs, certainly the most medieval, Schassburg is located about sixty-five miles south of Bistrita. Its castle lies on the strategic hillside location which dominates the valley of the Tirnava River. It is surrounded by thick defensive walls of stone and brick three thousand feet long, with fourteen battlement-capped towers, each named for the guild which bore its cost — the tailors, jewellers, furriers, butchers, goldsmiths, blacksmiths, barbers, and ropemakers. With its narrow, tortuous, cobblestone streets and innumerable stairways linking the famous clock tower to the higher towers on the crest of the hill, the fortified town served the needs of a prosperous German merchant community that traded with Nuremberg and other German cities. The town functioned as a depot for goods moving back and forth between the German West and Constantinople; in addition it served the northeast trade route to Poland, the Baltic Sea, and the German cities linked to the Hanseatic Customs Union. The house in which Dracula and his brother Radu were born is identified by a small plaque mentioning the fact that their father, Dracul, lived there from 1431 to 1435. The building is a three-story stone construction of dark yellowish hue with a tiled roof and small windows and openings suitable for the small garrison assigned to Vlad Dracul. Recent restoration on the

Dracula's birthplace in Sighisoara, Transylvania. The plaque on the house states that Vlad Dracul, Dracula's father, lived here in 1431.

Two views of present-day Sighisoara.

second floor revealed a painted mural depicting three men and a woman seated at a table. Only the central figure has survived fully intact. The portrait is that of a rotund man with a double chin, a long, well-waxed moustache, arched eyebrows, and a finely chiseled nose. The similarity of the brown, almond-shaped eyes to those of the famous portrait of Dracula preserved at Ambras Castle suggests that this may be the only surviving portrait of Dracula's father, Vlad Dracul.

Dracula's mother, Princess Cneajna, of the Musatin dynasty of neighboring Moldavia, raised young Dracula with the help of her ladies-in-waiting within the household. His father's mistress, Caltuna, bore Dracul a second son named Vlad. She eventually entered a monastery and took the name Eupraxia. Her son later became known as Vlad the Monk, because he followed in his mother's footsteps, pursuing a religious vocation.

Dracula thus spent his youth in a peculiarly Germanic atmosphere; his father exercised authority over all the local German townships and defended all of Transylvania against potential Turkish attacks. Vlad

Portrait of Dracula at Castle Ambras, near Innsbruck, Austria. The artist is unknown, but this appears to be a copy painted during the second half of the sixteenth century from an earlier original. The original portrait was probably painted during Dracula's imprisonment at Buda or Visegrad after 1462. This painting is part of the original collection of Ferdinand II, who owned Castle Ambras in the sixteenth century; it was first listed in the collection in 1621.

Dracul owed his authority to the Holy Roman Emperor Sigismund of Luxembourg, at whose court in Nuremberg he was educated by Catholic monks. His political ambitions took shape when on February 8, 1431, two important events took place in Nuremberg: his induction into the prestigious Order of the Dragon, along with King Ladislas of Poland and Prince Lazarevic of Serbia, and his investiture as Prince of Wallachia. The German Emperor Sigismund of Luxembourg and his second wife, Barbara von Cilli, had founded the Order of the Dragon in 1387 as a secret military and religious confraternity with the goal of protecting the Catholic Church against heretics, such as the Hussites who then posed a threat to Central Europe. Another objective of the Order was the organization of a crusade against the Turks, who had overrun most of the Balkan peninsula. The second investiture, presided over by the Emperor himself, bound Dracul to the hazardous task of seeking the insecure Wallachian throne (which included the Transylvanian duchies of Amlas and Fagaras) ruled at the time by Prince Alexandru Aldea, Dracula's half brother. This was to mark the beginning of a lengthy feud between rival members of the princely Basarab family, one featuring numerous crimes.

When the recently invested "Dragon" was finally able to make good his title of prince by expelling Alexandru Aldea from Wallachia during the winter of 1436–37, the seat of Wallachian power continued to be close to the Transylvanian border, where Dracul drew his support. Historically, Transylvania had always been linked to both the Moldavian and the Wallachian principalities. After the Roman legions evacuated the more recently conquered province of Dacia in A.D. 271, the bulk of the Romanized population withdrew to the mountains, seeking escape from the turmoils of eastern invasion in the Transylvanian plateau. In this way, the Daco-Romans survived untouched by the Gothic, Hunnish, Slavic, or even Hungarian and Bulgarian avalanches, which would surely have destroyed their Latin language and customs had they remained in the plain. Only after the torrent of invasions had receded did these Romanians descend into the plain, but cautiously, maintaining their mountain hideout. Each generation of Romanians from the thirteenth century onward advanced a little farther into the plain. Eventually they reached the Danube and the Black Sea to the south, the Prut and the Dniester to the northeast — in other words, the limits of modern Romania, and also in part the former limits of ancient Dacia. In the case of Wallachia, nothing is more typical of its tendency to turn to Transylvania for security, and nothing better demonstrates the reticence in abandoning the mountains as a haven of shelter, than the choice of the early capitals of the principality. The first, early fourteenth-century capital, Cimpulung, borders the Transylvanian Alps.

Dracula's capital, Tirgoviste, lies somewhat lower in the hills, but still provides easy access to the mountains. The choice of this site marks a period of increased self-confidence in the country's history. Rumor had it that Dracula's younger brother, Radu the Handsome, owing to his lengthy sojourn in the Turkish capital, also wanted to be close to Constantinople, as he was not immune to the pleasures of the sultan's harem. Gossip accused him, largely because of his good looks,

Dracula's main palace at Tirgoviste. The city of Tirgoviste was his capital.

The Chindia watchtower at Tirgoviste; a nineteenth-century reconstruction. Apart from its role as an observation post, it also enabled Dracula to watch the impalements in the courtyard below.

of being one of the minions in the male harem of Mehmed, heir to the Ottoman throne, thus requiring him to be constantly at his master's disposal. In any case, Radu's reign marked the reversal of the heroic stage in Wallachia's history and the beginning of conditional surrender to the sultan. It was conditional, since the relationship of Wallachia to Constantinople continued to be regulated by treaty, with the local princes as vassals to the sultan.

When secure on his throne, Dracul, a wily politician, sensed that the tenuous balance of power was rapidly shifting to the advantage of the ambitious Turkish sultan Murad II. By now the Turks had destroyed both Serbs and Bulgars and the sultan was contemplating a final blow against the Greeks. Thus, Dracul began the first of his numerous deceptions, treacherously signing an alliance with the Turks against the successors of his patron, the Holy Roman Emperor Sigismund, who died in 1437. In 1438, in admittedly difficult circumstances, Dracul and his son Mircea accompanied Sultan Murad II on one of his frequent incursions of Transylvania, murdering, looting, and burning on the way, as was the Turkish practice. This was the first of many occasions when the Draculas, who considered themselves Transylvanians, returned to their homeland as enemies rather than as friends. But the Transylvanian cities and towns, though cruelly raided and pillaged, still believed that they could get a better deal from a fellow citizen than from the Turks. This provides an explanation for the eagerness of the mayor and burghers of the town of Sebes to surrender specifically to the Draculas, on condition that their lives be spared and that they not be carried into Turkish slavery. Dracul, sworn to protect the Christians, was at least on this occasion able to save one town from complete destruction.

Many such incidents made the Turks suspect the true allegiance of the Romanian prince. Accordingly, Sultan Murad II beguiled Dracul into a personal confrontation in the spring of 1442. Insensitive to the snare, Dracul crossed the Danube with his second son, Dracula, and his youngest son, Radu, only to be "bound in iron chains" and brought into the presence of the sultan, who accused him of disloyalty. In order to save his neck and regain his throne, after a brief imprisonment at Gallipoli, Dracul swore renewed fidelity to Murad II, and as proof of his loyalty, he left Dracula and Radu as hostages. The two boys were placed under house arrest in the Sultan's palace at Gallipoli and were later sent, for security reasons, to far off Egrigoz in Asia Minor. Dracula remained a Turkish captive until 1448; Radu stayed on and became the ally of Murad II and, because of his weaker nature, submitted more easily to the refined indoctrination techniques of his so-called jailors. He became a minion of the future Sultan Mehmed II and eventually the official Turkish candidate to the Wallachian throne, to which, in due course, he succeeded his brother, Dracula.

Dracula's reaction to these dangerous years was quite the reverse. In fact, his years of Turkish imprisonment offer a clue to his shifty nature and perverse personality. From that time onward Dracula held human nature in low esteem. Life was cheap — after all, his own life was in danger should his father prove disloyal to the sultan — and morality was not essential in matters of state. He needed no Machiavelli to instruct him in the amorality of politics. The Turks taught

Dracula the Turkish language, among other things, which he mastered like a native; acquainted him with the pleasures of the harem, for the terms of confinement were not too strict; and completed his training in Byzantine cynicism, which the Turks had inherited from the Greeks.

As related by his Turkish captors during those years, he also developed a reputation for trickery, cunning, insubordination, and brutality, and inspired fright in his own guards. This was in sharp contrast to his brother's sheepish subservience. Two other traits were entrenched in Dracula's psyche because of the plot into which father and sons had been ensnared. One was suspicion; never again would he trust himself to the Turks or to any man. The other was a taste for revenge; Dracula would not forget, nor forgive, those who crossed him — indeed, this became a family trait.

In December 1447, Dracul the father died, a victim of his own plotting. His murder was ordered by John Hunyadi, who had become angered by the Dragon's flirtations with the Turks. Dracul's pro-Turkish policies are easily accountable, if for no other basis than to save his sons from inevitable reprisals and possible death. Dracul's eldest son, Mircea, was blinded with red-hot iron stakes and buried alive by his political enemies in Tirgoviste. These killings and the particularly vicious circumstances attending his brother's death made a profound impression on young Prince Dracula shortly after his ascent to power. The assassination of Dracul had taken place in the marshes of Balteni near the site of an ancient monastery that still exists. There was, however, some justification for the Hunyadi-engineered assassination.

At the time of his imprisonment at Adrianople, Dracul had sworn that he would never bear arms against the Turks, a flagrant violation of his previous oath as a member of the Order of the Dragon. Once safely restored to his position as prince, and in spite of the fact that his two sons were hostages of the Turks, Dracul hesitantly resumed his oath to the Holy Roman Emperor and joined the anti-Turkish struggle. He was even absolved of his Turkish oath by the Papacy. This implied that he could participate in the Balkan crusades organized by Hunyadi against Sultan Murad II. Serbian Prince Brankovic's two sons were blinded by the Turks when Brankovic was disloyal to the sultan, and Dracul anticipated the same tragic fate awaited his own sons. He wrote disconsolately to the city elders of Brasov at the end of 1443: "Please understand that I have allowed my children to be butchered for the sake of the Christian peace, in order that both I and my country might continue to be vassals to the Holy Roman Empire." Indeed, it is little short of a miracle that the Turks did not behead Dracula and Radu. Dracula's elder brother, Mircea, not Dracul, had actually taken a more active lead in what is described as "the long campaign" of 1443. From the Wallachian point of view, this campaign proved an outstanding success. It led to the capture of the citadel of Giurgiu (built at great cost to Wallachia by Dracula's grandfather) and threatened Turkish power in Bulgaria. However, Hunyadi's Varna campaign of 1444, organized on a far more ambitious scale and reaching the Black Sea, was a disaster. The young, inexperienced King of Poland, Ladislas III, fell to his death along with the papal legate Juliano Cesarini. Hunyadi was able to flee and survived only because the Wallachians knew the terrain well enough to lead him to safety. In the inevitable recriminations which followed, both Dracul and Mircea held Hunyadi personally responsible for the magnitude of the debacle. A council of war held somewhere in the Dobrogea judged Hunyadi responsible for the Christians' defeat, and, largely upon the entreaties of Mircea, sentenced him to death. But Hunyadi's past services and his widespread reputation as the white knight of the Christian forces saved his life, and Dracul ensured him safe passage to his Transylvanian homeland.

Nonetheless, from that moment on the Hunyadis bore the Draculas and particularly Mircea a deep hatred. This vindictiveness was finally satisfied with Dracul and Mircea's assassinations. After 1447, Hunyadi placed the Wallachian crown in the more reliable hands of a Danesti claimant, Vladislav II. (The rival Danesti family traced back to Prince Dan, one of Dracula's great-uncles.)

What is far more difficult to account for is Dracula's attitude upon his escape from Turkish captivity in 1448. We know that the Turks, undoubtedly impressed by Dracula's ferocity and bravery and obviously opposed to the Danesti princes since they were thoroughly identified with the Hungarian court, tried to place Dracula on the Wallachian throne as early as 1448, while Vladislav II and Hunyadi were crusading south of the Danube. This bold coup succeeded for merely two months. Dracula, then about twenty years old, fearful of his father's Transylvanian assassins and equally reluctant to return to his Turkish captors, fled to Moldavia, the northernmost Romanian principality, ruled at that time by Prince Bogdan, whose son, Prince

Stephen, was Dracula's cousin. During these years of Moldavian exile, Dracula and Stephen developed a close and lasting friendship, each promising the other that whoever succeeded to the throne of his principality first would help the other to power swiftly — by force of arms if necessary. The Moldavian princely residence was then at Suceava, an ancient city where Dracula and Stephen continued their scholarly Byzantine ecclesiastical education under the supervision of erudite monks.

Dracula stayed in Moldavia until October 1451, when Bogdan was brutally assassinated by his rival, Petru Aron. Perhaps because of a lack of alternatives, Dracula then reappeared in Transylvania, where he threw himself upon the mercy of John Hunyadi. He was undoubtedly taking a chance, though by that time, owing to Turkish pressure, the reigning Danesti prince of Wallachia, Vladislav II, had adopted a pro-Turkish policy, thus estranging him from his Hungarian patrons. It was essentially history repeating itself at the expense of the Danesti.

It was in Hunyadi's interests once again to have a pliable tool, a prince in reserve, just in case the Danesti prince might turn to the Turks completely. Thus, mutual interest rather than any degree of confidence bound Dracula and John Hunyadi together from 1451

John Hunyadi (1387–1456), prince of Transylvania, hereditary count of Timisoara and Bistrita, governor-general and regent of Hungary. Father of King Matthias Corvinus, he was known as the white knight of the crusaders.

until 1456, when Hunyadi died at Belgrade. During this time, Hunyadi was Dracula's last tutor, political mentor, and, most important, military educator. Hunyadi introduced his protégé at the court of the Hapsburg king of Hungary, Ladislas V. He also met Hunyadi's son Matthias, his future political foe. Dracula could have had no finer instruction in anti-Turkish strategy. Like a chivalrous vassal he personally took part in many of Hunyadi's anti-Turkish campaigns fought in what became twentieth-century Yugoslavia. He was invested, as his father Dracul had been, with the duchies of Fagaras and Almas. In addition, Dracula also became the official claimant to the Wallachian throne. It was for this reason that he did not accompany his suzerain in the Belgrade campaign of 1456, when Hunyadi was finally felled by the plague. At the time Dracula had finally been granted permission to cross the Transylvanian mountains to oust the unfaithful Danesti prince from the Wallachian throne.

During the years 1451–56 Dracula once again resided in Transylvania. Abandoning the family home at Sighisoara, he took up residence in Sibiu, mainly to be closer to the Wallachian border. In Sibiu, Dracula was informed by the mayor of Sibiu and by many other refugees from the beleaguered capital of the Greek empire about an event which had the effect of a bombshell in the Christian world: Constantinople had fallen to the Turks and Emperor Constantine XI Paleologus (at whose court Dracula may briefly have been sent as a page in the 1430s) died in hand-to-hand combat defending the walls of his capital. One Romanian refugee, Bishop Samuil, informed Dracula that Sultan Mehmed II's next objective was the conquest of Transylvania and that he planned an attack on Sibiu itself, a strategic location that could serve as a base for later conquest of the Hungarian kingdom. Dracula at least could take comfort in the fact that Sibiu was considered the most impregnable city in Transylvania. This may have influenced his decision to stay there. Yet, in one of those acts that make a riddle of his personality, in 1460, barely four years after he left the city of Sibiu, Dracula mercilessly raided this region with a Wallachian contingent of twenty thousand men and killed, maimed, impaled, and tortured some ten thousand of his former fellow citizens and neighbors. He considered that the Germans of Sibiu had engaged in unfair trade practices at the expense of Wallachian merchants. Pillaging and looting took place on a more ferocious scale than had been the case with the Turks in 1438.

This leads us to consider one of the most ambivalent aspects of Dracula's Transylvanian career, when from friend he turned foe toward his former kinsmen and allies. (These will be described in detail in the review of the German horror stories.) This feud lasted roughly three years, from 1457 to 1460, during which Dracula was prince in neighboring Wallachia. The first lightning raid in the Sibiu area took place in 1457, when Dracula burned and pillaged townships and villages, destroying everything in his way. Only the city of Sibiu itself, at least that portion within its powerful defensive walls, was spared destruction. The purpose of the raid may have been to capture Dracula's half brother and political rival Vlad, the Monk, and to serve as a warning to the citizens of Sibiu not to give shelter and protection to rival candidates.

Another Transylvanian town that is linked with Dracula's name is Brasov (Kronstadt in German). Brasov has the dubious distinction of having witnessed on its surrounding hills more stakes bearing Dracula's victims rotting in the sun or chewed and mangled by Carpathian vultures than any other place in the principality. It was likely on one of the hills that Dracula is said to have wined and dined among the cadavers. It was likely on the same occasion that Dracula exemplified his perverted sense of humor. A Russian narrative tells of a *boyar* attending the Brasov festivity who, apparently unable to endure the smell of coagulating blood any longer, held his nose in a gesture of revulsion. Dracula ordered an unusually long stake prepared and presented it to him, saying: "You live up there yonder, where the stench cannot reach you." He was immediately impaled. After the Brasov raid, Dracula continued burning and terrorizing other villages in the vicinity of the city. He was not able, however, to capture the fortress of Zeyding (Codlea in Romanian), still partially standing today, but he executed the captain responsible for his failure.

During the winter of 1458–59 Dracula's relations with the Transylvanian Saxons took a turn for the worse in Wallachia. Dracula decided to increase the tariffs of Transylvanian goods to favor native manufacturers, in violation of the treaty he had signed at the beginning of his reign. He also obligated the Germans to revert to the previous custom of opening their wares only in certain specified towns, such as Cimpulung, Tirgoviste, and Tirgsor. This action suddenly closed many towns to German trade where the Saxons had made a profitable business, including those on the traditional road to the Danube. Since the Brasovians ignored these measures, Dracula proceeded to another act of terrorism.

Dracula's vindictiveness and violence extended through the spring and summer of 1460. In April he was finally able to catch and kill his opponent Dan III; only seven of Dan's followers were able to escape. In early July, Dracula captured the fortress of Fagaras and impaled its citizens — men, women, and children. Although statistics for that period are very difficult to establish (and the German figures must be viewed with caution), in the town of Amlas twenty thousand may have perished on the night of Saint Bartholomew, August 24, 1460, more than were butchered by Catherine de Médicis in Paris over a century later. Somehow Dracula's Saint Bartholomew massacre has escaped the eye of the historian while that of Catherine de Médicis has made her the object of great moral reprobation.

After 1460, Transylvanian raids and actions against the Germans in Wallachia subsided, and renewed treaties granting the Germans trading privileges were signed in accordance with previous obligations, as events conspired to turn Dracula's attention elsewhere. However, the Saxons exercised their revenge by being instrumental in Dracula's arrest "as an enemy of humanity" in the autumn of 1462, and more permanently by ruining his reputation for posterity.

In reviewing this catalog of horrors one must bear in mind that there were two sides to Dracula's personality. One was the torturer and inquisitor who used terror deliberately as an instrument of policy while turning to piety to liberate his conscience. The other reveals a precursor of Machiavelli, an early nationalist, and an amazingly modern statesman who justified his actions in accordance with *raison d'état*. The citizens of Brasov and Sibiu were after all foreigners who attempted to perpetuate their monopoly of trade in the Romanian principalities. They were intriguers as well. The Saxons, conscious of Dracula's authoritarianism, were eager to subvert his authority in Transylvania and grant asylum to would-be contenders to the Wallachian throne. It is far too easy to explain Dracula's personality, as some have done, on the basis of cruelty alone. There was a method to his apparent madness.

Although Dracula ruled the Romanian principality of Wallachia on three separate occasions and died near the citadel of Bucharest, his place of birth, his family homestead, and the two feudal duchies under his allegiance — Amlas and Fagaras — anchored his name to

Transylvania. Dracula loved the country of his birth and ultimately took residence in Sibiu after making peace with the Germans. Even his famous castle on the Arges River, though technically located on the Wallachian side of the border, skirts the Transylvanian Alps. To this extent the tradition borne out in Stoker's story is quite correct. Dracula's name is inexorably and historically connected with romantic Transylvania.

···· CHAPTER 4 ····

PRINCE OF WALLACHIA

BUT NO MATTER HOW CLOSELY Dracula was bound to Transylvania, his associations with Wallachia are a major part of his story. Dracula's ancestors came from Wallachia, the southernmost of the three Romanian provinces. It was here that he ruled three separate times: briefly in 1448; from 1456 to 1462; and for two months in 1476. It was here, too, that Dracula's capital was located: therein lay the center of his political power, the scene of many of his horrors, and the official headquarters of the Orthodox Church. He also built all of his monasteries in this province, and fought many campaigns against the Turks both on its southern frontier along the Danube and within the borders of his state.

On the northern frontier of Wallachia, facing Transylvania, Dracula erected his infamous castle. On a tributary of the Danube, the Dimbovita, he built yet another fortress covering 800 square meters. (Built of brick and river stone, some of the fortress walls are still visible in the heart of the old city of Bucharest.) Dracula was killed in 1476 close to Bucharest and was buried at the island monastery of Snagov, twenty miles north of the city. From Wallachia come sources concerning Dracula which confirm the narratives written in German, Russian, and Hungarian.

At the Military History Museum in Bucharest is an assortment of mementos from Dracula's time, and in a Bucharest park had been a model of the tyrant's castle. The document with the first mention of Bucharest is a manuscript signed by Dracula located at the library of the Romanian Academy. Ironically, the only existing life-size portrait of Dracula is at Castle Ambras near Innsbruck. Ferdinand II, Arch-duke of the Tyrol, who owned Castle Ambras during the sixteenth century, had a perverse hobby of documenting the villains and de-formed personalities of history. He sent emissaries all over Europe to collect their portraits and reserved a special room in the castle for dis-playing them. It made no difference whether the subjects were well known or comparatively obscure. What did matter was that they were actual human beings, not fictional ones. If such persons could be found alive, the archduke tried to settle them, at least temporarily, at his court, where paintings could be made of them on the spot. A few giants, a notorious dwarf, and the wolfman from the Canary Islands stayed on at Castle Ambras for some years. Dracula was already dead

The wolfman from Munich, in the collection at Castle Ambras. The wolfman was actually Petrus Gonsalvus from the Canary Islands, who went to Paris, refined his rough manners, and married. These portraits of the wolfman, his daughter, and his son form an extraordinary family series — one that Wilhelm V, Duke of Bava-ria, felt would make a welcome gift to his uncle Ferdinand II, who collected paint-ings of grotesque figures.

by the time this degenerate Hapsburg began his hobby, but the prince's reputation as a mass murderer was already largely established in the Germanic world because of the tales told by the Saxons of Transylvania. We do not know how or where Ferdinand's portrait of Dracula was painted or who the artist was.

The fascinating and rather frightening gallery of rogues and monsters at Castle Ambras, one of the first history museums in Europe, has hardly been disturbed since the days of its founding. The Dracula portrait hangs between that of the wolfman, Gonsalvus, and those of his two wolf children. A little to the left of Dracula is a portrait of Gregor Baxi, a Hungarian courtier who in the course of a duel had one eye pierced by a lance. The other eye degenerated, becoming bloodied and deformed. Baxi managed to survive this condition for one year, long enough for the portrait, showing the actual pale protruding from both sides of the head, to be completed. It is strangely appropriate that this portrait should be hung close to Dracula, whose eyes seem to gaze in satisfaction at this macabre scene. A visit to Castle Ambras, particularly to the Monster Gallery, as the modern-day guides insist on calling it, is a startling experience even for the most stouthearted.

At Castle Anif, near Salzburg, another Dracula portrait once existed. It was discovered at the close of the last century in rather unusual circumstances. A member of the Florescu family, Demeter, a jurist by profession, was traveling through Salzburg in 1885, and was by chance invited to dinner by Count Arco-Stepperg, the owner of Castle Anif. After dinner the count showed his guest the well-known collection of Oriental paintings in the large gallery of the castle. To his great surprise, Demeter saw among them a portrait of Dracula, which he immediately recognized, having seen the other portrait at Castle Ambras only a few days before. The owner was not able to explain to him how this painting had come into his family. In 1968, the authors of this book went back to Castle Anif. They showed the present owner, Count Moye de Son, the notes made by Demeter Florescu concerning his visit in 1885. Unfortunately, the Dracula portrait was no longer in the castle. The Arco-Stepperg family had died out, and inheritances had dissipated the collection.

Three other Dracula portraits exist. One, at the Vienna Art Gallery, is a miniature oil painting, probably a copy of the Ambras portrait. Another was discovered accidentally during the summer of 1970 by

A wooden cane carved with Dracula's likeness. Origin unknown. A Florescu family heirloom, the cane is now owned by Raymond McNally.

W. Peters, a German-born scholar of Romanian history. Entitled *St. Andrew's Martyrdom,* it shows Dracula — a symbol of evil for the fifteenth-century Austrian painter — as a spectator enjoying the scene. Crucifixion, after all, was just a variation of Dracula's favorite torture — impalement. A third painting dating back to the early seventeenth century was discovered by Dr. Virgil Candea in 1989 and is located in the library of the state of Wurtenberg in Stuttgart. The portrait on Dracula's tombstone at Snagov was likely destroyed by his political enemies.

Several primitive woodcuts of the prince survive in the German Dracula pamphlets, one of them depicting him in a military uniform. Whether these are true portraits is an open question since with time the German artists did their very best to deform Dracula's features.

It is a twist of history and fate that the Dracula portraits exist in the Germanic world while they are totally absent in Romania, underlining the fact that in his day Dracula was better known in Western and Central Europe than in his native land. Owing to the popularity of Stoker's novel outside Eastern Europe, this is still somewhat true today.

Saint Andrew's Martyrdom. *Dracula appears at the far left of this crucifixion scene. The fifteenth-century Austrian painter who executed this oil apparently was familiar with portraits of Dracula and was able to create an excellent likeness of the prince. Saint Andrew was the patron saint of the Transylvanian Saxons. Dracula is included as a tormentor of Saint Andrew because of his history of cruelty toward the Saxons. This painting was part of the collection housed at the Belvedere Palace in Vienna.*

The recently discovered Ochsenbach portrait of Dracula. It is presently located in the Library of the State of Wurtenberg in Stuttgart and dates from the early seventeenth century.

In Wallachia, Dracula is commemorated in popular ballads and peasant folktales, particularly in mountain villages surrounding Castle Dracula itself, the region where he is best remembered. Despite the perversions of time and transliteration, or the distortions of the vivid imaginations of the peasants themselves, it remains true that the popular epic plays an important role in constructing the past. Dracula was not defined as all-villain in Romanian folklore, in contrast to the German, Turkish, and, in part, Russian traditions. The German Transylvanians bore him a grudge because he massacred them; the Russians, because he abandoned the Orthodox faith; the Turks, because he fought them. Romanian folklore — which is, of course, the product of peasant imagery, not of the *boyar* chroniclers who labeled him the Impaler — has somehow attempted to explain away Dracula's cruel idiosyncrasies. Thus, it records him in Robin Hood–style, as cruel to the rich and a powerful friend of the poor. There is a little of the *haiduc*, the robber baron of the Balkans, in Dracula folklore. This peasant view of Dracula's deeds was probably a whitewash, an exaggeration; nevertheless it persisted. Moreover, Dracula was a brave warrior. The peasants were proud of his military accomplishments, no matter what methods he used to attain them. His main objective — ridding the country of the alien, non-Christian infidel — helped the peasants to excuse his impalement of the *boyars,* whose intrigues weakened the Wallachian state. It may also have helped them to forgive Dracula's attempts to eliminate those unfortunates, and the crippled, who could not usefully serve the state, especially in time of war. In Wallachian villages not far removed from Dracula's castle, there are peasants who claim to be descendants of the ancient warriors who fought for Dracula against the Turks, who defended him at his hour of need, guided him to safety across the mountains of Transylvania, and were rewarded by him.

The elderly peasants who still cultivate Dracula tales are a dying breed, and when the present generation is gone, the folklore may well die with them. We attempted to stimulate interest in Dracula tales and

Tîrgșor. The ruins of a fifteenth-century monastery built by Dracula. In 1922 Constantin Giurescu discovered an inscription indicating that Dracula was the founder of this monastery.

ballads, and made the first of a number of full-scale expeditions to tape record them in the fall of 1969.

In a sense, the whole of Wallachia (48,000 square miles), not just the castle region, is Dracula country, from the mountains to the Danube, from the plain to the Black Sea. The main sites are Dracula's capital of Tirgoviste, the ecclesiastical see at Curtea de Arges, his mountain castle a few miles up the road, the fortress of Bucharest, and his burial place at Snagov. Also of significance are Tirgsor (near Ploiesti), where Dracula killed his political enemy Vladislav II. As an act of atonement, Dracula built a monastery some years later at the precise location of the murder, in the middle of that once-important trading town. Many other places have been identified as having some links with the Impaler. Among them are: Comana, erected close to the Danube in gratitude for a victory over the Turks; the tiny grotto of Cetateni on the river Dimbovita, where Dracula found haven and refuge in his escape from the Turks in 1462; and the proud and iso-lated abbey of Tismana, where Dracula was a frequent distinguished visitor and patron. In addition, he gave land and privileges to other monasteries such as Govora, Cozia, and the abbeys of Rusicon and Filoteu on Mt. Athos in northern Greece, thus confirming the strong pietist inclinations noted earlier. Also to be included in a Dracula tour of Wallachia are: Braila, the largest commercial center in the country, burned by the Turks in 1462; the fortress of Giurgiu, built by his grandfather on the Danube, the scene of Dracula's most successful campaign; Chilia farther up the river, a strategic fortress that Dracula held precious enough not to yield even to his cousin Stephen of Mol-davia; the castle of Floci, a little beyond; and Enisala on the Black Sea, an older fortified bastion built by Dracula's grandfather, the remains of which can still be seen.

Apart from Dracula's famous castle on the Arges he erected minor fortifications such as the fortress of Gherghita in the Carpathians. Dracula monasteries are still being discovered. There are three vil-lages scattered throughout the country which bear the name Vlad Tepes. At times one has the impression that the stones want to tell the wayfarer their bloody story.

Although Dracula's reputation spread far beyond Wallachia, the seat of his power was confined to a triangle just south of the Carpathi-ans. At the apex, on the Arges River, a tributary of the Danube, was Castle Dracula. The base lay between the ancient ecclesiastical seat of

Curtea de Arges and Dracula's capital of Tirgoviste. Located between the two but closer to the mountains was Wallachia's first capital, the oldest city in the land, Cimpulung. To the north are two difficult mountain passes leading from Wallachia to Transylvania. One, by way of Turnu Rosu, reaches Sibiu, one of Dracula's Transylvanian residences; the other pass, closely guarded by the formidable German fortress of Bran, winds up the mountain to Brasov. This triangle just south of the Transylvanian border was the stage for Dracula's six-year rule of Wallachia.

In Dracula's time the capital city of Tirgoviste was more imposing than it is today, spreading beyond its actual walls. Like Versailles, Tirgoviste was not only the seat of power, but the nation's center of social and cultural life. Immediately surrounding the ostentatious palace — with its numerous components, its decorative gardens, and its princely church — were the Byzantine-style houses of the *boyars* and their more diminutive chapels. On a smaller scale, within the comparative security of the walled courtyard, the upper class attempted to ape the etiquette of the imperial court at Constantinople. Beyond these and interspaced with courtyards with stylish floral decorations, still a characteristic of modern Romanian cities, were the modest houses of the merchants, artisans, and other dependents of the princely and *boyar* courts. The three spiraled domes of the Orthodox churches and monasteries pierced the sky over the city. Tirgoviste, like Bucharest later on, was essentially a city of churches, remains of which survive to this day, reflecting the intense zeal and piety of an earlier age. The monasteries, with their cloisters, chapels, courtyards, and fortifications, added to the colorfulness of the city. In fact, one Venetian traveler compared Tirgoviste to a "vast gaudy flower house." The inner sanctuary, containing most of the aristocratic homes, was surrounded by the defensive ramparts characteristic of the feudal age, though these were built on a far less impressive scale than the walls of the German-inspired fortresses in Transylvania. One almost gains the impression that each *boyar* household was itself a small fortified bastion, capable of defense not only against the foe without but against the far more crafty enemy within. Suspicion reigned in the capital; anarchy was rampant; political assassination was frequent; and rapid succession of princes was the rule rather than the exception — all of which helps to account for some of Dracula's drastic measures against the *boyars*.

Shortly after ascending the throne in the spring of 1456, so runs one popular ballad, Dracula assembled several hundred of the great *boyars* in the hall of the Tirgoviste palace, along with the five bishops, the abbots of the more important foreign and native monasteries, and the archbishop. As Dracula surveyed the wily, dishonest expressions of the *boyars*, he knew that among the guests were his father's and brother's assassins. Then he delivered a most atypical speech for a Wallachian prince who was more often than not the *boyars'* tool. "How many reigns," he asked, "have you, my loyal subjects, personally experienced in your lifetime?" There were chuckles and grimaces in the audience, then a tense moment of silence. "Seven, my Lord," was the reply of one man. "I," said another, "have survived thirty reigns." "Since your grandfather, my liege," retorted a third, "there have been no less than twenty princes. I have survived them all." Even the younger men admitted having witnessed at least seven. In this manner, almost on a jocular note, each *boyar* stood his ground and tested the severity of the new ruler. The princely title and all that it implied had evidently been taken lightly. Dracula, his eyes flashing in a way that was to become characteristic, gave an order. Within minutes, his faithful attendants surrounded the hall. Some five hundred *boyars,* as well as their wives and attendants, were immediately impaled in the vicinity of the palace and left exposed until their corpses were eaten up by blackbirds. The lesson of this day did not escape the remaining *boyars*. Dracula was demanding either their total submission or exile to their respective estates. Woe to him who chose to disobey.

All that one can now see of Dracula's Tirgoviste are the remains of the princely palace, which was destroyed and rebuilt many times. Dracula's grandfather, the redoubtable Mircea the Old, laid the first foundation stone at the beginning of the fifteenth century. Nearby is the reconstructed sixteenth-century Chindeia watchtower built by Dracula himself to watch the atrocities. From the principal portico the tourist can still survey the whole city, if he has the heart to climb a steep and narrow winding staircase. Looking down on the courtyard below, one can clearly discern the remains of the palace's foundation, which indicate a structure of modest size. The cellar was probably used for the princely supply of wine. Here, too, would have been the prison or torture chamber where the unfortunate Gypsy slave or *boyar* opponent lucky enough to escape impalement was given the traditional bastinado. The notorious throne hall was evidently located on the ground floor. This was where Dracula, Dracul, and Mircea the Old were invested as princes of the land following a religious ceremony. Here Dracula also entertained the *boyars,* received audiences and petitions, and held official councils of state with the divan, an upper chamber which included every member of the higher aristocracy — bishops, abbots, and the metropolitan, or head of the Romanian Orthodox Church.

In this throne hall occurred a famous scene described in almost all the Dracula narrations: envoys of the Sultan had come to officially greet the prince and refused to take off their turbans when they bowed to him. Dracula asked them: "Why do you do this toward a great ruler?" They answered, "This is the custom of our country, my Lord." Dracula then answered, "I too wish to strengthen your law so that you may be firm," and he ordered that their turbans be nailed to their heads with small iron nails. Then he allowed them to go, telling them: "Go and tell your master that while he is accustomed to endure such shame, we are not. Let him not impose his customs on other rulers who do not wish them, but let him keep them in his land."

The point of this act of vengeance was not intended to teach the Turks a lesson in international good manners, for as a hostage of the Turks, Dracula was fully aware of their custom of wearing a turban on *all* occasions. Rather, given the poor relationship which existed between the two courts from 1461 onward, incidents such as these were deliberately aimed at provoking the Turks to war.

Many such cruel scenes occurred in the throne room of Dracula's palace at Tirgoviste. Some of the luckier victims escaped the pale by slavish adulation, confessions, and self-incrimination. Dracula took particular delight in ensnaring the unwary in a compromising statement. The following incident is typical: in September 1458, Dracula was entertaining a Polish nobleman, Benedict de Boithor, who had come as the ambassador of an alleged ally, King Matthias Corvinus of Hungary. The usual trivial conversation was pursued in the dining hall of the palace at Tirgoviste. At the end of the repast, a golden spear was brought in by some servants and set up directly in front of the envoy, who watched the operation cautiously, having heard of Dracula's reputation. "Tell me," said Dracula, addressing the Pole with some amusement, "why do you think that I have had this spear set up in the room?" "My lord," he answered with verve, "it would seem that some great *boyar* of the land has offended you and you wish to honor him in some way." "Fairly spoken," said Dracula. "You are the representative of a great king. I have had this lance set up especially in your honor." Maintaining his *savoir faire,* the Pole replied: "My Lord, should I have been responsible for something worthy of death, do as you please, for you are the best judge and in that case you would not be responsible for my death, but I alone." Dracula burst into laughter. The answer had been both witty and flattering. "Had you not answered me in this fashion," said Dracula, "I would truly have impaled you on the spot." He then honored the man and showered him with gifts.

Of Dracula's married life in this period, far too little is known. His first wife or mistress — it mattered little since all male descendants were considered legitimate claimants to the throne — was a Transylvanian commoner with whom he had fallen in love following his escape from the Turks in 1448. From the native Romanian Dracula tales, it would appear that their marriage was not a happy one for the prince was often seen wandering alone at night on the outskirts of the city, usually in disguise, seeking the company of the beautiful but humble women who in time became his mistresses. Such relationships indicated both Dracula's distrust of the *boyars* and his plebeian instincts.

But as one might expect, loving Dracula could be a dangerous thing, and so it turned out for one particular young woman. Romanian peasant tales state that the luckless mistress was assassinated by her suitor for infidelity, though she met a far more cruel death than Anne Boleyn. She was impaled and had her sexual organs cut out. Like a good medieval pietist, Dracula was most concerned with the survival of the soul in the afterlife. He had particular qualms concerning those victims for whose death he was personally responsible, and presumably he gave his mistress a Christian burial, a reflection of the morbid religiosity inspired by the enormity of his crimes.

He took the precaution of surrounding himself with priests, abbots, bishops, and confessors, whether Roman Catholic or Orthodox. He often spent long moments of meditation within the saintly confines of monasteries, such as Tismana in western Wallachia, where he was known as a generous donor. All the Draculas seemed intent upon belonging to a church, receiving the sacraments, being buried as Christians, and being identified with a religion. Even the famous apostate Mihnea in due course became a devout Moslem. Like the average penitent of pre-Lutheran times, these men felt that good works, particularly the erection of monasteries along with rich endowments and an appropriate ritual at the moment of death, would contribute to the eradication of sin. Mircea, Dracul, Dracula, Radu, Vlad the Monk, and Mihnea were collectively responsible for no less than fifty monastic foundations or endowments (Dracula alone was responsible for five). Even the degenerate Radu erected a monastery, Tanganul, and was probably buried there. Monastic interest was, of course, a perfect pretext for interfering in and controlling the affairs of both Catholic and Orthodox churches in Wallachia.

Dracula had a close relationship with the Franciscan monks in Tirgoviste and with the Cistercian monastery at Carta, and he frequently received monks from both orders at the palace. But the religious of various orders — Dominicans, Benedictines, Franciscans, and Capuchins — sought refuge in German lands after they had incurred Dracula's wrath by refusing to toe the line.

Dracula's crimes, the refinements of his cruelty, deserve a chapter unto themselves. Impalement, hardly a new method of torture, was his favorite means of imposing death. A strong horse was usually harnessed to each leg of the victim, while the stake was carefully introduced so as not to kill instantly. Sometimes Dracula issued special instructions to his torturers to have the pales rounded-off, lest gaping wounds kill his victims on the spot. Such quick death would have interfered with the pleasure he received from watching their agonies over time. This torture was often a matter of several hours, sometimes a matter of several days. There were various forms of impalement depending upon age, rank, or sex.

There were also various geometric patterns in which the impaled were displayed. Usually the victims were arranged in concentric circles on the outskirts of cities where they could be viewed by all. There were high spears and low spears, according to rank. Victims were impaled and left either feet up or head up, or they might be impaled through the heart or navel. Victims were subjected to nails driven into their heads, maiming of limbs, blinding, strangulation, burning, the hacking off of noses and ears, the hacking out of sexual organs in the case of women, scalping and skinning, exposure to the elements or to wild animals, and boiling alive.

Dracula's morbid inventiveness may well have inspired the Marquis de Sade, who was no doubt familiar with his crimes. In regard to the cruel techniques practiced in our so-called enlightened twentieth century, Dracula set another shining precedent. Prior to punishment he generally demanded confessions, the nature of which could result in his victims escaping some violence or even death. And often he scaled the severity of the punishment to the instinctively self-preservative wit of his potential victim. As with the Polish nobleman, there were instances when the doomed were able to save their lives with a happy or flattering phrase.

Beyond the suburbs of Tirgoviste lies an extensive network of lakes. These were used by Dracula mostly for fishing the stocked trout, and for lakeside picnics and orgies. Just outside Tirgoviste, high up in what is essentially an area of vineyards, lies an edifice far more handsome, with its pure Byzantine profile, than any existing church within the city itself. This is the Monastery of the Hill, known more traditionally as the Monastery of St. Nicholas of the Wines. Although it is reputedly one of the most beautiful ecclesiastical structures in Romania — second only to the Church of Arges, a few miles away — an atmosphere of gloom pervades it. At one time it served as a prison, later as an elite military academy — Romania's West Point. Today it is a retreat for elderly priests and monks. Inside, virtually every stone one steps on marks a tomb. No church in Romania speaks more eloquently about death.

The Monastery of the Hill (Dealu in Romanian) was initially built and endowed by Dracula's cousin, Prince Radu the Great (1495–1508). Prince Radu gained renown as a patron of learning and a builder of churches; his reward was a majestic tomb at the foot of the mountain altar. Tradition suggests that the body of Dracula's father was, on Dracula's orders, removed from the small unmarked grave in Balteni chapel and reburied in the more imposing wooden chapel long before the construction of the present Monastery of the Hill. It is also alleged that Dracula's brother Mircea was layed to rest next to his father at the altar. In the sixteenth century Michael the Brave, another of Dracula's indirect descendants (who is mentioned in Stoker's novel), found his last resting place at the Monastery of the Hill. His head was brought there after the prince's assassination by Radu Florescu, one of his faithful *boyars*.

· · · · CHAPTER 5 · · · ·

CRUSADER
AGAINST THE
TURKS

DURING THE WINTER OF 1461, Dracula hurled a challenge at none other than the proud conqueror of Constantinople, Sultan Mehmed II. The subsequent Danubian and Wallachian campaigns, which lasted from the winter of 1461 through the fall of 1462, undoubtedly constitute the most-discussed episode in Dracula's fascinating career. His resourcefulness, his feats of valor, his tactics and strategy brought him as much notoriety in Europe as his gruesome treatment of his own subjects. Whereas his impalements were recorded in popular narratives, his acts of heroism during the crusades against the Turks were enshrined in the official records of the time.

With the death of the great Hunyadi in 1456, the remaining Christian forces desperately needed leadership. The bitter squabbles that had led to Dracula's father's assassination continued unabated. This absence of Christian unity greatly helped the Turkish cause and contributed to the capture of Constantinople in 1453, three years before Dracula's second accession to the Wallachian throne.

With the disappearance of the last vestiges of Serbian and Bulgarian independence and the fall of the Greek Empire, circumstances of geography placed Wallachia at the forefront of the anti-Turkish crusade. Moldavia, Wallachia's ally, lay safely in the hands of Dracula's cousin Stephen, who emerged as a hero in the post-Hunyadi Christian world. Following the assassination of his father, Bogdan, Stephen had accompanied Dracula to his exile in Transylvania. There, while both were sojourning in the castle of the Hunyadis at Hunedoara, Dracula made a formal compact with Stephen: whoever succeeded to the throne first would help the other gain the sister principality. In 1457, exactly one year after his accession to the throne, Dracula, true to his promise, sent a Wallachian contingent to help Stephen reconquer the crown of his ancestors. In this way, Dracula helped launch the brilliant career of the greatest soldier, statesman, and man of culture that the Romanian Renaissance produced. For Stephen the Great, or Saint Stephen as he is now called following his canonization by the Orthodox Church in 1972, was both a soldier and a lover of the arts. The number of monasteries that still survive in the region of Suceava, Stephen's capital, are eloquent testimony to the cultural and architectural brilliance of his age.

When Dracula finally ascended the throne in June 1456, both Chinese and European astronomers documented an unusual celestial appearance — a comet "as long as half the sky with two tails, one pointing west the other east, colored gold and looking like an undulated flame in the distant horizon." The comet later became an object of study for British astronomer Edmund Halley and has been known ever since as Halley's comet. In the fifteenth century, as today, superstitious people looked upon the sighting of a comet as a warning of natural catastrophies, plagues, or threats of invasions. With the death of Hunyadi at Belgrade, such auguries seemed likely to be fulfilled. Yet Dracula's seers and astrologers interpreted the comet as a symbol of victory. A Romanian numismatic specialist recently discovered a small silver coin minted by the prince showing the Wallachian eagle on one side and a star trailing six undulating rays on the other, a crude depiction of the famous comet.

After the fall of Constantinople, the surviving powers of Central and Eastern Europe were all committed to liberating the Balkan lands conquered by the Turks. One of the great Renaissance figures, Enea Silvio Piccolomini, an astute diplomat and expert on Eastern Europe, became Pope Pius II in 1458. He saw the portents of danger for the whole Christian world in the imperialist ambitions of Sultan Mehmed II. Pius II launched his crusade at the council of Mantua in 1459, warning the incredulous rulers in attendance that unless Christians banded together to oppose Mehmed, the Sultan would destroy his enemies one by one. The pope asked Christians to take up the cross and raise 100,000 gold ducats.

Following the death of Hunyadi and the assassination of his eldest son, Ladislaus, a struggle for the Hungarian crown ensued between the Hunyadis and the Hapsburgs. Dracula had remained loyal to the Hunyadis throughout his struggles with the Transylvanian Germans, initially to Ladislaus and after his assassination to Hunyadi's younger son, Matthias, and brother-in-law, Michael Szilagy. On the opposing side were the Hapsburgs: Albert I who had ruled briefly, his wife Elizabeth, and Ladislaus V. The sacred Crown of Saint Stephen, hidden at the Fortress of Visegrad, waited for the next legitimate Hapsburg to claim it. The Holy Roman Emperor Frederick III was so preoccupied with internal affairs that his empire was not likely to respond to the papal appeal. Hunyadi's son, Matthias, managed to become king of Hungary in 1458. Dracula, who had met Matthias as a young man, had expected him to join the crusade. He was as disappointed in that respect as the pope. Matthias never gave his full support to the papal crusade against the Turks because of his shaky hold on the Hungarian throne. The Holy Roman Emperor Frederick III; George of Podebrady, king of Bohemia; Casimir IV of Poland; the grand duke of Moscow, Ivan III; the rulers of the Italian republics; and a number of Eastern potentates, all of whom had attended the council, merely sent kind words of encouragement to the pope. All were embroiled in their own petty squabbles and chose to dismiss the papal appeal out of hand.

Dracula was the only sovereign who responded immediately to the papal plea. His courageous action was rewarded with favorable comments from the official representatives of Venice, Genoa, Milan, Ferrara, and even Pope Pius II. While still disapproving of some of the cruel tactics he used, they all admired Dracula's courage and praised his willingness to fight for Christianity.

In spite of his oath to the Hungarian king and the pope, Dracula's relationship with the Turks remained accommodating. He fulfilled his obligation of vassalage, which included payment of the tribute and an occasional visit to Constantinople. The first indication that there might be problems in preserving amicable relations came from Dracula himself. In a letter dated September 10, 1456, written to the city elders of Brasov, Dracula revealed his real thinking, only days after his inauguration as prince:

> I am giving you the news . . . that an Embassy from the Turks has now come to us. Bear in mind and firmly retain what I have previously transacted with you about brotherhood and peace . . . the time and

the hour has now come, concerning what I have previously spoken of. The Turks wish to place on our shoulders . . . unbearable burdens and . . . to compel us not to live peaceably [with you]. . . . They are seeking a way to loot your country passing through ours. In addition, they force us . . . to work against your Catholic faith. Our wish is to do no evil against you, not to abandon you, as I have told you and sworn. I trust I will remain your brother and faithful friend. This is why I have retained the Turkish envoys here, so that I have time to send you the news.

There follows a typical precept which anticipates Machiavelli:

You have to reflect . . . when a prince is powerful and brave, he can make peace as he wishes. If, however, he is powerless, some more powerful than he will conquer him and dictate as he pleases.

Taking into account the overall tense Turkish-Wallachian situation resulting from Dracula's double allegiance, the reasons for the final breakdown of relations and for the opening of hostilities must be sought in Turkish attempts to turn infringements of existing treaties to their advantage. The tribute had been paid regularly by Dracula only during the first three years of his reign. From 1459 to 1461 and onward, however, because he was preoccupied with the problems of the Transylvanian Saxons, Dracula had violated his obligation and failed to appear at the Turkish court. This is why when negotiations resumed, the Turks asked for the payment of the unpaid tax.

There was another surprising new demand which had never been stipulated before and represented a clear infraction of previous treaties. This entailed a request for child tribute — no fewer than five hundred young boys destined for the janissary corps. This infantry elite was composed of recruits from various provinces of the Balkans under the Sultan's control. Indeed, Turkish recruiting officers had occasionally invaded the Wallachian plain, where they felt the quality of young men was best. Dracula had resisted such incursions with a force of arms, and any Turks who were caught were apt to find themselves on the stake. Such violations of territory by both sides were added provocations and only embittered Turkish-Wallachian relations. Raiding, pillaging, and looting were endemic from Giurgiu to the Black Sea. The Turks had also succeeded in securing control of various fortresses and townships on the Romanian side of the Danube.

Further complicating matters, Radu the Handsome, who had faithfully resided at Constantinople since his liberation in 1447, was encouraged by the Turks to consider himself a candidate to the
Wallachian throne. Before relations broke down, Sultan Mehmed II
gave Dracula a final chance. He invited him to come to Nicopolis on
the Danube to meet Isaac Pasha, the ruler of Rumelia and the sultan's
representative, who was instructed to persuade Dracula to come to
Constantinople in person and explain his vassalage violations of the
last few years. Dracula said he was prepared to come with gifts to Constantinople, agreed to discuss nonpayment of the tribute and the frontier adjustments, but was still unwilling to contribute the child levy. In
truth, under no circumstance would he proceed to the Sultan's court
because he remembered how his father had been tricked. The official
pretext for his refusal to go to Constantinople was fear that if he did
his enemies in Transylvania would seize power in his absence.

Since there was no basis for genuine and sincere negotiations, one
must view the sultan's reaction with a certain understanding. Dracula's refusal to go to Constantinople confirmed the Turks' suspicions
that he was simultaneously negotiating an alliance with the Hungarians. Thus the Turks laid plans for an ambush. The men entrusted to
carry out the plot could not have been better chosen — a clever
Greek devil, Thomas Catavolinos, and Hamza Pasha, the chief court
falconer, governor of Nicopolis, a man known for his subtle mind.
Their ostensible pretext was to meet with Dracula to discuss a mutu-
ally acceptable frontier and to persuade him to come to Constantinople. Since they knew Dracula would refuse the latter, their secret
instructions were to capture the Wallachian prince dead or alive.

We are fortunate to possess a comprehensive and dramatic account
of the precise circumstances by which Dracula outfoxed his opponents. The story is told by Dracula himself in a letter dated February
11, 1462, addressed to King Matthias Corvinus:

> In other letters I have written to Your Highness the way in which the
> Turks, the cruel enemies of the Cross of Christ, have sent their en-
> voys to me, in order to break our mutual peace and alliance and to
> spoil our marriage, so that I may be allied only with them and that I
> travel to the Turkish sovereign, that is to say, to his court, and, should
> I refuse to abandon the peace, and the treaties, and the marriage
> with Your Highness, the Turks will not keep the peace with me. They
> also sent a leading counselor of the Sultan, Hamza Pasha of Nicopo-

lis, to determine the Danubian frontier, with the intent that Hamza
Pasha should, if he could, take me in some manner by trickery or
good faith, or in some other manner, to the Port and if not, to try
and take me in captivity. But by the grace of God, as I was journey-
ing towards their frontier, I found out about their trickery and sly-
ness and I was the one who captured Hamza Pasha in the Turkish
district and land, close to a fortress called Giurgiu. As the Turks
opened the gates of the fortress, on the orders of our men, with the
thought that only their men would enter, our soldiers mixing with
theirs entered the fortress and conquered the city which I then set
on fire.

In that same letter Dracula describes the subsequent campaign that
took place along the Danube up to the Black Sea during the winter of
1461, which constituted a de facto opening of hostilities without so
much as a formal declaration of war. Thus, Dracula can be looked
upon as the aggressor.

The Danubian campaign was the initial successful phase of the
Turkish-Wallachian war. Dracula was on the offensive, attempting to
duplicate Hunyadi's successful amphibious warfare of the 1440s.
Much of the campaign took place on Bulgarian soil controlled by the
Turks. From the mention of place names it is possible to reconstruct
the progress of Dracula's forces along the Danube, and Dracula tells
precisely the number of casualties inflicted:

I have killed men and women, old and young, who lived at Oblucitza
and Novoselo where the Danube flows into the sea up to Rahova
which is located near Chilia from the lower [Danube] up to such
places as Samovit and Ghighen [both located in modern Bulgaria].
[We killed] 23,884 Turks and Bulgars without counting those whom
we burned in homes or whose heads were not cut by our soldiers . . .
thus Your Highness must know that I have broken the peace with the
sultan.

There follow some startling statistics of people killed: at Oblucitza and
Novoselo, 1,350; at Dirstor (Durostor, Silistria), Cirtal, and Dri-
dopotrom, 6,840; at Orsova, 343; at Vectrem, 840; at Turtucaia, 630;
at Marotim, 210; at Giurgiu itself, 6,414; at Turnu, Batin, and Novi-

grad, 384; at Sistov, 410; at Nicopolis, Samovit, and Ghighen, 1,138; at Rahova, 1,460. To further impress King Matthias with the accuracy of this account, Dracula sent to him his envoy, Radu Farma, with two bags of heads, noses, and ears.

The winter campaign ended on the Black Sea coast, within sight of the powerful Turkish invasion force that had crossed the Bosporus for a full-scale invasion of Wallachia. With his flank unprotected, Dracula was compelled to abandon the offensive. He had burned all the Turkish fortresses he could not actually occupy. Beyond that he could not go; the momentum of the offensive had been spent.

The Danubian campaign had established Dracula's reputation as a crusader and warrior for Christianity. Throughout Central and Western Europe Te Deums were sung, and bells tolled from Genoa to Paris in gratitude for endowing the crusade with a new lease on life and taking over the leadership of the great Hunyadi. Dracula's bold offensive also sent a new hope of liberation to the enslaved peoples of Bulgaria, Serbia, and Greece. At Constantinople there was an atmosphere of consternation, gloom, and fear, and some of the Turkish leaders, fearing the Impaler, contemplated flight across the Bosporus into Asia Minor.

Mehmed II decided to launch his invasion of Wallachia during the spring of 1462; Dracula had given the sultan no alternative. To defy the sultan by spoiling a probable assassination plot was one thing; to ridicule him and instill hopes of liberation among his Christian subjects was quite another, one far more dangerous to his recently established empire. In any event, Mehmed wished to reduce Wallachia to a Turkish province. With this formidable task in mind, the sultan gathered the largest Turkish force that had been amassed since the fall of Constantinople in 1453. The main contingent, led by the sultan himself, was carried across the Bosporus by a vast flotilla of barges. The other major force, collected at Nicopolis in Bulgaria, was to cross the Danube, recapture the fortress of Giurgiu, and then unite with the main force in a combined attack on Tirgoviste.

Dracula hoped for reinforcements from Matthias of Hungary in order to correct the disparity of numbers; he had, according to the Slavic narrative, no more than 30,900 men. Dracula appealed to his countrymen; as was the custom when the independence of the country was threatened, able-bodied men, including boys from age twelve upward, and even women were conscripted. An eyewitness Turkish chronicler states that the crossing of the Danube was completed on the night of the sixth day of the fast of Ramadan (Friday, June 4, 1462), the Turkish soldiers being transported in seventy boats and barges. Other Turkish eyewitnesses give us detailed and graphic accounts of the whole operation. The crossing was made possible by Turkish cannon fire being directed against Wallachian emplacements on the right bank:

[When night began to fall,] we climbed into the boats and floated down the Danube and crossed to the other side several leagues lower from the place where Dracula's army was standing. There we dug ourselves in trenches setting the cannons around us. We dug ourselves into the trenches so that the horsemen could not injure us. After that we crossed back to the other side and thus transported other soldiers across the Danube. And when the whole of the infantry crossed over, we prepared and set out gradually against the army of Dracula, together with the artillery and other impedimenta we had taken with us. Having stopped, we set up the cannon, but until we could succeed in doing this, 300 soldiers were killed. The Sultan was very saddened by this affair, seeing a great battle from the other side of the Danube and being unable personally to come there. He was fearful lest all the soldiers be killed, since the Emperor had personally not crossed. After that, seeing that our side was weakening greatly, having transported 120 guns, we defended ourselves with them and fired often, so that we repelled the army of the prince from that place and we strengthened ourselves. Then the Emperor having gained reassurance, transported other soldiers. And Dracula seeing he could not prevent the crossing, withdrew from us. Then, after the Emperor had crossed the Danube following us with a whole army, he gave us 30,000 gold coins to be divided among us.

Soon after, there were preliminary skirmishes along the marshes of the Danube, aimed essentially at delaying the juncture of the two great Turkish armies. Dracula abandoned the river and began his withdrawal northward. From this point, Dracula resorted to what is known as strategic retreat, a device invariably used by an outnumbered army. The idea was to draw the enemy force deep into Dracula's territory. The Romanians depended on the varieties of the terrain for their defense: the marshy soil near the Danube, the dense Vlasie forest extending deep into the plain, and the impenetrable mountains. According to Romanian tradition, the "mad" forest and the mountains were "brothers of the people" that ensured survival of the nation through the ages. As the Wallachian troops gave up their native soil to the Turks, Dracula used scorched-earth tactics in wearing down his enemies, creating a vast desert in the path of the invading army. As Dracula's army withdrew northward, abandoning territory to the Turks, they depopulated the area, burned their own villages, and set fire to the cities, reducing them to ghost towns. *Boyars,* peasants, and townspeople alike accompanied the retreating armies, unless they could find shelter in isolated mountain hideouts or inaccessible island monasteries such as Snagov, where the wealthy sought refuge. In addition, Dracula ordered the crops systematically burned, poisoned all the wells, and destroyed the cattle and all other domestic animals that could not be herded away into the mountains. His people dug huge pits and covered them with timber and leaves in order to trap men, camels, and horses. Dracula even ordered dams to be built to divert the waters of small rivers to create marshes that might impede the progress of the Turkish cannons by miring them down. Contemporary sources confirm the scenario of desolation that greeted the Turkish armies. For instance, a Greek historian states, "Dracula removed his entire population to the mountains and forest regions, and he left the fields deserted. He had all beasts of burden herded up into the mountains. Thus, after having crossed the Danube and advancing for seven days, [Mehmed] II found no man, nor any significant animal, and nothing to eat or drink." A compatriot added, "Dracula had hidden the women and children in a very marshy area, protected by natural defenses, covered with dense oak forest. And he ordered his men to hide themselves in this forest, which was difficult for any newcomer to penetrate." On the Turkish side, the comments are very much the same. A veteran of the campaign complained that "the best of the Turks could find no springs . . . [no] drinkable water." Mahmud Pasha, one of the commanders who was sent ahead of the main army with a small contingent, thought that he had finally found a place to rest. "But even here," the veteran wrote, "for a distance of six leagues there was not a drop of water to be found. The intensity of the heat caused by the scorching sun was so great that the armor seemed as if it would melt like a lighted candle. In this parched plain, the lips of the fighters for Islam dried up. The Africans and Asians, used to desert conditions, used their shields to roast meat." Certainly a factor contributing to the sufferings and death endured by the Turkish army was the fact that the summer of 1462 was one of the hottest on record.

Along with the scorched-earth measures, Dracula used guerrilla tactics in which the element of surprise and intimate knowledge of the terrain were the keys to success. An Italian traveler reported that Dracula's cavalry would often emerge from relatively unknown paths and attack foraging Turkish stragglers who had departed from the main force. At times Dracula would even attack the main force when it least expected and, before they could rally, he would return to the forest without giving his enemy an opportunity to give battle on equal terms. Stragglers who remained behind the main body of the Turkish force were invariably isolated and killed, most likely by impalement. A most insidious tactic, almost unheard of in this period, was a fifteenth-century form of germ warfare. Dracula would encourage all those affected by diseases, such as leprosy, tuberculosis, and the bubonic plague, to dress in Turkish fashion and intermingle with the soldiers.

The night attack of June 17, 1462. This is a painting by the nineteenth-century Romanian artist Theodor Aman.

Should they somehow survive their illness after successfully contaminating and killing Turks, the infected Wallachians would be richly rewarded. In that same vein, Dracula set free hardened criminals, who were then encouraged to kill Turkish stragglers.

The attack known as the Night of Terror is a dramatic example of Dracula's daring and mastery of surprise tactics. In one of the many villages leading to Tirgoviste, near the forest encampment of the Turks, Dracula held a council of war. The situation of Tirgoviste was desperate, and Dracula presented a bold plan for saving his indefensible capital. The council agreed that only the assassination of the sultan would sufficiently demoralize the Turkish army to effect a speedy withdrawal.

The outcome of this plan was admirably recorded by a Serbian soldier who experienced the whole impact of Dracula's audacious onslaught. His account described the complex Turkish camp: the sound of vigilant guards occasionally called to order, the smell of lamb roasting over glowing fires, the noise of departing soldiers, the laughter of women and other visitors, the plaintive chant of Turkish slaves, the noise of the camels, the countless tents, and finally, the elaborate gold-embroidered tent of the sleeping sultan in the very heart of the camp. Mehmed had just retired after a heavy meal. Suddenly came the hooting of an owl, Dracula's signal to attack, followed by the onrush of cavalry. The invaders penetrated the defensive layers of guards, frantically galloping through the tents housing half-asleep soldiers. The Wallachian sword and lance — with Dracula in the lead — cut a bloody swath. "*Kaziklu Bey!*" — "the Impaler!" — cried rows of awestruck Turkish soldiers, moaning and dying in the path of the Romanian avalanche. Finally Turkish trumpets called the men to arms. A body of determined elite guardsmen gradually assembled around the sultan's tent. Dracula had calculated that the sheer surprise and impetus of the attack would carry his cavalry to the sultan's bed. But as he was within sight of his goal, the sultan's guard rallied, held the Wallachian offensive, and actually began to push the attackers back. Realizing that he was in danger of being surrounded and captured, Dracula reluctantly gave the orders to retreat. He had killed several thousand Turks, wounded countless more, created havoc, chaos, and terror within the Turkish camp; but he had lost several hundred of his bravest warriors and the attack had failed. Sultan Mehmed had survived and the road to Tirgoviste lay open.

The grand vizier Machumet caught a Wallachian and, threatening him with torture, began to question him as to Dracula's whereabouts and ultimate plans. The prisoner remained silent and was eventually sawed in half. Overawed by such a display of courage, the grand vizier told the sultan, "If this man had been in command of an army he could have achieved great power."

The Turks eventually reached Tirgoviste but found neither men nor cattle, food nor drink. Indeed, the Wallachian capital presented a desolate spectacle to the incoming Turks. The gates of the city had been left open, and a thick blanket of smoke shut out the dawning light. The city had been stripped of virtually all its holy relics and treasures, the palace emptied of all that could be taken, and the rest burned. Here, as elsewhere, all the wells had been poisoned. The Turks were greeted by a few desultory cannon shots fired by the few Wallachian defenders who still manned the battlements. Mehmed II chose not to secure the capital but continued on his march in quest of the elusive Impaler. Just a few miles to the north, the sultan was greeted by an even more desolate spectacle: in a narrow gorge, one mile long, he found a veritable "forest of impaled cadavers, perhaps 20,000 in all." The sultan caught sight of the mangled, rotting remains of men, women, and children, the flesh eaten by blackbirds that nested in the skulls and rib cages. In addition, the sultan found the corpses of prisoners Dracula had caught at the beginning of the campaign the preceding winter. On a much higher pike lay the carcasses of the two assassins who had tried to ensnare Dracula before hostilities had begun. Over the course of several months the elements and the blackbirds had done their work. It was a scene horrible enough to discourage even the most hardhearted. Overawed by this spectacle, Mehmed II ordered the Turkish camp to be surrounded by a deep trench that very night. Soon, reflecting on what he had seen, the sultan lost heart. As one historian recorded it, "Even the sultan, overcome by amazement, admitted that he could not win the land from a man who does such things, and above all knows how to exploit his rule and that of his subjects in this way. A man who performs such deeds would be capable of even more awesome things!" The sultan then gave orders for the retreat of the main Turkish force and started eastward for a port on the Danube where the fleet had anchored.

After the withdrawal of Mehmed's contingent, the character of the war changed radically. Indeed this last chapter should be described more properly as a civil rather than a foreign war, even though Turkish soldiers were still involved. Before departing, Sultan Mehmed formally appointed Radu as commander-in-chief with the mission of destroying Dracula and taking over the princely office. The Turkish contingent, under the command of the pasha of Silistria, was to support Radu's actions, but the new commander was to rely primarily upon native support. The Turks had deliberately fostered this conflict in order to confuse the Wallachians and avoid the impression of a national war against a common foe, in effect abandoning their erstwhile plan to conquer Wallachia by reducing it to an obedient vassal state. What they had failed to do by force of arms they accomplished by diplomacy. Thus, in the final analysis, it was less a matter of tactics than of politics. The last battles pitted Dracula not so much against the Turks as against the powerful Romanian *boyars* who ultimately and decisively rallied to the cause of Radu. "The Romanian *boyars* realizing that the Turks were stronger, abandoned Dracula and associated themselves with his brother who was with the Turkish Sultan." So ended an account by a Serbian janissary.

There was another more compelling reason for the Turkish withdrawal. The plague had made its appearance within the sultan's ranks and the first victims of the dreaded disease were recorded at Tirgoviste. Perhaps Dracula's attempt at bacterial warfare had worked.

Dracula's desperate appeal for help from his kinsman Stephen was answered with treachery. In June, the Moldavian ruler attacked the crucial Wallachian fortress of Chilia from the north, while powerful Turkish contingents attacked it from the south simultaneously. Yet this extraordinary double assault was unsuccessful. The Turks abandoned the siege. Stephen was wounded by gunfire from the fortress and withdrew to Moldavia. He did not renew the attack on Chilia until 1465, and that time he captured it, while his cousin Dracula was safely in a Hungarian jail many miles farther up the Danube at Visegrad.

During the last phase of the Turkish-Wallachian war, Dracula ruled from his castle on the upper Arges, the prince's final place of refuge from the advancing Turks. Since the primary chronicler of the Turkish campaign returned to Constantinople with the sultan and the main bulk of the army, historians must rely on popular ballads from the castle region for information.

The peasants in the villages surrounding Castle Dracula relate numerous tales concerning the end of Dracula's second reign in the fall of 1462. All these stories end when Dracula crossed the border into Transylvania and became prisoner of the Hungarian king. They start anew around 1476, when Dracula returned to Wallachia for this third reign. One of the more classic narrations of Dracula's last moments of resistance to the Turks in 1462 runs as follows: after the fall of Tirgoviste, Dracula and a few faithful followers headed northward; avoiding the more obvious passes leading to Transylvania, they reached his mountain retreat. The Turks who had been sent in pursuit encamped on the bluff of Poenari, which commanded an admirable view of Dracula's castle on the opposite bank of the Arges. Here they set up their cherrywood cannons. The bulk of the Turkish soldiers descended to the river, forded it, and camped on the other side. The bombardment of Dracula's castle began, but it had little success owing to the small caliber of the Turkish guns and the solidity of the castle walls. Orders for the final assault upon the castle were set for the next day.

That night, a Romanian slave in the Turkish corps who, according to local tale, was a distant relative of Dracula, forewarned the Wallachian prince of the great danger that lay ahead. Undetected in the moonless night, the slave climbed the bluff of Poenari and, taking careful aim, he shot an arrow at one of the distant, dimly lit openings in the main tower, which he knew contained Dracula's quarters. Attached to the arrow was a message advising Dracula to escape while there was still time. The arrow extinguished a candle within the tower opening. When it was relit, the slave could see the shadow of Dracula's wife, and could faintly discern that she was reading the message.

The remainder of this story could only have been passed down by Dracula's intimate advisors within the castle. Dracula's wife apprised her husband of the warning. She told him she would rather have her body eaten by the fish in the Arges River below than be led into captivity by the Turks. Dracula knew from his own experience at Egrigoz what that imprisonment would entail. Realizing how desperate their situation was and before anyone could intervene, Dracula's wife rushed up the winding staircase and hurled herself from the tower. Today this point of the river is known as *Riul Doamnei,* the Princess's River. This tragic folktale is practically the only mention of Dracula's first wife.

Dracula immediately made plans for his own escape; no matter how unfavorable the circumstances, suicide was not an option. He ordered the bravest leaders from the neighboring village of Arefu to be brought to the castle, and during the night they discussed the various routes of escape to Transylvania. It was Dracula's hope that Matthias of Hungary, to whom he had sent many appeals since that first letter in February 1462, would greet him as an ally and support his reinstatement on the Wallachian throne. Indeed, it was known that the Hungarian king, along with a powerful army, had established headquarters just across the mountains at Brasov. To reach him was a matter of crossing the Transylvanian Alps at a point where there were no roads or passes. The upper slopes of these mountains are rocky, treacherous, often covered with snow or ice throughout the summer. Dracula could not have attempted such a crossing without the help of local experts. Popular folklore still identifies various rivers, clearings, forested areas, even rocks which were along Dracula's escape route. We have tried to use them to reconstruct Dracula's actual passage, but the task has been difficult since many of the place names have changed over the years. As far as we have been able to reconstruct the escape, Dracula, a dozen attendants, his illegitimate son, and five

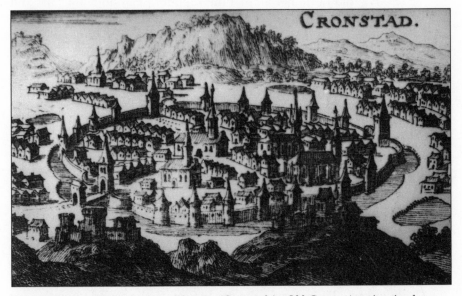

Seventeenth-century engraving of Brasov (Cronstad in Old German) as it existed in Dracula's time, showing the city walls and defensive towers as well as Timpa Hill, where Dracula committed many atrocities.

guides left the castle before dawn by way of a staircase which spiraled down into the bowels of the mountain and led to a cave on the banks of the river. Here the fleeing party could hear the noises of the Turkish camp just a mile to the south. Some of the fastest mounts were then brought from the village; the horses were equipped with inverted horseshoes so as to leave false signs of an approaching cavalry.

During the night the castle guns were repeatedly fired to detract attention from the escape party. The Turks at Poenari replied in kind. Because of the noise, so the story goes, Dracula's own mount began to shy, and his son, who had been tied to the saddle, fell to the ground and in the confusion was lost. The situation was far too desperate for anyone to begin a search, and Dracula was both too battle-hardened and too coldhearted to sacrifice himself for his son.

This tragic little vignette had a happy outcome, though. The boy, not yet in his teens, was found the next morning by a shepherd who took him to his hut and raised him as though he were one of his own family. When Dracula returned as prince fourteen years later, the peasant, who had found out the true identity of his ward, brought the boy to the castle. By that time he had developed into a splendid young man. He told his father all that the shepherd had done for him, and in gratitude Dracula richly recompensed the peasant with tracts of land in the surrounding mountains. It is possible that the son stayed on in the area and eventually became governor of the castle.

When the fleeing party finally reached the crests of the mountains, they were able to view the Turks' final assault to the south, which partially destroyed Castle Dracula. To the north lay the fortified walls and towers of Brasov, where it was hoped the armies of King Matthias were maneuvering to come to Dracula's aid. At a place called Plaiul Oilor, or Plain of the Sheep, Dracula's party, now quite safe from the Turks, retired and made plans for the northward descent.

Summoning his brave companions, Dracula asked them how best he could recompense them for saving his life. They answered that they had simply done their duty for prince and country. The prince, however, insisted: "What do you wish? Money or land?" They answered: "Give us land, Your Highness." On a slab of stone known as the Prince's Table, Dracula fulfilled their wishes, writing upon the skin of some hares caught the day before. He bestowed upon the five guides vast tracts of land on the slope of the mountain as far as the eye could see. This included sixteen mountains and a rich supply of tim-

ber, fish, and sheep, all in all perhaps 20,000 acres. He further stipulated in the deed that none of this land could ever be taken away from
them by prince, *boyar*, or ecclesiastical leaders; it was for their families
to enjoy through the generations.

Ancient tradition has it that these rabbit skins are still carefully hidden by the five men's descendants, but despite many efforts and in-
ducements, no descendant has been willing to shed light on the exact
whereabouts of these alleged documents. Still, we have reason to suppose that somewhere hidden in an attic or buried underground, the
Dracula rabbit skins still exist. One Romanian historian attempted to
find the scrolls, but the peasants of the area remained secretive and
intractable. Even large sums of money would not persuade them to
share such precious souvenirs of Dracula's heroic age.

CHAPTER 6

CASTLE DRACULA

THERE ARE TWO ROUTES from the ancient capital city of Tirgoviste to Castle Dracula and the mountains of Transylvania. One of them proceeds north along the Dambovita River to Cimpulung, then to Rucar at the Transylvania border, and through the mountains, by way of the pass at Bran. This was the route traveled by Dracula during his raids against Brasov, which lay just across the mountains, on the edge of the Transylvanian plateau. The second route is slightly more cumbersome. It takes one west to the river Olt, a tributary of the Danube, north to the episcopal city of Ramniculul-Valcea, and then into Transylvania, via the pass of Turnu Rosu, known to Germans as Roterturm.

The first of the two routes is the more scenic. In Cimpulung one finds a city of transition between the Germanic and Romanian worlds. It still has traces of what it was in the thirteenth century, a Teutonic burgh, and in that sense it belongs to the civilization of Central Europe.

Among the medieval customs continued here is the celebration of the Feast of Saint Elias, an Orthodox portrayed on icons in a chariot whipping evil creatures out of the sky; the protector of the peasants, who often come from neighboring areas to sell their wares and partake of the traditional entertainment. Dracula often sojourned at Cimpulung on his way to the north, but only a few local stories are linked to his name.

There are many rustic villages on the route from Cimpulung to Bran. On a mountain overlooking the village of Cetateni din Vale are the remains of a castle and a small church. This castle is not Dracula's but was built, according to popular legend, by Wallachia's first prince, Basarab I. Inside the grotto, three monks still observe a ritual which has been held there at midnight since earliest times, an index of the ageless piety of the region. Peasants in gaily embroidered dress still come from as far as fifty miles away, often making the difficult ascent barefoot, to attend the midnight service in this musty, incense-filled, cavernlike place where faded icons portray martyrs and saints. According to local legend, Dracula himself climbed this mountain when fleeing from the Turks in 1462 and took sanctuary within the grotto before continuing on to his own castle.

The region between Cimpulung and Bran is the heart of Romania's historic area. Here a national life was born at the close of the thirteenth century. There is hardly a mountain, a river, a torrent, or any other landmark, natural or artificial, that in some way or other does not evoke the stormy past so often recalled in the historical ballads of the peasants. Each village church, disintegrating castle, or fortified manor challenges the historian to seek the reason for its survival in an area where so much has been destroyed by invading hordes.

The peasants along this route are mostly *mosneni*, or free peasants. Never having experienced serfdom, most of them are probably descendants of the warriors who fought in Dracula's army — the bulk of Dracula's military forces consisted of freeholders since they were more trustworthy than the *boyars*. Even during the period of the Communist regime, peasants in this area proudly remained the owners of their soil, for collectivization proved unworkable in these mountainous districts. Their wooden houses are more ambitious than those found elsewhere; the scale larger, the styling somewhat Tyrolean in character, but the courtyards more extensive, with porches, more artistically carved. These peasants still tend cattle and sheep, and they take any surplus grapes, apples, and pears from their orchards to the market of Cimpulung.

Apart from the German townships, the Hungarian frontier was fairly peaceful in Dracula's time, and relationships with Buda were cordial for a while. In a sense, Hungarian-Romanian relations had to be friendly. Struggling with the Turks on the Danube, Dracula was hardly able to challenge the formidable guns and fortifications of Castle Bran, which dominated the valley of the Dambovita.

Castle Bran was allegedly founded by a Teutonic knight in the thirteenth century. Given the number of times it was besieged, burned, or

Castle Bran.

partially razed, it is a miracle that so much of it is extant. In 1225 it came into the hands of the Hungarian kings, and then successively belonged to the Wallachian prince Mircea, the emperor Sigismund, John Hunyadi, his son King Matthias Corvinus, the city of Brasov, the former royal family, and now the Romanian Ministry of Culture. Dracula was undoubtedly a guest of Hunyadi at Bran and later a prisoner of his son Matthias.

With its vast halls, dark corridors, multilevel battlements, high water tower, numerous inner courtyards, Gothic chapel, and rustic Germanic period furnishings, Bran has an atmosphere which conveys, more than any other existing castle in Romania, the legacy of the age of Dracula. In the middle of the inner courtyard lies a well, and next to it, hidden by a covering of stone, is a secret passage. Following a winding staircase that sinks one hundred fifty feet down into the mountain, one emerges into a cell near the bottom of the well. Beyond the cell is a heavy oak door which opens to another passageway leading to the safety of a mountain knoll and farther on to the citadel of Brasov. The purposes of this intricate passageway were manifold: protection of the castle's water supply; a place of refuge; a place for

Castle Bran: at left, the courtyard; at right, a secret underground passageway.

torture and detention; and finally, a secret means of escape. Dracula was apparently impressed by the features of this passageway, for very similar arrangements were later contrived in his own castle on the Arges.

The analogies between Stoker's Castle Dracula and the real Castle Bran seem to some too close to be merely coincidental. Since the earlier edition of this book, Bran has often been erroneously described by officials of the Romanian Tourist Ministry as Castle Dracula, perhaps because it ranks among the most picturesque castles of Transylvania, and possibly because Dracula's actual castle on the Arges is both difficult to access and rather unphotogenic. Successive Dracula tours (some of them sponsored by Dracula societies), Dracula films, and other commercial ventures have for that reason made extensive use of Castle Bran. Even more recently it was rumored that Michael Jackson's agents leased the Teutonic fortress for a substantial sum, presumably as a suitable backdrop for the singer, who was very popular in Romania.

The second major route to Transylvania follows the valley of the

Mountain pass near Castle Dracula.

river Olt via the pass at Turnu Rosu linking it to Dracula's favorite city, Sibiu. Turnu Rosu is often mentioned in documents concerning Dracula. The fortress, built on a much smaller scale than Bran, lies on a high bluff on the left side of the pass as one proceeds north. Only the ruins of its main towers are still visible. The fortress was built by the Saxon citizens of Sibiu around 1360, on the site of an old Roman castle, to guard the southern approaches of the city and as part of an outward defensive network against Turkish attack. Turnu Rosu means the Red Tower, commemorating its heroic role in a specific battle, when its walls were reddened by the blood of barbarian assailants. Although the castle was almost entirely destroyed on this occasion, the Turks were never able to capture the Red Tower. Nor for that matter was Dracula.

The road to Castle Dracula passes through the Citadel of the Arges (Curtea de Arges in Romanian), once the site of the princely church (Biserica Domneasca), the burial place of many of Romania's early princes. (This is to be distinguished from the far more ambitious seventeenth-century necropolis the Cathedral of the Arges.) Here in the princely church, Dracula and his ancestors were annointed princes of the land by the head of the Orthodox church in the presence of the *boyar* leaders. Generally, however, Dracula avoided the citadel and all it represented, for he got along no better with church officials than he did with the *boyars,* who often intrigued against him in Tirgoviste. Castle Dracula, merely twenty miles to the north of this ecclesiastical capital, acted as a powerful deterrent to potential revolt. In fact, this center of church authority was generally submissive during Dracula's lifetime.

Wallachian chronicles, as well as popular folklore, place Castle Dracula high up on a rock on the left bank of the Arges, just beyond the small communities of Arefu and Capatineni. By a strange irony, Castle Dracula is also known in the chronicles as the fortress of Poenari, the name of another village located on the opposite bank of the river. In fact, one of the oldest of these chronicles credits Dracula with just two accomplishments: "The Impaler built the castle of Poenari, and the monastery of Snagov, where he lies buried." Small wonder that there has been such difficulty in identifying the horrible tyrant and persecutor of the Germans with the castle and monastery founder recorded by the Romanians. Romanian histories, drawing upon the early chronicles, speak of "a castle known as Poenari, converted by

Castle Dracula in ruins. The original caption for the photograph, taken in 1930, identified Dracula's mountain retreat as "the fortress of Poenari in the district of the Arges." The authors later identified the ruins as those of Castle Dracula.

Dracula into an impregnable retreat." Local tradition, however, disputes this idea of a *single* castle, maintaining that Dracula's castle was located on the left bank of the Arges, and that the Castle of Poenari — a much older fortress, no longer extant — was located on the right bank. If this tradition is correct, one can only assume that early chroniclers confused the two structures and later historians perpetuated the mistake.

It will take the work of the archaeologist to prove this matter. For the time being, we are inclined to agree with tradition, and with the elders of Arefu, Capatineni, and Poenari that within the narrow gorges of the Arges at a distance of about one mile from each other, there were *two* castles.

Of the two villages, Arefu, where Dracula's castle actually is located, and Poenari, which chroniclers have taken to be the actual site, the latter was by far the more important. In the Middle Ages, Poenari was a princely village; over the years the castle built within its confines became the seat of control of all the neighboring villages, including Arefu. Deeds made by several princes to monasteries and individual *boyars*, both before and after Dracula's time, all speak of land endowed to the Castle of Poenari. Moreover, Poenari is the only castle remembered in the documents of the thirteenth, fourteenth, and fifteenth centuries. Local peasant tales clarified the problem their own way, but the key to the confusion is that Dracula's castle was literally built out of the bricks and stones of the castle of Poenari. Before describing this reconstruction, let us briefly survey our findings about the older Castle of Poenari.

There are no visible remains of the castle, but peasants from Poenari told us about the remains of a low-lying wall at the foot of the hill which might have formed part of the outward defense of a very ancient fortress. That fact could not, however, be scientifically corroborated. They also stated that when excavations were made not too many years ago in the local church, the workers came across bricks and stones that date back to the time of the Dacians, the pre-Roman ancestors of the Romanians. We were also led to some local mud houses, the chimneys of which contained stones remarkably like the Dacian stones found under the church. In addition, a small museum organized by the local priest displays an amazing array of stones, coins, weapons, and other artifacts, some of which date to Roman and pre-Roman times. The hypothesis of a local priest, Rev. Jon Stanciulescu, seems quite plausible: the original Castle Poenari was built upon the site of the ancient Dacian fortress of Decidava. After all, the center of Dacian power, Sarmisegetuza, which was destroyed by Trajan's Roman legion in A.D. 106, was only one hundred miles to the northwest. In accordance with this theory, Decidava was rebuilt by Romanian princes at the close of the thirteenth century to resist Hungarian and Teutonic incursions from the north, and given the name of the village which surrounds it — Poenari. It thus figures as a Wallachian fortress with extensive land holdings and occupied a strategic point on the Transylvanian frontier. Poenari survived until Dracula's time, though it was badly battered by Turkish and Tartar invaders. In 1462, when pursuing Dracula, the Turks stumbled across the decaying fragments of the fortress and completed its destruction. What is left of Poenari is likely to be found in the foundation of the village church, in peasant chimneys, in the local museum, and in the remaining walls and towers of Castle Dracula itself.

We must turn now to a further complication in the story of the real Castle Dracula. In a strict sense, Dracula was not its founder. When he came to the throne in 1456, the ruins of *two* fortresses faced each other across the Arges: on the right bank, the ruins of the ancient medieval fortress of Poenari; on the left, the remnants of Castle Arges. One of the two structures deserved to be rebuilt. Dracula chose the Castle Arges, which had greater strategic advantage, being sited at a higher point along the river. The Castle Arges was probably founded by the earliest Romanian princes and was definitely not a Teutonic fortress. In a sense it represents one of Romania's first bastions on Wallachian soil. Structurally it bears little resemblance to the much more formidable German or Transylvanian fortresses, such as Bran or Hunedoara, located in Transylvania proper. In fact, like the Wallachian castle at Cetateni, it is built on a modest scale and bears some of the features of Byzantine fortifications.

Local tales tell that the ancient Romanian prince Basarab withdrew to his citadel on the Arges following his encounters with the Turks around 1330. It was considerably fortified by his successors and, like so many other castles in the region, had a stormy history even before Dracula's time. On one occasion at the close of the fourteenth century, the Tartars, who had penetrated the heart of Wallachia, pillaging, burning, and looting on the way, reached the ecclesiastical see of Curtea de Arges farther down the river. The prince, his bishops, and *boyars* fled to the Castle Arges. In pursuit along the right bank of the river, the Tartars reached the village of Capatineni within sight of the castle, crossed the river, and camped in a clearing on the left bank. When they stormed the fortress the next morning, they found not a man within its walls. The prince, his bishops, and *boyars* had fled through a secret passage that led to the banks of the river. The Tartars in their vengeance left the castle so badly damaged that it was in need of reconstruction. This reconstruction, in effect a new construction, was Dracula's contribution. According to local tradition, Dracula is known as the founder of the Castle Arges or the Castle of the Impaler — Castle Dracula. Historical chronicles are incorrect only in confusing the names.

The story of the construction of Dracula's castle is very succinctly described in one of the ancient Wallachian chronicles:

So when Easter came, while all the citizens were feasting and the young ones were dancing, he surrounded and captured them. All those who were old he impaled, and strung them all around the city; as for the young ones together with their wives and children, he had them taken just as they were, dressed up for Easter, to Poenari, where they were put to work until their clothes were all torn and they were left naked.

As much as any Romanian document, this one establishes Dracula's reputation for cruelty in his own country, for these enslaved workers were neither Turkish nor Saxon invaders, but Dracula's own subjects. Despite the passage of time and many generations, on occasion local traditions and historical sources agree on aspects of Romania's grim history. The story of Dracula's motivation for reconstructing the famous castle on the Arges, which follows, is one of the best instances of coinciding accounts.

Shortly after his ascent to power, Dracula wished to examine the precise manner of his brother Mircea's death, having heard only rumors about the murder. Thus he ordered Mircea's body exhumed from the unmarked grave in the public burial ground in Tirgoviste. Upon opening the coffin he found his brother lying face down, his body twisted as if gasping for breath. This grizzly discovery seemed to confirm the rumor that Mircea had been buried alive.

Dracula's cup of indignation was filled to the brim, and his servants witnessed a mad rage equal to those of Ivan the Terrible. There was always great cunning in his dementia, however, and Dracula now planned a revenge worthy of the crime.

Earlier in the course of his journey from Transylvania, Dracula had made a survey of the region of the two castles on the upper Arges and was struck by their commanding strategic position. The punishment of the *boyars* and the reconstruction of the castle Arges on the left bank immediately became linked in his mind. "Thus," states a ballad, "our new Prince Dracula assembled those of high and low of birth for all to join in the Easter festivities." All attended the Easter vigil service on the eve of the observance, the most important religious celebration of the year. The following morning there were to be festivities, including a lavish banquet in the princely gardens surrounding the city walls. In addition to the roasted lambs, sweetened cakes, and wines provided by the palace, both *boyars* and merchants were to bring provisions of their own.

On Easter morning the *boyars* came to the meadows, mounted on fine horses and riding in carriages. The merchants followed in carts or on foot. The metropolitan and the bishops wore their imposing ecclesiastical robes. Some of the *boyars* wore the Hungarian or Central European nobleman's dress, though others preferred the more ornate Byzantine style. The merchants and artisans dressed more simply, some of them wearing peasant dress essentially identical to that still worn today. Many of the men wore the Dacian costume — an embroidered shirt, trousers held by a wide leather belt, a wool-lined and embroidered vest, and soft pigskin laced sandals. The *boyars'* wives gathered in small circles, usually in accordance with their rank or court function, and brought handsome Persian or Oriental carpets to rest on. Gypsy fiddlers organized both the music and the mirth.

The merchants, craftsmen, and guild representatives, equally conscious of rank, formed small groups of their own. Unperturbed by the feast of the wealthy *boyars,* the middle estate carefully instructed their apprentices how to settle their less expensive carpets, how to handle their wine, how to serve a table in genteel fashion. On such occasions, they had entertainment of their own at a more modest level.

After the feast, as was customary, the children enjoyed the swings, carousels, and various games provided by a specifically organized fair. Their elders rested on the grass, and the younger folk, both *boyars* and artisans, joined in the *hora,* a traditional Romanian folk dance. Minstrels and jesters sang or played for the prince, the *boyars,* and their ladies. In this fashion, the evening wore on until the sun had set behind the Carpathians.

Observers related that Dracula seemed preoccupied throughout the day, rarely conversing with the *boyars,* nor joining in the dances, as was his wont. While the partying was at its height, he conversed secretly with the captains of the guard, issuing instructions and posting men under trees and bushes surrounding the meadows. As dusk turned into evening, stern words of command were issued. Within seconds, Dracula's soldiers isolated most of the older *boyars* and rich merchants — all easily identifiable by their gaudy costumes — from the rest of the revellers and had them impaled in the courtyard of his palace. The younger *boyars* and merchants, along with their wives and children, were enclosed in a prepared paddock and then manacled to each other.

The operation had been so well organized that few *boyars* had the time to flee and seize weapons. In any case, because of the large quantity of wine they had consumed, many of them were in a state of torpor. The occasion could not have been better chosen. Dracula was intent upon teaching his *boyars* a lesson in submission they would never forget — if they survived.

Now convinced of the unreliability of his own capital, Dracula had determined to build a new castle; it would be closer to Transylvania, on some secure elevation far from any well-traveled highway, or any of the traditional passes, or any powerful Germanic fortresses. The northern slopes along the Arges River satisfied him on all these points. He made up his mind to rebuild Castle Arges with the bricks and stone from the older Castle Poenari on the Arges's southern slopes. Moreover, the outer walls of the new complex were to be doubled in thickness. Castle Dracula was to be made virtually impregnable, able to resist the heaviest cannon fire from the Turks. This scenario also neatly explains why Poenari has been identified as Castle Dracula.

The fifty-mile trek from Tirgoviste was a painful one, particularly for the *boyar* women and children. Those who survived it received no rest until they reached Poenari. The region was particularly rich in lime deposits and possessed good clay, and on Dracula's orders ovens and kilns for the manufacture of bricks had already been prepared. The concentration camp at Poenari must have presented a strange sight to the local peasants, with the *boyars* arriving in what was left of their Easter finery. As construction began, some of the prisoners formed a work chain relaying the bricks and stones down the hill from Poenari; others worked up the mountain across the valley; yet others made bricks. The story does not tell us how long the reconstruction took, nor the number of those who died during its course. People were fed simply to keep them alive; they rested just long enough to restore their energy. The chronicles relate that they toiled until their tattered clothes literally fell off their bodies. Months later, Dracula had succeeded in both of his aims: the powerful *boyar* class and the principal merchants had been savagely humiliated, and Dracula had his castle retreat.

The path leading from the valley to the top of the mountain where Castle Dracula is located is not difficult by any standards of modern alpinism. The actual climb takes about one hour. The first surprise, as one reaches the small wooden bridge which leads to the main gate, is the smallness of the structure, particularly when compared with the vast areas occupied by Castle Bran or Castle Hunedoara. However, the plan of Castle Dracula was limited by the perimeter of the mountain-top. The view is superb, almost majestic, both to the south and east to west. One can see dozens of villages scattered among the hills immediately surrounding the valley of the Arges. To the south, barely visible in the sun-scorched Wallachian hills, lies the city and ecclesiastical capital known as Curtea de Arges. To the north, the snowcapped mountains of Fagaras divide Transylvania from Wallachia proper. It is perhaps inevitable that Dracula's perch reminds today's visitors of Hitler's retreat at Berchtesgaden.

The castle was built on the plan of an irregular polygon, dictated by the shape of the summit, approximately 100 feet wide and 120 feet long. It is built in the style of a small mountain fortress of Byzantine and Serbian — rather than Teutonic — design. From what little remains, one can detect two of the five original towers resting under a heavy overgrowth of every variety of Carpathian wildflower, greenery, and fungus. The central main tower, probably the oldest, is in the shape of a square. The other two are in the classic cylindrical form. The thickness of the walls, reinforced with brick on the outside, confirms the popular account. These walls, protected by conventional battlements, were originally quite high, and from afar give the impression of forming part of the mountain itself. They were, in due course, able to withstand Turkish cannon fire.

Crossing the castle's threshold, one can clearly see that within the fortress there was little room for extensive maneuvering. Each tower could have housed only twenty to thirty soldiers and an equal number of retainers and servants. Within the main courtyard it would have been difficult to drill more than one hundred men. In the center of that courtyard was the well. According to folklore, there was also a secret passage leading to a separate tunnel into the bowels of the mountain and emerging in a cave on the banks of the Arges. This was probably the escape route Dracula used in the autumn of 1462. The tunnel, say the peasants, was built solidly and reinforced with stones joined by grooves and boards to prevent any cave-ins. A few feet away from the tunnel's entrance are the remains of a vault, which may well constitute the only vestige of a chapel on the site.

Whatever else there was within the fortress has disappeared without a trace. The houses of the attendants, the stables, the animal pens, the outhouses that were customarily erected in small fortifications of this nature, and the cell where Dracula's treasure was stored can be readily imagined. As can the drawbridge, which evidently existed before the present slender wooden bridge. The towers had some openings, for the peasant ballads speak of candlelight visible at night in the various towers.

Castle Dracula, although continuing to serve as a strategic defensive rampart for roughly a century following the prince's death, soon ceased to command the attention of local folklore. The last surviving story concerning the castle refers to the last stage of Dracula's campaign against the Turks in the fall of 1462, when the castle was partially dismantled.

At the end of the fifteenth century, Castle Dracula was used as a prison for political offenders. There is a document which relates that during the reign of Vlad the Monk in the late fifteenth century a *boyar* "was thrown into the dungeon of Dracula's former castle." The governor of the castle at that time was a *boyar* called Gherghina, who was a brother-in-law of Vlad the Monk and one of the few *boyars* who had remained loyal to Dracula. In 1522 the local peasants apparently revolted against their governor and the Battle of Poenari took place. Shortly thereafter the castle was taken over by the Hungarian king, who exchanged it for two other fortresses in Transylvania.

The peasants of the area often talk about the castle but rarely dare visit it. In the eyes of the superstitious, the spirit of Dracula still dominates the place. On one of our visits we found a peasant with a tattered Bible guarding the castle at night; he read it constantly while on duty to ward off lingering evil spirits. A few years ago, during the Communist regime, he asked us to provide a new Bible to replace his yellowed New Testament — a request which the U.S. embassy in Bucharest counseled us politely to refuse. Bible traffic was considered dangerous until the revolution of 1989.

In the vivid imagination of the peasantry, evil spirits abound in abandoned fortresses where treasures were once stored. The brilliant gold, silver, and russet hues that brighten the night sky are believed to be due to the treasure stored in a castle, and celestial specters take the shape of real creatures, some good and some bad. The cursed bat is a figure of woe in Romanian folklore and dominates the castle battlements at night. Peasants relate strange tales of people with bat-inflicted wounds becoming demented and wishing to bite others, then dying, usually within a week. These are symptoms of rabies, not vampirism. These stories mix nicely with the Dracula vampire myth and provide a rational basis for Stoker's horror tale.

Eagles that nest in the castle area are probably attracted by the number of smaller prey animals. Around the ramparts can be found rabbits, rats, snakes, the occasional stray sheep, mountain goats, many foxes, even mountain lynx and the Romanian bear. But the most dangerous visitor by far is the wolf. In his novel, Stoker mentions wolves howling as they accompany Dracula's carriage. If hungry enough during the winter, wolves will attack men. Wild dogs often howl at night also — particularly, as legend would have it, during a full moon — sending shivers through the hearts of the most valiant. These are some of the legitimate reasons why spending a night on the site of Dracula's castle has become a sport. Although the sophisticated, adventuresome students from the University of Bucharest and elsewhere are occasionally willing to try their luck and brave the spirit of Dracula, one can hardly blame the superstitious peasants of the area for shunning it. In a manner that has almost become a horror film cliché, when a stranger approaches peasants to ask directions to the castle, they usually turn away and emphatically refrain from giving help. If the tourist persists, they simply shrug their shoulders in quiet disbelief that anyone should be so bold as to tempt the spirit of evil, or they mutter *nu se poate,* an approximation of the German *verboten.*

Beyond such superstitions is a strange belief somewhat reminiscent of the medieval German obsession that the great Barbarossa would arise someday to save Germany. This sense of Dracula's immortality was expressed by a famous Romanian poet of the nineteenth century, Mihai Eminescu, who in a period of great political turmoil coined the phrase, "Where are you Dracula, now that we need you?" This appeal to the Impaler could quite aptly have been made during recent Romanian history. In fact, the late dictator Ceausescu may have uttered a similar invocation during the last frenzied days before his execution in December 1989.

Present-day visitors to the castle prefer to view it from a safe distance, usually from the opposite knoll where Castle Poenari once stood. Such a perspective offers not only the castle itself, but the picturesque mountain scenery surrounding it. Because of the abrupt ridge and the heavily forested area, it is almost impossible to photograph the castle at a closer vantage, except by helicopter.

All that is visible of the castle today are the brick and stone stumps of three main towers. As late as 1912 a visitor reported seeing remains of the other two towers, the sunken well, and the secret passageway. One year later, on January 13, 1913, the peasants in the area reported a violent earth tremor throughout the region. To some it seemed that the spirit of Dracula had suddenly awakened from centuries of slumber. At noon, when the tremor was over, the main tower of the castle was no more. Its bricks and stones had toppled down the precipice into the Arges. This earthquake wrought far more destruction on the castle than either the Turks or the ages of neglect. Two more severe earthquakes, in 1940 and 1976, substantially contributed to the castle's deterioration.

No traces remain of whatever else stood within the fortress. Only within recent years has general interest in Dracula the national hero and the observance in 1976 of the five hundredth anniversary of Vlad's death made the castle into a tourist attraction. To avoid further decay, the Commission on Historic Monuments decided to shore up

A nineteenth-century pencil sketch of Castle Dracula showing the tower walls before their destruction by earthquakes.

the existing towers and battlements. The walls have been rebuilt to what was probably their original size, and two of the five towers are quite visible now. To facilitate the climb, steps have been constructed in lieu of the winding path.

With increased tourism there have been the inevitable changes. Along the road at the foot of the mountain, posters indicate the castle's location. Were Dracula able to view the recent changes to his

Above: Castle Dracula Hotel at the Borgo Pass.

Left: Dracula the hero: statue of Dracula built by the National Tourist Office of Romania to attract attention to the gateway to the famous castle on the Arges. The statue is located in the village of Capatineni.

mountain hideout, his belated notoriety, the tourism, and the attending commercialization, the prince who loved solitude and distrusted men would surely be disturbed. In spite of this, the spirit of the authentic Dracula still lingers on in this majestic site. More in character with the historical prince, the surrounding area lies entombed in a morass of alpine overgrowth in summer and layers of snow in winter, a dignified mantle for his principal shrine.

· · · · CHAPTER 7 · · · ·

DRACULA HORROR STORIES
OF THE FIFTEENTH
CENTURY [1]

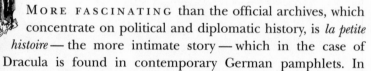

MORE FASCINATING than the official archives, which concentrate on political and diplomatic history, is *la petite histoire* — the more intimate story — which in the case of Dracula is found in contemporary German pamphlets. In modern parlance, these pamphlets not only created bad press for Dracula, but also became bestsellers in the extensive medieval Germanic world from Brasov to Strasbourg. The Saxons' desire for vengeance was realized, at least after Dracula's death, by defaming his character for centuries to come. Although this is controversial, the experiences of and stories told by Transylvanian Saxon refugees may well lie at the basis of all the accounts of Dracula's misdeeds.

To date, many accounts concerning Dracula have been found, in places as diverse as the Strasbourg public archives, the Benedictine monastery of St. Gall (now known as the Stiff Library) in Switzerland, and the Benedectine monastery of Lambach near Salzburg. Most are printed, some illustrated with crude woodcuts, and four are in manuscript form. Such pamphlets were the principal medium for transmitting stories and images to the general public in the fifteenth century.

Most of the stories concerning Dracula are tales of horror with some sort of moral for the reader. Though distortion is unquestionable, their amazing accuracy of historical, geographical, and topographical detail leads scholars to accept much in them as fact. The

---

[1] The appendixes contain translations of the German St. Gall Manuscript; several tales, including a few variants, from Romanian folklore; and the oldest Russian manuscript about Dracula.

Wie facht sich an gar ein grausem

liche erschrockenliche hystorien von dem wilden wütrich.
Dracole wayde. Wie er die leüt gespißt hat. vnd gepraten.
vnd mit den haüßtern, yn einem kessel gesoten. vñ wie er die
leüt geschunden hat vñ zerhacken lassen als ein kraut. Itez
er hat auch den mütern ire kind gepraté vnd sy habēs müs
sen selber essen. Vnd vil andere erschrockenliche ding die in
dissem Tractat geschribem stend. Vnd in welchem land er
geregiret hat.

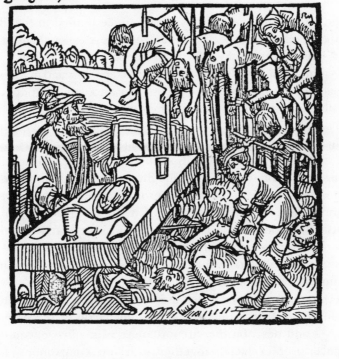

*From the pamphlet published by Ambrosius Huber in 1499 at Nuremberg. The text
above the impalement scene states:*

> *Here begins a very cruel frightening story about a wild bloodthirsty man,
> Dracula the voevod. How he impaled people and roasted them and with
> their heads boiled them in a kettle, and how he skinned people and hacked
> them into pieces like a head of cabbage. He also roasted the children of moth-
> ers and they had to eat their children themselves. And many other horrible
> things are written in this tract and also in which land he ruled.*

German stories about Dracula can be considered bona fide historical sources; they constitute a credible account of Dracula's life and
times, particularly when they coincide with the formal diplomatic dispatches.

Those responsible for starting the legend were hardly gothic authors but German Catholic monks from Transylvania, refugees who
fled the country because of Dracula's brutal attempt to destroy the
Catholic institutions and confiscate their wealth. Like all fugitives,
they had a story to tell, and, as so often happens in these instances,
the story exaggerated their plight.

The oldest surviving manuscript was once housed in the library at
the monastery of Lambach, near Salzburg; the original has been lost,
but a copy was made by a German scholar, W. Wattenbach, in 1896
(one year before the publication of Stoker's *Dracula*). Other manuscripts are now located at the British Museum and the public library
in Colmar, France, as well as in the Stiff Library in St. Gall, Switzerland.

The separate segments of the St. Gall narrative, all very similar in
style and composition, initially strike the reader as very brief sum-
maries of horror stories, undoubtedly among the first of their kind.
They seem to be designed for an unsophisticated audience. Dracula is
portrayed as a demented psychopath, a sadist, a gruesome murderer,
a masochist, "one of the worst tyrants of history, far worse than the
most depraved emperors of Rome such as Caligula and Nero." Among
the crimes attributed to this Dracula are impalement, boiling alive,
burning, decapitation, and dismemberment.

Recent research has enabled us to reconstruct the route followed by
the author of that manuscript — Brother Jacob of the Benedectine
order — and describe the circumstances of his first encounter with
Dracula. Brother Jacob, together with two companions, Brothers
Hans and Michael, were chased out of their abbey, called Gorrion
(present-day Gorjni grad in Slovenia), for refusal to abide by the new
rules adopted by the order. Forced into exile, the monks crossed the
Danube and fled north to Wallachia, where they found asylum in a
fifteenth-century Franciscan monastery still extant in Tirgoviste, not
very far from Dracula's palace. A chance encounter with Dracula took
place outside the princely palace. Dracula, always suspicious of visiting
ecclesiastics (particularly Catholics), invited the monks to his throne
room. He first ironically addressed Brother Michael, wishing to ascer-

tain whether God had a place reserved for him in paradise notwith-
standing the many victims he had sent to death. "In a way," added the
prince, "could one in the eyes of God be considered a saint, if one has
shortened the heavy burdens of so many unfortunate people on this
earth?" What concerned Dracula most was the expiation of his sins
after death, a concern implicit in his attention to good works as a
means of atonement: construction of and gifts to monasteries, services
for the dead. Obviously intimidated by the awesome Impaler, Brother
Michael attempted to assuage Dracula's fears of hellfire. "Sire, you can
obtain salvation," replied the monk, "for God in His mercy has saved
many people." Thus, with hypocritical words Brother Michael succeeded in saving his own neck. But Dracula needed additional reassurance from the other monks. He therefore summoned Hans the
Porter, asking him more bluntly this time, "Sire monk, tell me truly,
what will be my fate after death?" The latter, who had the courage of
his convictions, was forthright in his answer and reprimanded the
prince for his crimes: "Great pain and suffering and pitiful tears will
never end for you, since you, demented tyrant, have spilled and
spread so much innocent blood. It is even conceivable that the devil
himself would not want you. But if he should, you will be confined to
hell for eternity." Then, with a pause, Brother Hans added: "I know
that I will be put to death by impalement without judgment for the
honesty of my words devoid of flattery, but before doing so, give me
the privilege of ending my sermon." Annoyed yet fearful, Dracula allowed the friar to proceed: "Speak as you will. I will not cut you off."
Then followed what surely must have been one of the most damning
soliloquies that Dracula ever allowed anyone to utter in his presence:
"You are a wicked, shrewd, merciless killer; an oppressor, always eager
for more crime; a spiller of blood; a tyrant; and a torturer of poor
people! What are the crimes that justify the killing of pregnant
women . . . ? What have their little children done, . . . whose lives you
have snuffed out? You have impaled those who never did any harm to
you. Now you bathe in the blood of the innocent babes who do not
even know the meaning of evil! You wicked, sly, implacable killer!
How dare you accuse those whose delicate and pure blood you have
mercilessly spilled! I am amazed at your murderous hatred! What im-
pels you to seek revenge upon them? Give me an immediate answer to
these charges!" These extraordinary words both amazed and enraged
Dracula. He contained his anger, however, and replied calmly, re-

asserting his own Machiavellian political philosophy, "I will reply willingly and make my answer known to you now. When a farmer wishes to clear the land he must not only cut the weeds that have grown but also the roots that lie deep underneath the soil. For should he omit cutting the roots, after one year he has to start anew, in order that the obnoxious plant does not grow again. In the same manner, the babes in arm who are here will someday grow up into powerful enemies, should I allow them to reach manhood. Should I do otherwise, the young heirs will easily avenge their fathers on this earth."

Hans knew his fate was sealed but insisted on having the last word: "You mad tyrant, do you really think you will be able to live eternally? Because of the blood you have spilled on this earth, all will rise before God and His kingdom demanding vengeance. You foolish madman and senseless, unhearing tyrant, your whole being belongs to hell!" Dracula became mad with anger. The monk had pricked him where it hurt most, in his conscience and in his belief that because he was appointed prince by God, who, in His mercy, would have pity on his soul. He seized the monk with his own hands and killed him on the spot. Forsaking the usual procedure, he forced the monk to lie down on the floor and repeatedly stabbed him in the head. Writhing in pain on the bloodstained floor, Hans died quickly. Dracula had him hanged by his feet from a cord. He then hoisted the unfortunate wretch on a high stake in front of the Franciscan monastery. For good measure he impaled his donkey as well.

One can well imagine the effect of this gruesome sight on the remaining monks. Terrified, they quickly abandoned the monastery. Brother Michael, whose cowardice had saved his life, and Brother Jacob, his surviving companion, crossed into Transylvania, then sought refuge in various Benedictine houses in lower Austria and at St. Gall in Switzerland. There they related their unsavory adventures to other monks, the tales obviously colored by the anguish of a close escape. It was in this manner that the first Dracula horror story was born at the end of 1462.

Brother Jacob settled at Melk, a large abbey on the Danube. This abbey, the inspiration for Umberto Eco's detective thriller *The Name of the Rose*, still occupies its commanding position on a hill dominating the river and is one of the most palatial Benedictine houses in Europe. It was at Melk that Brother Jacob met other Benedictine refugees from Transylvania. Dracula's horrors undoubtedly became a highlight of conversation among the Romanian and German monks attached to this grandiose monastery, and some of these stories were inserted into the annals of the abbey. It was also at Melk that Brother Jacob met the court poet of the emperor Frederick III, Michel Beheim, who lived at Wiener Neustadt, just a few miles from the abbey. By that time Beheim's skill at writing history in verse was well established. Among his many historical poems was a history of the Varna crusade, highlighting the role of Dracula's brother Mircea. Information of Brother Jacob's misadventures at Dracula's court whetted Beheim's appetite for yet another poem on the extraordinary Dracula family. The courtier sought out the monk in the summer of 1463. The poem was likely completed in that year.

This poem represents by far the most extensive contemporary account of Dracula's life story. Over a thousand lines, the original manuscript is housed in the library of the University of Heidelberg, where most of Beheim's other original manuscripts are kept. He entitled the poem *Story of a Bloodthirsty Madman Called Dracula of Wallachia* and read it to the Holy Roman Emperor Frederick III during the late winter of 1463. This story of Dracula's cruelties was evidently to the emperor's taste, for it was read on several occasions from 1463 to 1465 when he was entertaining important guests.

The progressive popularization of the Dracula story, however, was due to the coincidence of the invention of the printing press in the second half of the fifteenth century and the production of cheap rag paper. The first Dracula news sheet destined for the public at large was printed in 1463 in either Vienna or Wiener Neustadt. Later, money-hungry printers saw commercial possibilities in such sensational stories and continued printing them for profit. This confirms the fact that the horror genre conformed to the tastes of the fifteenth-century reading public as much as it does today. We suspect that Dracula narratives became bestsellers in the late fifteenth century, some of the first pamphlets with a nonreligious theme. One example of the many unsavory but catchy titles is: *The Frightening and Truly Extraordinary Story of a Wicked Blood-thirsty Tyrant Called Prince Dracula.*

No fewer than thirteen different fifteenth- and sixteenth-century Dracula stories have been discovered thus far in the various German states within the former empire. Printed in Nuremberg, Lübeck, Bamberg, Augsburg, Strasbourg, Hamburg, etc., many of them exist in several editions.

Woodcut portrait of Dracula from Ioan Bogdan's 1896 publication Vlad Tepes, *where its source is identified as a fifteenth- or sixteenth-century German pamphlet that was in Budapest.*

The following excerpt from the title page of a German pamphlet is a lurid preview of what lay in store for the reader:

> The shocking story of a MONSTER and BERSERKER called Dracula who committed such unchristian deeds as killing men by placing them on stakes, hacking them to pieces like cabbage, boiling mothers and children alive and compelling men to acts of cannibalism.

By way of further enticement, the anonymous pamphleteers promised many other shocking revelations, plus mention of the country over which Dracula ruled. For dramatic purposes, the frontispiece of several pamphlets included a woodcut depicting the tyrant Dracula dining happily amid a forest of his impaled victims. Others simply showed Dracula's face, but with distorted features. One printed in 1494 has a woodcut portraying a bleeding, suffering Christ.

The deeds attributed to Dracula in the German narratives are so appalling that the activities of Stoker's bloodsucking character seem tame by comparison. The following excerpt is an example of "Dracula's unspeakable tortures unequaled by even the most blood-thirsty tyrants of history such as Herod, Nero and Diocletian."

Once he had a great pot made with two handles and over it a staging device with planks and through it he had holes made, so that a man would fall through the planks head first. Then he had a great fire built underneath the heads and had water poured into the pot and boiled men in this way.

The woodcuts graphically demonstrate that there were many methods of impalement: the stake penetrating the navel, the rectum, or piercing the heart — as vampires might say it — causing instant death. The "berserker" was not deterred by age, sex, nationality, or religion. Pamphlets mention the killing of native Romanians, Hungarians, Germans, Turks, and Jews; Gypsies, it seems, incurred Dracula's wrath on frequent occasions. Catholics, Orthodox Christians, Moslems, and heretics also perished. Mothers and even sucklings were executed; sometimes children's heads were impaled on their mother's breasts. There was, it seems, a stake in constant readiness at Dracula's palace.

The German writers relate that aside from impaling his victims, Dracula decapitated them; cut off noses, ears, sexual organs, limbs; hacked them to pieces; and burned, boiled, roasted, skinned, nailed, and buried them alive. In one verse Beheim described Dracula as dipping his bread in the blood of his victims, which technically makes him a living vampire — a reference that may have induced Stoker to make use of this term. According to the German sources he also compelled others to eat human flesh. His cruel refinements included smearing salt on the soles of a prisoner's feet and allowing animals to lick it off. If a relative or friend of an impaled victim dared remove the body from the stake, he was apt to hang from the bough of a nearby tree. Dracula terrorized the citizenry, leaving cadavers at various strategic places until beasts or the elements or both had reduced them to bones and dust.

How credible are these stories? Were they based on concrete historical fact, were they the product of sadistic propagandists seeking to awe or amuse, or were they written by monks simply to offer diversion from the daily fare of religious literature? Or, as some critics of these anecdotes have suggested, were they in fact contrived on orders of the Hungarian court to destroy Dracula's reputation and justify the harsh treatment subsequently meted out to him in prison? It would then follow that a common model inspired all the fifteenth-century Dracula narratives, whether German or not.

The Hungarian court had strong reasons for discrediting Dracula and having him safely removed from power. Aside from other factors, his strong autocratic rule threatened Hungarian hegemony in Transylvania. However, even granting that a common German anti-Dracula model may have inspired the accounts of the official Hungarian court chronicler, Antonio Bonfinius, one finds it hard to account for the similarity of the many other Dracula narratives written in a variety of languages and circulating over widely scattered geographic and political regions. For instance, the Russian Dracula manuscript closely coincides with the German stories. Yet to assume that all of these were mere translations of an original German source is to credit the fifteenth century with twentieth-century efficiency of transmission. In addition, the Russian and other narratives are sufficiently different in their explanation of the crimes to account for a single source.

One major argument against the theory of a common horror story prototype is provided by the oral ballads and traditions that contain anecdotes similar to those mentioned elsewhere, yet explain away the Impaler's crimes by providing rational motives. The Romanian peasants could understand neither German nor Slavonic, nor read or write even their own language. The Romanian Dracula narratives were stories composed in his lifetime, simply transmitted orally from one generation to another, very much in the manner of the Viking sagas. Not until the twentieth century were they formally committed to print, and it is safe to assume that a few Romanian anecdotes still go unrecorded.

One can pursue the argument against a single source by pointing out that identical stories about Dracula appeared in the reports of official chroniclers, diplomats, and travelers; in the folklore of neighboring states; and in a great number of languages: Italian, French, Latin, Czech, Polish, Serbian, and Turkish, obviously written by independent observers or commentators or sung by peasants.

To the determined skeptic, a sound yardstick of credibility is provided by the reports of diplomats stationed in the nearby capitals of Buda and Constantinople. Diplomats reporting to their home governments are usually wary of embellished facts, and their dispatches have to be terse and to the point. Here is a quote from the papal legate at Buda, Nicholas of Modrussa, reporting to Pope Pius II in 1464, referring to a specific massacre in which Dracula killed 40,000 men and women of all ages and nationalities:

He killed some by breaking them under the wheels of carts; others stripped of their clothes were skinned alive up to their entrails; others placed upon stakes, or roasted on red-hot coals placed under them; others punctured with stakes piercing their heads, their breasts, their buttocks and the middle of their entrails, with the stake emerging from their mouths; in order that no form of cruelty be missing he stuck stakes in both the mother's breasts and thrust their babies unto them. Finally he killed others in various ferocious ways, torturing them with many kinds of instruments such as the atrocious cruelties of the most frightful tyrant could devise.

A contemporary papal nuncio, Gabriele Rangone, bishop of Erlau, reported in 1475 that by that date Dracula had personally authorized the murders of 100,000 people. This figure, if true, is equivalent to at least one-fifth of the total population of Dracula's principality, though the number obviously includes Turks, Germans, and other enemies.

In fairness to the narratives of the German monks, one should note that by mentioning precise locations in Transylvania and elsewhere, dates, historical figures, cities, districts and townships, and specific fortresses and churches, a measure of credibility is added to their accounts. In addition, they provide a fairly accurate geopolitical and topographical description of Transylvania. With pinpoint accuracy one German pamphlet, published in Nuremberg in 1499, refers to individual sections of Brasov, or Kronstadt (Kranstatt in Low German dialect cited below).

And he led away all those whom he had captured outside the city called Kranstatt near the chapel of St. Jacob. And at that time Dracula . . . had the entire suburb burned. Also . . . all those whom he had taken captive, men and women, young and old, children, he had impaled on the hill by the chapel and all around the hill, and under them he proceeded to eat at table and enjoyed himself in that way.

This particular horror occurred outside the fortifications of Brasov in April 1459, undoubtedly one of Dracula's most dramatized atrocities. Dracula's famous meal among the impaled cadavers was immortalized in two woodcuts, one printed at Nuremberg in 1499, the other at Strasbourg in 1500. The mention of smaller townships, individual villages, monasteries, and fortresses further strengthens the historicity of the accounts. Although identification is at times difficult since most German names in use during the fifteenth century have been replaced by Romanian ones, and some ancient townships have now disappeared, it has been possible with the help of sixteenth-century maps to retrace Dracula's path of destruction through Transylvania.

Among the sources to which the historian can turn to verify the authenticity of the German accounts is the rich primary documentation in the archives of Brasov and Sibiu, fortified cities that figure prominently in all the German accounts. The Sibiu archive includes, among other items, one missive by Dracula himself, bearing the awesome signature DRAKULYA, a nickname that he adopted to demonstrate that he considered himself son of the crusading Dragon.

As the criminal investigator seeking the truth about a suspect looks for a motive, so the historian testing the veracity of these German stories looks for Dracula's motivation to commit his horrible deeds. Undoubtedly there was the occasional irrational streak in his character, but we have found all along that such moments were often accompanied by a keen awareness of the problem he was attempting to resolve. Some of his motives mentioned in the various German horror stories are best summarized below.

Revenge. The killing of Dracula's father and brother, Dracul and Mircea, related in the first episode of the St. Gall manuscript, are authentic historical facts. The assassinations both took place in 1447. Dracula's investigation into Mircea's murder prompted his enslavement of the nobles and citizens of Tirgoviste, which led to the construction of Castle Dracula.

The execution in 1456 of Vladislav II, Dracula's predecessor, can also be credited to revenge, since Vladislav was in part responsible for the assassination of Dracula's father.

Inter-family feuds. The struggle between the two rival factions of the Wallachian princely family, the Draculas and the Danestis, was a struggle for survival; it helps account for many of Dracula's massive raids. For example, it was because of the defection and betrayal of his half brother, Vlad the Monk, that Dracula destroyed cities and villages in his own enclave.

Protection of Transylvanian commerce. Most of Dracula's vindictiveness against the German Saxon population of Transylvania was due to an ill-defined but rising patriotism, directed in this instance against the commercial monopoly exercised by the German Transylvanian Saxons in all Romanian provinces. For instance, the incident mentioned by Beheim of Dracula's arrest of German youths traveling in Wallachia illustrates this intense belief in the national sovereignty of his state. In 1459 after secretly recalling his own Wallachian merchants from Transylvania, Dracula apprehended four hundred German-speaking Transylvanian trainees who had come to Wallachia in order to learn the Romanian language. He had them assembled in a room and burned alive. Dracula undoubtedly saw these apprentices less as trainees than as spies sent by the Saxon merchants of Brasov and Sibiu to learn about native methods of production.

Establishment of personal authority. As previously related, when Dracula first came to rule in 1456 Wallachia was beset by internal anarchy, *boyar* intrigue, rival factions, and Hungarian political pressure. The mass *boyar* impalement is vividly described in Beheim's poem and recounted in other sources. (The killings resulted from the lighthearted answers of the *boyar* council to Dracula's question: "How many reigns have you my loyal subjects personally experienced in your lifetime?") Thus Wallachia was immediately and horribly instructed that the princely title, and all that it implied, was not to be taken lightly. Moreover, the property of the victims was distributed to Dracula adherents, who formed a new nobility with a vested interest in the survival of the regime.

Affirmation of national sovereignty. Some of Dracula's motives to commit atrocities against the Turks were surely personal in nature, the result of the suffering he experienced during his imprisonment in Egrigoz when he was a boy. But he was impelled by national concerns, as well.

Dracula's defiance of the Turks included the famous scene in the throne room of Tirgoviste, when Turkish representatives failed to remove their turbans. This story, concluding with Dracula's moralizing about the impropriety of imposing Turkish customs upon another nation, clearly indicates his intention of affirming full national sovereignty over limited sovereignty.

Another indication of the veracity of the German stories is what they omit. For example, Beheim's poem includes an invaluable, detailed description of Dracula's last days of freedom in the fall of 1462, when he appealed to the Hungarian king for help and protection following his flight to Castle Dracula. It does *not* include an account of Dracula's subsequent imprisonment in Hungary; an understandable omission since German Transylvanian witnesses could hardly have been present in Buda.

In addition to anecdotes which can easily be placed in a geographical or historical context are a number which cannot be connected to any specific place or date, but which are nevertheless mentioned in the various German texts and form an integral part of the story.

The authenticity of such anecdotes can be substantiated because they occur in all three variants, German, Slavonic, and Romanian, and, for reasons explained, they could not have derived from a common literary model. In terms of content, moral and political philosophy, and even specific methods of punishment, they coincide fairly closely with those anecdotes that do have historical validity. They reveal characteristics of Dracula which correspond with traits expounded in the other anecdotes. They describe events and policies which can be verified.

One story tells of a famous fountain in a deserted square in Tirgoviste where travelers habitually would rest and refresh themselves. Dracula ordered a golden cup to be permanently stationed here for all to use. Never did that cup disappear throughout his reign. He was, after all, a "law and order" ruler.

A second anecdote tells of a foreign merchant who spent the night at an inn and, being aware of the reputation of Dracula's country for honesty, left his treasure-laden cart in the street. Next morning, to his amazement, he found that one hundred sixty gold ducats were missing. He immediately sought an audience with the prince. Dracula simply replied, "Tonight you will find your gold." To the citizens of Tirgoviste he gave the ultimatum: "Either you find the thief or I will destroy your town." Certain of success in advance, Dracula commanded that one hundred sixty substitute ducats plus one extra one be placed in the cart during the night. Duly the thief and the original ducats were found. Having proved the honesty of his capital, Dracula desired to test the ethics of the foreigner. Fortunately, he was honest and admitted to the additional ducat. While impaling the thief, Dracula told the merchant that such would undoubtedly have been his fate had he proved dishonest.

Both of these stories are in keeping with contemporary references to Dracula's attempt to set a strict code of ethics in his land — a most difficult thing to implement in a society known for its Byzantine cynicism and absence of moral standards, but not an impossible one, since

Dracula enforced public morality by means of severe punishment. Narratives about burning the poor and the sick are more difficult to rationalize. Perhaps because of the exigencies of war Dracula could ill afford to feed useless mouths. Regarding the poor, Dracula may have imagined he was sending them to Paradise where they would suffer less, in accordance with Scripture. In the case of the sick, one might argue it was a form of mercy killing or perhaps an attempt to rid the country of the plague or other disease.

Throughout the various sagas one also notes a sadistic sexuality: the ritual and manner of impalement, a husband's forced cannibalism of his wife's breasts, and similar horrors. Here, again, Dracula employs morbid measures to impose puritanical morality. The extent of Dracula's indignation against an unfaithful woman almost surpasses belief. Dracula ordered her sexual organs to be cut out. She was then skinned alive and displayed in public, her skin hanging separately from a pole in the middle of the marketplace. The same punishment was applied to maidens who did not keep their virginity, and to unchaste widows. In other instances, Dracula was known to have nipples cut from women's breasts, or a red-hot iron stake shoved through the vagina until the instrument emerged from the mouth.

What explanation might successfully reconcile Dracula's apparent attraction to women with the savagery of his sexual crimes? One obvious conjecture suggested by the phallic use of the stake is some sort of sexual inadequacy, most likely partial impotence.

There are other, general considerations which must be kept in mind when evaluating Dracula's criminality. One is the proverbial concern of viewing a man's actions according to the standards of his time. Dracula's age was that of the spider king, Louis XI; Ludovico Sforza the Moor; the Borgia pope, Alexander VI; his son Cesare; and Sigismondo Malatesta. One could go on and on enumerating their brutal contemporaries. The point is that the Renaissance, for all its humanism, was marked by extraordinary inhumanity.

Impalement, though never before or since practiced on so wide a scale, was not Dracula's invention. It was known in Asia and practiced by the Turks. One recorded instance in the West is attributed to John Tiptoft, Earl of Worcester, during the War of the Roses, and he had learned it from the Turks.

Dracula's cruel traits were not unique in his family, either. We know little about his father, except that he was a crusader of the Order of the Dragon. Dracula's eldest legitimate son is remembered as Mihnea the Bad. Also, Dracula spent more years in prison than he did on the throne; his first imprisonment, by the Turks, began when he was no more than fifteen. But most of his experiences seemed to reinforce one fact: life was insecure — and cheap. His father was assassinated; a brother was buried alive; other relatives were killed or tortured; his first wife killed herself; subjects conspired against him; his cousin, a sworn friend, betrayed him; Hungarians, Germans, and Turks pursued him. When reviewing Dracula's life in light of his imprisonment and the chaos of his early years, it becomes all too clear that horror begets horror.

CHAPTER 8

THE HISTORICAL DRACULA, 1462–1476: IMPRISONMENT AND DEATH

DRACULA'S TWELVE YEARS OF IMPRISONMENT in Hungary constitute the most obscure phase of his extraordinary career. Romanian oral and written sources are understandably silent about the prince's experiences at that time, since they took place far from the Transylvanian and Wallachian regions. Turkish chroniclers had no means of being apprised of Dracula's fate because technically the Turks were at war with Hungary. The German publicists, having triumphed in their anti-Dracula cause, were less interested in the subject; Dracula was safely removed from the Wallachian throne, which was all they desired.

Dracula succeeded in escaping from his castle, besieged by the Turks. He managed to descend the treacherous Transylvanian slopes at the head of a small mercenary force, and they went to seek support from his formal ally King Matthias Corvinus of Hungary to whom he had written asking for military help. The German court poet Michel Beheim narrates the Dracula story only to the point of his imprisonment by the Hungarian king in 1462 and recounts the following dramatic events:

The king of Hungary declared himself ready to come to the aid of Dracula with a large army and set in motion from the city of Buda. He took the shortest route to Transylvania. The king also sent reassuring messages to Pope Pius II to the effect that he would soon attack the Turks on the Danube.

Bonfinius, Matthias's historian, reaffirmed this information. "The king," he wrote, "was proceeding to Wallachia in order to liberate

94

Left: King Matthias Corvinus, son of John Hunyadi, king of Hungary.

Below left: Solomon's tower, Visegrad; one of the places where Dracula was confined while a prisoner of King Matthias.

Below right: An artist's impression of King Matthias's summer palace at Visegrad on the Danube. Dracula was held here under house arrest from 1462 to 1474. The castle walls extend to the Danube, where Solomon's tower is located. The king's palace is on the summit of a hill. Even if Dracula was detained at the tower, he would have been present at the palace when important delegations visited.

Dracula from the Turks . . . and he would give a relative of his to the Wallachian prince as a wife." When he learned that Matthias had reached Brasov, Dracula, still wary of the king's intentions, took up residence in the Scheii district, the Romanian section of town which lay outside the city gates. The two men met in what is now the town hall, still standing in the heart of the city. They maintained a pretense of negotiations during a five-week period.

After weeks of fruitless talks, Dracula suggested to Matthias that they finally act and embark on a campaign to liberate Wallachia from Turkish control under Dracula's brother Radu. The king gave him a body of soldiers under the leadership of Jan Jiskra of Brandys, a former Slovak Hussite leader. Jiskra had little love for Dracula and resented his support of the Hunyadis during the internal strife in Hungary, while he had espoused the imperial cause. The small contingent, composed of a few remaining mercenaries and of Hungarians and Slovaks, was ostensibly to provide the vanguard for a larger Hungarian force that was supposedly to have followed under the command of Matthias. On December 5 the party reached the fortress of Konigstein, at the basin of the Dimbovita, high up in the Carpathians, where Dracula had established his headquarters a few weeks before while awaiting Matthias's arrival at Brasov.

Dracula's contingent and their war wagons were slowly lowered down from the high fortress to the Valley of the Saxons below. To the north loomed the majestic, lofty, snow-covered Carpathian Mountains; from the castle walls there was a sheer thousand-foot drop straight down a wall of stone, rendering the castle wholly inaccessible from the valley below. It was only on the next day, when almost all of Dracula's soldiers had been lowered by ropes and pulleys to the lush valley below, that the Slovak mercenary seized them. Dracula, unable to resist, separated from his soldiers, was captured under secret orders from the Hungarian king. Far below in the valley, his men cried out in vain for their captured leader. There was nothing they could do to save him.

Jiskra brought Dracula back to Brasov, but once they were within the city walls the Slovak was replaced by a more trustworthy Hungarian bodyguard. The royal retinue and its important prisoner then left for Alba Iulia, where Dracula was imprisoned in the fortress. It was only there that some form of judicial inquiry into Dracula's conduct was set in motion to justify the arrest. Then they proceeded by way of

Medias, Turda, Cluj, and Oradea, and crossed the frontier of Hungary near Debrecen. They finally reached Buda around Christmas of 1462.

Despite all the precautions that had been taken by King Matthias, the arrest of Dracula only months after he had been universally greeted as a hero in the successful war against Mehmed created a good deal of consternation among the European powers — particularly in Venice and Rome, where large sums had been spent in the name of crusading. The arrest became a concern for all those powers that had a stake in the anti-Ottoman struggle. Matthias was badly in need of a legitimate explanation for his drastic action.

Some extraordinary documents provided the king with the most damning justification for Dracula's arrest. Three letters bearing Dracula's signature, written from a place called Rothel and dated November 7, 1462, appeared, only copies of which have survived. One of these letters was addressed to Mehmed himself, another to the renegade vizier Mahmud, and the third to Prince Stephen the Great of Moldavia. All three seem to reveal an unaccountable change of attitude and policy on Dracula's part. In the first, Dracula addressed Sultan Mehmed in abject and servile terms such as "emperor of emperors" and "lord and master." Dracula "humbly begged forgiveness for his crimes," and offered his services to the Turks to campaign alongside the sultan, to conquer Transylvania and Hungary, and "offered even to help in seizing the person of the Hungarian king." Because of the style of writing, the meek rhetoric of submission — incompatible with what we know of Dracula's character — clumsy wording, and poor Latin, most historians consider these letters to be forgeries. It was hardly conceivable that Dracula would have been foolish enough to write letters of treason while he was in Hungarian territory, far removed from the Ottoman forces to whom he appealed. The clinching argument is that, in spite of various attempts at locating Rothel, no satisfactory identification has thus far been made.

We believe that the Rothel letters were clever forgeries aimed at blackening Dracula's reputation and making him appear a traitor to the Christian cause. The authors of these forgeries could have been the same German Saxons who had previously placed the tales of horror at the disposal of the Hungarian king. It was also in this manner that the first anti-Dracula tracts found their way into the diplomatic concerns at Venice, Milan, Vienna, and Rome. The Rothel letters and other damaging evidence against Dracula were later included in the

Commentaries of Pope Pius II. It was one of the first demonstrations of the effective use of propaganda in diplomacy. Thus Matthias had a valid pretext for giving up the campaign and breaking his alliance with Dracula, enabling him to keep the papal subsidies for political ambitions of his own. King in name only, he had never been officially invested with the holy Hungarian crown of Saint Stephen, which would have legitimized his rule. The crown, which commanded a high price, was safely hidden by Emperor Frederick III, a rival candidate. Matthias signed a secret peace treaty with Sultan Mehmed and recognized Radu the Handsome as prince of Wallachia. Above all, he had valid reasons for condemning Dracula as "an enemy of humanity." Without the formality of a trial, which the Saxon leaders would have wished, Dracula was now to endure a lengthy period of imprisonment.

The final stage in Dracula's career must be divided into two phases: his lengthy period of Hungarian captivity, which extended over twelve years (1462–1474); and his liberation and third reign, which lasted barely two years, from 1474 to 1476.

The period of Hungarian imprisonment or house arrest is the least documented segment of Dracula's whole career. Nevertheless, it is possible to construct a fairly accurate picture of what Dracula's life was like during the years 1462–1474. His presence in Buda and his positive achievements in the Turkish campaign did not pass unnoticed in the reports of representatives from the court of the Papacy, Venice, Milan, Genoa, Ferrara, and other Italian republics. Nicholas of Modrussa, the papal legate who met Dracula at that time, wrote lengthy dispatches to Pope Pius II describing Dracula's physical appearance and even attempting to rehabilitate his reputation. However, the man who showed the greatest interest was the representative of the grand duke of Moscow, Fedor Kurytsin, who came with a large retinue to the Hungarian capital in 1482. He met King Matthias, the court historian, Antonio Bonfinius, countless officials, diplomats, Transylvanian merchants, and bankers. He was also introduced to Dracula's Hungarian widow and his three children Vlad, Mircea, and a third son whose name was not recorded. Kurytsin also made a point of reading the German narratives that were still circulating at court and showed an obsessive interest in this remarkable man who had died six years earlier.

Like a good journalist, he later traveled to Transylvania, saw Dracula's cousin Stephen in Moldavia, and consulted with the soldiers who defended the prince in his last hours. He finally committed his account to paper, calling it *The Story of the Romanian Prince Dracula.* Scholars have found no fewer than twenty copies of this document. Though deprecating Dracula's crimes and assailing him for his conversion to Catholicism, Kurytsin's report was a political pamphlet that had a deep and long impact on Russian political theory. Dracula served as a role model in the manner of Machiavelli's *The Prince,* a ruler who threatened torture and death to advance the principles of justice and morality. Ivan the Terrible was also acquainted with Kurytsin's Dracula pamphlet and may have modeled some of his crimes, including impalement of Russian *boyars,* on those of Dracula.

By way of contrast, the 1474–1476 period was richly documented. We have Dracula's personal correspondence and that of his chancellery officials, written in Latin, to the Hungarian king and to various Transylvanian officials. In addition, there is the fairly rich external diplomatic correspondence for these years from the usual vantage points, such as Venice, Buda, and Constantinople. Only the circumstances leading to Dracula's assassination and burial are obscure, but they can be pieced together by reference to local tradition in the vicinity of the island monastery of Snagov.

Controversy and lack of documentation center upon the actual site of Dracula's imprisonment. The Russian story seems to be precise enough on the location, stating that he was imprisoned for twelve years at Visegrad, the summer palace of King Matthias on the Danube above Buda. Both the palace and the fortress prison at Visegrad did, of course, exist in Dracula's time, and the ruins still survive. The palace is located twenty miles up the Danube, on the famous scenic bend, high up on a hill with a commanding view of the river. Solomon's tower, where political prisoners were held, lies at the foot of the hill, on the banks of the Danube, and has been completely restored. Within this large complex was centered the flowering culture of the Hungarian Renaissance. Matthias evidently liked to think of himself as a true patron of learning and the arts, like the Medicis, and used Visegrad to impress foreign visitors with the material splendors of his age, reflected in the countless artistic treasures housed in the main palace.

Careful investigation in the local library and archives did not, however, reveal the name of Dracula on the roster of eminent political detainees at Solomon's tower. This in itself does not necessarily invalidate the veracity of the Russian narrative. One way of accounting for the absence of official documentation is to understand that Dracula was less a political prisoner than a hostage of the Hungarian king. Matthias even produced Dracula to awe Turkish ambassadors who were still terrified of him.

Among the references to Dracula's lifestyle in prison is a short anecdote told in the Russian narrative claiming that even when he was in jail, he could not give up his bad habits. After catching mice and having birds bought at the market, he tortured and impaled them. Some critics consider this story apocryphal. Indeed a later one, concocted by his enemies and asserting that he "drank the blood of his animal victims," was just another way of blackening Dracula's reputation.

Dracula's remarriage while under arrest poses formidable problems. We do know from Dracula's own letter to the Hungarian king in June 1462 that a marriage contract with the Hungarian royal family was in the offing. The Russian story tells us that the lady in question was "a sister of the king," though more likely it was Ilona Szilagy, Matthias's cousin, the daughter of Michael Szilagy, Dracula's one-time ally.

In the Russian story the question of Dracula's remarriage is linked to Dracula's abandonment of Orthodoxy and his conversion to Roman Catholicism, which the Russian account severely condemns. Only after Dracula's formal renunciation of Orthodoxy did the king give him the hand of his kinswoman in marriage and decide to name him the official candidate to the Wallachian throne. One way of making sense of this complicated story is by realizing that Matthias must have given Dracula a kind of Hobson's choice: either convert to Catholicism in order to marry into the Hungarian royal family and be considered an acceptable candidate to the Wallachian throne, or die in jail. Some Orthodox apologists express righteous indignation about Dracula's decision to abandon "the true faith," but could he really afford to do otherwise? Surely, taking his ambition into account, the deal was tempting enough. To Dracula, the throne of Wallachia was certainly worth a Catholic mass.

What is more difficult to gauge is the precise date of Dracula's conversion and remarriage. The Russian narrative confirms that the episode occurred "after the death of the Wallachian prince previously recognized by Matthias." In that event, the date of Dracula's remarriage and conversion would coincide with the end of his imprisonment, after more than twelve years. It is difficult, however, to envision Dracula wooing a princess and fathering children behind prison bars. The Russian story comes to our aid in affixing a plausible date. The narrative adds that "Dracula had two sons of this marriage and that he only lived for a short time afterwards." Since Dracula died in December 1476, by deducting ten years one can trace Dracula's remarriage and liberation back to 1466; this allows for a period of only four years of imprisonment, from 1462 to 1466, at Visegrad. Such an interpretation, we think, seems reasonable enough.

Dracula was, insofar as we can judge from the oil portrait at Castle Ambras, a rather handsome man. The Saxon woodcuts seen on the cover of some of the German pamphlets are crude in technique and doubtless distorted and deformed his true features. A second oil painting, a miniature in Vienna, depicts the face of a powerful man. The large dark green eyes have great intensity; the nose is long; the mouth is large, ruddy, and thin-lipped. Dracula appears clean-shaven except for a long, well-waxed mustache; his hair was dark and slightly grayed; and his complexion a deadly, almost sickly white. He is wearing the Hungarian nobleman's tunic with an ermine cape and a diamond-studded Turkish-style fur-lined headdress.

The description left by Modrussa corresponds fairly well with the painting:

> He was not very tall, but very stocky and strong, with a cruel and terrible appearance, a long straight nose, distended nostrils, a thin and reddish face in which the large wide-open green eyes were enframed by bushy black eyebrows, which made them appear threatening. His face and chin were shaven but for a mustache. The swollen temples increased the bulk of his head. A bull's neck supported the head, from which black curly locks were falling to his wide-shouldered person.

When Dracula was released from jail following his remarriage, he was "given a house in Pest, opposite Buda," where he lived with his Hungarian wife and where likely the two sons referred to in the Russian narrative were born: Mihail (Mihnea), and one unnamed son who died in 1482. We know almost nothing of his life in Pest beyond an anecdote that obviously caused a good deal of mirth at the Hungarian court. The story describes an incident in which a thief broke into Dracula's house. A captain of the Hungarian guards pursued him, crossing the threshold of Dracula's house without a formal search warrant. Dracula stabbed the unfortunate official to death on the spot. When the municipal authorities went to complain about this strange behavior to the Hungarian king, Dracula justified himself in his inimitable and characteristic manner: "I did no evil; the captain is responsible for his own death. Anyone will perish thus who trespasses into the house of a great ruler such as myself. If this captain had come to me and had introduced himself, I too would have found the thief and either surrendered him up or spared him from death." When reports of the incident reached the Hungarian king, he is said to have smiled at the audacity of his new in-law. The authenticity of this entire episode is sufficiently guaranteed by what we know of Dracula's character.

From the point of view of the Hungarian king, Dracula's conversion and marriage into his family reestablished the status quo. No matter what his past sins, Dracula could resume the role of leader of a crusading Catholic army, and he was given the rank of captain. The king, now legally invested with the holy Hungarian crown of Saint Stephen, could justify the use of the remaining funds and prepare his protégé for an opportunity to reassert his authority in Wallachia and lead the crusade against the Turks.

From the moment of Dracula's remarriage and conversion, his active candidacy to the Wallachian throne was a *fait accompli*. Radu, always considered the instrument of the Turks, was defeated by Stephen the Great in the spring of 1473. His successor, Basarab III (Laiota), became prince and ruled until the beginning of November 1475. He was, however, totally unreliable from the Hungarian point of view. It was evidently in Hungarian interests to make official Dracula's investiture as leader of the crusade. He was by far the ablest and the most distinguished strategist available in the Christian camp. As such, the newly created captain moved from Hungary to Transylvania to receive the command of the frontier district of that province, a situation not very different from that which he enjoyed during the days of Hunyadi.

The first military action against the Turks in which Dracula participated took place in 1474 when he was placed in charge of a Hungarian contingent, collaborating with the forces of Vuk Brancovic, the

Serbian despot. The papal nuncio, the bishop of Erlau, reported the brutalities committed against the Turks, stating that Dracula was spearing the Turks with his own hand and impaling the separate pieces on stakes. Dracula was using his old devices to frighten his enemies.

Dracula's cousin, Stephen of Moldavia, had had his own conflicts with Matthias. He recalled the vow that he and Dracula had made years before: whichever of them was on the throne would help the other gain his legitimate succession. Dracula had certainly been faithful to that promise, helping Stephen obtain his rightful position in 1457. In the meantime, for reasons of political expediency, Stephen had broken his vow and sided with the Turks on their attack of Dracula's fortress at Chilia on the Danube, an act of treachery for which the Moldavian prince paid with a wound in the thigh from which he never recovered. Evidently Stephen now wished to make amends. From this moment to the end of Dracula's career the cousins remained loyal to each other. Forgetting previous differences and promising each other aid and support, a formal compact was signed in the summer of 1475 by Matthias, Dracula, and Stephen. This alliance was to be the cornerstone of the renewed anti-Ottoman crusade sponsored by the new pope Sixtus IV.

Dracula and his family spent the winter of 1475–76 in Sibiu. In January 1476, the Hungarian Diet formally gave its support to Dracula's candidacy to the Wallachian throne. By February, Dracula's hold on Transylvania was so firm that Basarab retaliated by writing to the citizens of Sibiu that he no longer considered himself their friend because Dracula was living among them.

By the summer, twenty years after his last restoration, serious plans were made to regain his throne, which was still officially occupied by Basarab (Laiota). Supreme command of the expedition was given by Matthias to Stephen Bathory, a member of the famous Hungarian noble family from Transylvania. In mid-November, as a few *boyars* stood by, the metropolitan at Curtea de Arges reinvested Dracula, still feared as a merciless criminal by both Saxons and *boyars*, as prince of Wallachia. He was intrigued against by supporters of rival claimants, hated by the Turks and Basarab, and all of them vowed to kill him. Thus, when Bathory's Hungarian force and Stephen's contingent left the country, Dracula was exposed to great danger for he had had little time to consolidate his strength. His failure to bring his wife and sons with him to Wallachia suggests that he was aware of the danger. It was an irony, and in a sense Stephen's expiation for his previous infidelity, that the only contingent Dracula could now completely trust was a small Moldavian guard two hundred strong.

The Slavic account of Dracula's assassination runs as follows:

> Dracula's army began killing Turks without mercy. Out of sheer joy, Dracula ascended a hill in order to see better his men massacring the Turks. Thus, detached from his army and his men, some took him for a Turk, and one of them struck him with a lance. But Dracula, seeing that he was being attacked by his own men, immediately killed five of his would-be assassins with his own sword; however, he was pierced by many lances and thus he died.

Like a lion at bay, Dracula must have defended himself formidably. All but ten of the two hundred Moldavians perished at the side of their new master.

Dracula's death undoubtedly took place in the course of battle, but likely the assassin was either Basarab, one of his *boyars,* or a Turkish soldier. According to both Bonfinius and a Turkish chronicler, Dracula was then beheaded. His head was sent to Constantinople, where it remained exposed as proof that the dreaded Impaler was really dead. It took about a month for this calamitous news to reach Western Europe; only in February 1477 did the envoy of the duke of Milan at Buda, Leonardo Botta, write to his master, Ludovico Sforza, that the Turks had reconquered Wallachia and that Dracula had been killed.

····CHAPTER 9····

SNAGOV:
THE MYSTERY OF THE
EMPTY GRAVE

STRANGE IS THE FATE of the Dracula epic. The legend was born in Transylvania; it spread westward to the
German lands and eastward to Russia. The heroic moments
took place on the Danube; the dramatic ones at the castle and
in Hungary. According to tradition, Dracula's final resting place
was the isolated island monastery of Snagov, which perhaps more than
any other structure connected with Dracula's name, religious or otherwise, bears the imprint of his tortured personality. A visit today reveals motor launches, sailboats, beaches, restaurants, lovely villas, and
former president Ceausescu's summer palace (where Michael Jackson
resided in the fall of 1992). It requires some effort of the imagination
to think back to that bloody era when Dracula once stalked this vicinity. Once you enter the chapel with its faded Byzantine frescoes of heroes and saints and listen to the gory stories of one of the local
historians, this is quite another matter. What makes the bloodstained
history of Snagov unique is that, unlike castles which are essentially
edifices built for war, Snagov was a monastery, admittedly a fortified
monastery, but nevertheless a place of worship. According to the old
Romanian chronicles, the monastery of Snagov was closely associated
with Dracula even though his grandfather, Prince Mircea, built it originally.

There exists a Snagov saga which is vivid and still alive among the
peasants of the villages surrounding the lake. In the imagination of a
few village elders, the awesome figure of the Impaler still dominates
the little church and preoccupies their superstitious minds. Dracula
has succeeded in stamping his personality profoundly upon the bricks

and stones of the only surviving chapel which he allegedly built and in which, according to tradition, he lies buried.

As archaeological excavations on the island and popular folklore have confirmed, the monastery of Snagov originally covered an area much larger than that presently occupied by the church one can see today. The original monastic complex occupied the full length of the island. It was fortified by the original walls extending to the edge of the lake. In times of peril, both princes and *boyars* stored their treasures at Snagov. In addition to three original chapels (the largest of which is the Chapel of the Annunciation, built by Vladislav II in 1453), the complex was composed of a princely residence, cloisters for the monks, houses for the *boyars*, stables for their mounts, a prison, a mint, and a printing press. Snagov, in fact, like many medieval fortresses, was a little town all its own, naturally limited by the size of the island. Today nothing is left of this vast structure except the chapel.

The original monastery is a much older ecclesiastical building that can be traced back to the fourteenth century. Snagov was certainly not the first ecclesiastical edifice in Romania founded by one prince and completed by another; as often happens in the erection of larger buildings, the name that history associates with it is less that of the original founder than that of the one who completed it.

Much of the popular folklore in the Snagov area is clearly fictitious. One popular ballad relates that Dracula had a vision of God telling him to establish a place of prayer near the scene of his father's assassination at Balteni. Other stories are more specific and may contain an element of truth. One ballad relates that Dracula's contribution was the completion of another church on the island monastery just to compete with his enemy Vladislav II, who had constructed the Chapel of the Annunciation. It is far more likely that Dracula converted Snagov from a poorly defended monastery into an island fortress. With his morbid desire for a refuge, he could find no better natural fortification than the island, surrounded by the dense Vlasie forest and commanding views on all sides. Even in winter, when the lake is frozen, a cannon shot from the island could break up the ice and thus drown an incoming enemy. It was no mere accident that the fortress-monastery fell into the hands of Radu's partisans during the Turkish campaign of 1462. It was known that the monastery was used at the time by Dracula and his *boyars* to hide treasure in the vault of the

Above and opposite: Contemporary views of Snagov.

church. According to later peasant stories, after Dracula's death the monks, fearful for their lives, threw the gold into the lake to avoid tempting the Turks. Some narratives relate that the treasure was hidden in barrels by Dracula's henchmen. The barrels were then sent to the bottom of the reed-covered lake, one of the deepest in Romania. Dracula, of course, impaled those responsible for this service, fearing that his soldiers might reveal the secret location which is still being sought to this day. It is likely that Radu and his *boyar* partisans also used the monastery to store their wealth.

Popular narratives also make mention of other crimes Dracula perpetrated on the island. Apparently his intention had been to transform the monastery into a prison and establish a torture chamber for political foes. In a tiny cell the prince would invite his intended victims to kneel and pray to a small icon of the Blessed Virgin. While the prisoners were praying, Dracula released a secret trap door, sending them deep into a ditch below, where a number of pales stood erect waiting. The discovery of several decapitated skeletons lends further credence to the theory that the monastery was used as a place of punishment.

Other members of Dracula's immediate family were also connected with Snagov. Perhaps simply for reasons of filial piety, Dracula's son, Mihnea, repaired the monastery after the extensive damage done to it by the Turks during the campaign of 1462 and endowed it with additional land. Vlad the Monk, Dracula's half brother and political enemy, was at one time abbot of the monastery. He took the religious name of Pahomie. Vlad the Monk's second wife, Maria, following the example of her mother-in-law, also took the veil and the same religious name — Eupraxia. She lived at Snagov for several years, together with her sons. One of these, Vlad V, or Vladut, spent his early years at the monastery before becoming prince in 1510. His son, yet another Vlad, known to history as Vlad VII the Drowned, briefly ruled between 1530 and 1532 and may well have died swimming in the lake.

A great deal of violence has occurred at Snagov since Dracula's time. A small portion of the tragedy of Snagov is enshrined in its walls and on the cold stone floor of the small church. One can still read the terse inscriptions in the original Slavonic giving the names of the victims each successive century has added to the unwritten list compiled by the Draculas. Death came to these *boyars* in different ways and for various reasons, but chiefly their deaths were politically motivated.

In spite of the monks' ongoing prayers, the monastery was not spared punishment. It was burned and partially destroyed by the Turks shortly after Prince Radu's inauguration in 1462. In addition to destruction wrought by man, natural disaster added to the tragedy of Snagov. Shortly after Dracula's death a violent storm erupted with winds of hurricane velocity. Of the two churches then standing, the Chapel of the Annunciation was torn, steeple and all, from its foundations and blown into the lake. Local tradition has it that the beautifully sculptured oak door was all that survived. It floated on the waters of the lake and was later blown to the opposite bank, where it was found by some nuns. They used this providential gift to replace a much less decorative door at their convent. The Snagov door has since been deposited at the Bucharest Art Museum where it is displayed as an extraordinarily ornate example of fifteenth-century woodcarving. As for the submerged tower, peasants say to this day that whenever the lake is unduly agitated one can hear the muffled metallic sound of the bell buried deep underwater.

The carved door from the ancient church at the Snagov monastery. When a violent storm ripped apart the church, this door was salvaged for use at a convent.

At the close of the seventeenth century, the monastery had a fine reputation as a place of learning. It contained one of Romania's first printing presses, the result of the labor of one of the erudite monks of the period, Antim Ivireanu, who printed Romanian and Arabic versions of the Testaments. Because of Antim's excellence as a teacher, two famous travelers came to the island; Paul of Alep and his father, Patriarch Macarie of Antioch. Writing in Arabic, these men compiled the first reliable travelogue of Snagov, which mentions the two churches still in existence and a bridge connecting the monastery to the mainland. From their account one might almost believe that Snagov had finally become exempt from tragedy and was launched to a brilliant new cultural phase. This presumed change of fortune, however, was never to occur. Antim, for reasons still obscure, was poisoned and died in exile from Snagov. His books were dispersed, and the main printing press taken to Antioch.

The period of Greek rule in the eighteenth century gave Snagov some respite. It was then placed under the custody of the Greek patriarchates, which at that time were taking over many of the country's ancient ecclesiastical foundations, and the taxes collected by the monks were sent to Constantinople or Antioch, making the monks unpopular with the natives. This may explain why the peasants burned the wooden bridge linking Snagov to the mainland, hindering communications and travel to and from the monastery for a time until the bridge was eventually rebuilt.

The worst indignity to the monastery occurred in the mid-nineteenth century when General Paul Kiselev, the Russian-born governor-general of Wallachia, ordered the conversion of Snagov into a state prison. In that capacity, Snagov experienced at least one tragedy, when chained criminals were crossing to the island and the flimsy pontoon bridge broke under their weight. Fifty-nine helplessly weighted prisoners were sent to the bottom of the lake. A cross on the lake's edge, at the precise spot where the bridge reached the mainland, recalls the tragic occasion.

At the end of its prison history, which lasted barely twenty years, Snagov, which had always housed a few monks, was virtually abandoned. By 1867 it was formally closed. A few monks stayed on; no abbot was appointed. Sunday masses were occasionally said by priests from neighboring villages. During this period this one-time sanctuary was often violated by pillagers. Nothing was left untouched — people took the bricks and stones of the remaining outside walls to build their houses, stole all the wood they could find, and tore doors down from their hinges. Roofing material disappeared; invaluable stained glass windows were broken. Inside, the church suffered equally: pews, pulpits, icons, crosses, chalices, Bibles, holy vases, and other religious valuables and manuscripts were all stolen. Tombs were violated, inscriptions torn off, and the buried remains of *boyars* and princes exhumed and combed for gold and weapons.

By 1890 the administrator of state domains described the ancient monastic complex as nothing but an empty shell. Seven years later, the year Stoker published *Dracula* in London, concerned historians, lovers of old monuments, and archaeologists began the difficult task of saving what was left of the neglected Snagov chapel. Because of the government's apathy, the battle to save Snagov was as difficult a struggle as any the monastery had ever confronted. The necessary sums were finally voted and the restoration of the church began at the turn of the century, a restoration which was done with serious attention to historical and architectural accuracy. The Commission on Historic Monuments, guided by specialists in fifteenth-century ecclesiastical architecture, reconstructed the monastery exactly the way it was sup-

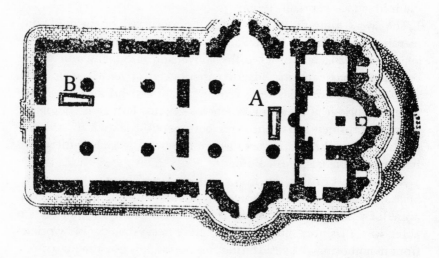

Floor plan of existing church at Snagov. A: altar tomb. B: grave on the north side.

posed to have been in Dracula's time. Like any puzzle long abandoned, there are pieces missing. It is conceivable that the government may someday decide to restore the monastery and rebuild the second chapel as it was in the days of Vladislav II.

In 1940 there was a massive earthquake in Bucharest which sent many historic buildings toppling to the ground. The tremor tore the nave of the chapel at Snagov in two. Further damage was done by the tremor of 1976, and by minor earthquakes since.

Today an eerie serenity seems to surround the church where Dracula is supposed to be interred. Only an abbot, a nun, and a peasant woman look after it. The abbot is a learned man who knows the history of the fifteenth century and Dracula's connection with the monastery. During one of our visits we met another monk who resided on the island, did not wear the religious garb, and spent much time in prayer. When questioned by us, he confessed that he had committed a crime and been assigned by the patriarch to the island monastery for expiation of his sins. Here old traditions die slowly.

Snagov is a place of prayer and terror, famous names and infamous acts. Even if one does not believe that Dracula lies buried here, the very atmosphere of this antique site forms an ideal setting for the last phase of the search for the historical Dracula. Where is the precise location of Dracula's tomb within the monastery? Does it in fact lie there as popular tradition has it?

In 1931 genealogist George Florescu and archaeologist Dinu Rosetti were assigned by Romania's Commission on Historic Monuments to dig around the monastery and elsewhere on the island. Their findings, published in a fascinating monograph, *Diggings Around Snagov,* included various artifacts showing that the island was the site of an ancient settlement. A great number of skulls and skeletons were dug up, helping to confirm popular traditions about the crimes committed at Snagov from the fifteenth century onward. Numerous gold and silver coins of all kinds were also excavated, indicating the use of Snagov as a treasury and mint by *boyars* and princes alike.

One particular site investigated by the Florescu-Rosetti team was the stone beneath the altar, which, according to tradition, marked the place where Dracula lay buried. Popular legend had various explanations as to why this was the location of his grave. The monks who interred Dracula's headless body placed it close to the altar — the

Above: Stone over the tomb traditionally assigned to Dracula, near the altar of the existing church at Snagov.

Left: This photo dates from the 1930s, the time of the excavations by Florescu and Rosetti. No casket was found, only a large hole containing the bones of various animals.

obvious location for a prince — and marked it with an inscription and a painted fresco, so that his troubled soul could have the advantage of the prayers of the celebrants. However, when the stone was finally removed, to the consternation of the archaeologists, neither a casket nor a headless skeleton was found; there was instead a deep, empty hole which held the bones of oxen and other animals.

Further exploration inside the entrance on the northern side of the church revealed an unmarked stone of exactly the same size as the altar tombstone. It was found to contain a casket still partially covered by a purple shroud embroidered with gold. Both coffin and covering had mostly rotted away. Within lay a skeleton. It was covered in fragments of a faded purple garment of silk brocade, very similar to the Hungarian-style shirt worn by Dracula in the Ambras portrait. The sleeves, originally crimson, were clearly discernible, with large round silver buttons; one sleeve had a small ring sewn on it. Not far away were the remains of a crown worked in cloisonné, with terra cotta–colored claws, each holding a turquoise gem.

The ring on the sleeve was a symbol of the long-dead customs of courtly love in Western Europe, when mounted knights in armor engaged in jousts attempting to unhorse their opponents. The winner was awarded a trophy or a symbol from an admiring lady who witnessed his triumph. But whose ring was it? Dracula's, his Hungarian wife's, or some unknown lady's? Whoever bestowed this tender token of courtly love, it is a strange item to find in the grave of such a prince. Professor Rosetti, in more recent research, believes that the ring resembled others found in the Nuremberg area, and was part of a clasp attached to the symbol of the Order of the Dragon, in which Dracul had been invested in 1431. Unfortunately, all of the grave's contents have mysteriously disappeared from the History Museum of Bucharest where they had been stored. This curious disappearance has given rise to the reports of many Dracula grave finds, including one in America, all of them unsubstantiated so far.

The presence of animal bones in the grave near the altar and the loss of all tangible evidence, including a casket, continues to mystify historians, leading many to suspect a hoax. The debate continues today.

As in the case of the mysterious disappearance of the body of Alexander I of Russia, dozens of opinions have been voiced, but not much scientific progress has been made. We are inclined to accept the

idea that the actual grave was the one near the altar, the one sanc-
tioned by local folklore — always a useful guide in resolving enigmas
connected with Dracula. Village traditions about tombstones have led
to the identification of historic personalities in many other instances.
For example, in the old church of Curtea de Arges, it was long ob-
served that the faithful persisted in standing at a certain place to the
right of the altar for no other reason than that it was the place where
their elders worshipped and lit their candles. An enterprising young
archaeologist excavated that particular spot and discovered the unmarked tomb of one of Wallachia's early princes. At Snagov for many

*Three views of the 1931 excavations at
Snagov showing graves other than
Dracula's.*

years the peasants similarly stood close to the altar. We also believe that Dracula's remains may have been reinterred near the entrance of the church, presumably in the seventeenth century by Greek monks with little respect for the hero-prince. They deliberately, contemptuously, placed what the Greeks considered "his unworthy remains" at the entrance of the chapel for the faithful to trample upon. It was likely at this time that all inscriptions and Dracula's portrait were removed from the original gravestone. As an additional gesture of contempt, animal bones were thrown into the empty grave, thereby compounding a hoax with a sacrilege. "Dracula's remains," states an expert on the problem, Reverend Ion Dumitriu, "lie at the rear of the chapel of Snagov . . . without trace of either an inscription or memento, under a cold stone that gets yearly trampled by the weight of the tourists. All this to wipe away forever the memory of that prince." His theory jibes with the dates of certain repairs made to the altar area during the late 1700s.

Even had the tomb not been desecrated in this particular way, one might still reasonably assume that since the original site of the tomb was near the altar, the tombstone being larger and more ambitious than others (presumably with an inscription and a portrait), it was obvious prey for grave robbers during the mid-nineteenth century, following the closing of Snagov as a state prison. In that case, Dracula's actual remains, casket and all, could simply have disappeared.

In any event, historical common sense suggests that Dracula, who was after all a prince in spite of his misdeeds and was remembered fondly for his heroism, would be given an honored burial place, even though with an enemy prince in power it was dangerous for the monks who interred him to honor him in that manner.

On these grounds we accept the veracity of the traditional location of Dracula's grave, even though controversy lingers on. However, there is really no need to strain after explanations concerning the transfer of Dracula's remains or, if the second grave is not Dracula's, to account for the disappearance of his body. They seem almost to suggest themselves. Given Dracula's insidious reputation, the horror in which his name was held by his political enemies, and the crimes committed on the island at various times, it is unreasonable to expect that his tomb would have survived intact. All the well-considered explanations about the disappearance of Dracula's remains and his possible reburial have only added to the mystery that continues pending new archaeological investigation.

Some Romanians still say that Dracula will rise again in time of great need to save the Romanian people. Perhaps that is why Ceausescu, in desperation following his ouster in December 1989, directed his helicopter first to Snagov. He certainly needed Dracula's help — he may even have tried to contact the spirit of the great undead.

Spurred on by the German horror stories, the Dracula riddle assumed a far more universal dimension in the West and still lives on in the idea that Dracula is undead, like the vampire. So, in our further search for Dracula we now turn to the vampire link, in part manufactured by Western literature. However, vampire belief unassociated with Dracula also formed part of the body of world folklore, including the folktales of Eastern Europe and particularly Transylvania, the home of many ethnic groups. It is this belief that attracted and fascinated Bram Stoker, who studied it scientifically, focusing his attention on a number of travelogues that noted the superstitions of Transylvanians.

···· CHAPTER 10 ····

VAMPIRISM:
OLD WORLD FOLKLORE

THE NOTION BEHIND VAMPIRISM traces far back in time — to man the hunter, who discovered that when blood flowed out of a wounded beast or a fellow human, life, too, drained away. Blood was the source of vitality. Thus men smeared themselves with blood and sometimes drank it. The idea of drinking blood to renew vitality thereupon entered history. To the vampire, indeed, "The blood is the life," as Dracula, quoting from Deuteronomy 12:33, tells us in Stoker's novel, though the actual biblical passage is a warning *against* drinking human blood.

Vampire belief is universal; it has been documented in ancient Babylon, Egypt, Rome, Greece, and China. Vampire accounts exist in completely separate civilizations, where any direct borrowing would not have been possible. The vampire is known by various names — *vrykolakes, brykilakas, barbarlakos, borborlakos,* or *bourdoulakos* in modern Greek; *katakhanoso* or *baital* in the ancient Sanskrit; *upiry* in Russian; *upiory* in Polish; *blutsäuger* in German, etc. Early Chinese were afraid of the *giang shi,* a demon who drinks blood. In China, it was reported that vampires existed there in 600 B.C. Depictions of vampires are found on ancient Babylonian and Assyrian pottery going back thousands of years before Christ. The belief flourished in the New World as in the Old. Ancient Peruvians believed in a class of devil worshippers called *canchus* or *pumapmicuc,* who sucked blood from the sleeping young in order to partake of their life. Aztecs sacrificed the hearts of prisoners to the sun in the belief that their blood fed the sun's continuing energy.

In ancient Greece there were *empusa* or *lamia* akin to the vampire

— horrible winged demon-women who lured handsome youths to their death in order to drink their blood and eat their flesh. Lamia was once the beloved of Zeus who was driven insane by Zeus's jealous wife, Hera. Lamia killed her own children and goes about at night killing human children for revenge.

The first woman on earth was Lilith, or Lilitu, according to ancient Semitic belief. In the Talmud, the book of Jewish laws, customs, and tradition, Adam had a wife before Eve named Lilith. But she was disobedient to Adam and challenged his authority. In a state of anger she left Adam, though three angels, Sanvi, Sansanvi, and Semangelaf, tried to convince her to stay. Because of her disobedience, her children were killed and she was transformed into a night-roaming monster. Eve then came into the picture and bore Adam children. Extremely jealous, Lilith went about taking her revenge by killing the sons and daughters of Adam and Eve. Since humans are all descended from Adam and Eve, everyone must defend himself against Lilith's attacks. The medieval Jews had special amulets to guard against the attacks of Lilith, one made for male children and another for female. Traditionally, these depicted the three angels who attempted to persuade Lilith not to leave Adam.

Early in the Christian era the learned Bhavabhūti wrote classic Indian tales, including twenty-five stories of a vampire who animates dead bodies and is seen hanging upside down from a tree like a bat. The female Hindu god Shiva shares many similarities with the vampire, such as being creator and destroyer at the same time. Behind the vampire is the Oriental concept of eternal return, in which nothing is ever really destroyed but comes back in endless recreations and reincarnations. The vampire takes blood from the living, but should she mix her blood with that of her victim, that person in turn becomes an undead, having survived mortal death.

Proof that vampires were considered to be essentially female, without male organs, comes from Saint Augustine and the early church fathers. For example, Augustine writes that demons have "bodily immortality and passions like human beings" but cannot produce semen. Instead they gather semen from the bodies of real men and inject it into sleeping women to cause pregnancy. Saint Clement testifies that the demons have human passions but "no organs, so they turn to humans to make use of their organs. Once in control of suitable organs, they can get whatever they want."

During the eighteenth century, a vampire of renown named Peter Poglojowitz emerged from a small village in Hungary. Following his death in 1725 his body was disinterred. They found fresh blood flowing from his mouth and his body appeared to be without any signs of *rigor mortis* or decay. So the local peasants thought he was a vampire and burned his body.

In 1732 the case of the Serbian vampire Arnold Paole from Medvegia stimulated eighteenth-century scientific research into vampires. At the height of rationalism in 1751 a Dominican scholar, Augustin Calmet, wrote a treatise about vampires in Hungary and Moravia.

Vampire beliefs are particularly strong today throughout southeastern Europe, especially among the modern Greeks. The southerly Cyclades island of Santorini is infamous for its vampires. Many authors noted this fact as early as the seventeenth century. In fact, if a suspected vampire were uncovered on mainland Greece, the body was customarily shipped off to Santorini because the people there had a long history and vast experience in dealing with vampires. An old Greek saying is "bringing vampires to Santorini" in the sense of "like bringing coals to Newcastle," a redundant act.

Orthodox practices of excommunication bolstered belief in the vampire. When Orthodox Christian priests or bishops issue an order of excommunication, they add the curse "and the earth will not receive your body!" This signifies that the body of the excommunicated person will remain "uncorrupt and entire." The soul will not rest in peace. In this case a nondecaying body is the sign of evil. Those Orthodox Christians who have converted to Roman Catholicism or Islam are doomed to wander the earth and not enter Heaven. It is worth recalling in this context that the historical Dracula, having converted to Roman Catholicism toward the end of his life, "forsook the light of orthodoxy" and "accepted the darkness" of heresy and was hence a candidate to become an undead, a vampire.

One theory about the prevalence of vampire belief in Transylvania suggests that since the Tibetan Mongols had a belief in both the vampire and the bat god, they may have come in contact with those Asians who eventually migrated in large numbers to Transylvania. Both the Hungarians (Magyars) and the Szekelys of Transylvania moved initially from Asia into Europe. In this context it is revealing to note that Stoker has Dracula claim Szekelys descent. Another theory concerning the reasons for the apparent richness of vampire belief in Transylvania comes from the fact that so many different ethnic groups inhabit the area, leading to an elaborate mix of folklore from the Germans, Hungarians, Gypsies, and Romanians.

Romanians in particular have many names for a variety of vampires. For example, the most common term, *strigoi* (or the feminine form, *strigoaica*), is an evil creature who sleeps during the daylight hours, flies at night, can change into animal form such as a wolf, dog, or bird, and sucks the blood from sleeping children. The female is more dangerous than the male. She can also spoil marriages and harvests, stop cows from giving milk, and even cause fatal disease and death. The Romanian *pricolici* is an undead who can appear in human, dog, or wolf forms. Among Romanians vampires are always evil, their journey to the other world has been interrupted, and they are doomed to prey upon the living for a time.

In Transylvania, garlic is the powerful weapon to deter vampires. Windows and doors are anointed with garlic to keep them away. In addition, farm animals, especially sheep, are rubbed with garlic for vampires might just as well attack animals for their blood as humans.

Peasants consider garlic to be a medicinal plant. They eat it to ward off the common cold and various diseases. Anything that wards off disease is considered to be good or "white" magic, hence garlic can ward off devils, werewolves, and vampires.

A vampire's grave can sometimes be detected by holes around the gravesite big enough for a snake to pass through. To prevent the vampire from emerging from the grave, one must fill these holes with water. The thorns of wild roses are sure to keep vampires at bay. Poppy seeds are strewn on the path from the cemetery to the town because vampires are compulsive counters and must pick up all the thorns. This practice can prevent the vampire from reaching the village before dawn, at which time he must return to his coffin.

The ultimate way to destroy a vampire is to drive a stake through the heart or the navel during the daylight hours when the vampire must rest in his coffin. The stake should be made of wood from an ash or an aspen tree. In some areas of Transylvania iron bars — preferably heated red-hot — are used. As an added safeguard, the vampire's body is burned. Sometimes a fir tree is plunged into the body of the vampire in order to keep it in the grave. A derivation of this is the fir tree ornament that one finds over graves in Romania today.

Most Romanians believe that life after death will be much like life on earth. As there is not much faith in a purely spiritual world, it seems reasonable that after death an undead will walk the earth in much the same way as a living person. The walking dead are not always vampires, however. In fact, the Romanian term for undead, *moroi*, is more prevalent than the term for vampire or blood-drinker, *strigoi*. But both the undead and the vampire are killed in the same way. *Strigoi* are literally demon birds of the night. They fly only after sunset, and they eat human flesh and drink blood.

Belief in vampires is still prevalent in Dracula country particularly among the older generation. In 1969, at the foot of Castle Dracula, in the small village of Capatineni, lived a Gypsy named Tinka. She was the *lautar,* or village singer, and was often called upon to sing old stories at weddings, balls, and funerals.

Tinka told us two stories about the undead. One of them concerned her father. When he died thirty years before, he was duly laid out, but the next day the villagers discovered that the old man's face was still ruddy, and his body still flexible, not rigid. The people knew that he was an undead, and a stake was driven through his heart.

The other story concerned an old woman in the village. After her death many of her close relatives died. So did various animals around her home. The people realized that she was an undead and they exhumed her coffin. When the lid was removed, they found that her eyes were open and that she had rolled over. They also noticed that the corpse had a ruddy complexion. The villagers burned her body.

Belief in the walking dead and the blood-sucking vampire may never entirely disappear. It was only in the past century — 1823, to be exact — that England outlawed the practice of driving stakes through the hearts of suicides. Today, it is in Transylvania that the vampire legends have their strongest hold. Examining the following superstitions, it is chilling to imagine their potency six hundred years ago.

In Eastern Europe vampires are said to have two hearts or two souls; since one heart or one soul never dies, the vampire remains undead.

Who can become a vampire? In Transylvania, criminals, bastards, witches, magicians, excommunicated people, those born with teeth or a caul, and unbaptized children can all become vampires. The seventh son of a seventh son is doomed to become a vampire.

How can one detect a vampire? Any person who does not eat garlic or who expresses a distinct aversion to garlic is suspect.

Vampires sometimes strike people dumb. They can steal one's beauty or strength, or milk from nursing mothers.

In Romania, peasants believe that the vampires and other specters meet on Saint Andrew's Eve at a place where the cuckoo does not sing and the dog does not bark.

Vampires are frightened by light, so one must build a good fire to ward them off, and torches must be lit and placed outside the houses.

Even if you lock yourself up in your home, you are not safe from the vampire, since he can enter through chimneys and keyholes. Therefore, one must rub the chimney and the keyholes with garlic, and the windows and doors as well. The farm animals must also be rubbed with garlic to protect them.

Crosses made from the thorns of wild roses are effective in keeping the vampire away.

Take a large black dog and paint an extra set of eyes on its forehead with white paint — this repulses vampires.

According to Orthodox Christian belief, the soul does not leave the body to enter the next world until forty days after the body is laid in the grave. Hence the celebrations in Orthodox cemeteries forty days after the burial.

Bodies were once disinterred between three and seven years after burial; if decomposition was not complete, a stake was driven through the heart.

If a cat or other evil animal jumps or flies over a body before it is buried, or if the shadow of a man falls upon the corpse, the deceased may become a vampire.

If the dead body is reflected in a mirror, the reflection helps the spirit to leave the body and become a vampire.

In Hungarian folklore one of the most common ways of identifying a vampire was to choose a child young enough to be a virgin and seat the child on a horse of a solid color that was also a virgin and had never stumbled. The horse was led through the cemetery and over all the graves. If it refused to pass over a grave, a vampire must lie there.

Usually the tomb of a vampire has one or more holes roughly the size through which a serpent can pass.

How to kill a vampire? The stake, made from a wild rosebush, ash or aspen wood, or of heated iron, must be driven through the vampire's body and into the earth in order to hold him securely in his grave. The vampire's body should then be burned, or reburied at the crossroads.

If a vampire is not found and rendered harmless, it first kills all members of its immediate family, then starts on the other inhabitants of the village and the animals.

The vampire cannot stray too far from his grave since he must return to it at sunrise.

If not detected, the vampire climbs up into the belfry of the church and calls out the names of the villagers, who instantly die. Or, in some areas, the vampire rings the death-knell and all who hear it die on the spot.

If the vampire goes undetected for seven years, he can travel to another country or to a place where another language is spoken and become a human again. He or she can marry and have children, but they all become vampires when they die.

Romanians slit the soles of the feet or tie together the legs or knees of suspected vampires to try to keep them from walking. Some bury bodies with sickles around their necks, so that in trying to rise the vampire will cut his own head off.

Whitethorn was sure to keep vampires away since it was believed that Christ's crown of thorns was made from whitethorn. Vampires would become entrapped in the thorns and become disoriented.

Silver, thought to be a pure alloy, was believed to thwart vampires as well as werewolves. So crosses or icons were often made of silver.

Did the peasants of the fifteenth century consider Vlad Tepes a vampire? When questioned about current beliefs, peasants living in the region around Castle Dracula revealed that there is no longer a connection between Vlad Tepes and the vampire in their folklore. The peasants are not aware of Stoker's *Dracula*. The elderly do believe passionately, however, in vampires and the undead.

As our culture has become more urban, a bias against peasant superstition has evolved. This is reflected in our use of the word "urbane" to describe something positive, broadminded, and rational, and the word "provincial" to designate something unsophisticated, narrow-minded, and ignorant. One tends to regard peasant culture as primitive and unscientific. Even Karl Marx conceded that capitalism had at least saved a majority of the population from "the idiocy of rural life."

Far from being incessantly preoccupied with doubt and fear, h w-ever, peasants spend most of the day in very practical pursuits necessary for their subsistence.

Some evolutionists assume that primitive people have no capacity to comprehend natural explanations, that since primitive man lives at a low technological level he must have a thought process opposite to that of modern man. The assumption is that primitive, rural man is "prelogical," like an innocent or a child.

But not all of modern Western man's beliefs are logical and scientific. Attitudes toward death and life have always been complex for all men, encompassing hate and love, attraction and repulsion, hope and fear. Belief in vampires is a poetic, imaginative way of looking at death and at life beyond death.

Primitive beliefs are not any stranger than modern scientific beliefs. Nightly on our TV sets there is some variation of the man in the white coat who stands amid Bunsen burners and test tubes and declares, "Scientific tests have proved that in nine out of ten cases . . ." whereupon everyone in the audience genuflects to the new god Science. If it is scientific then it must be true, and only the scientifically proven fact can be true. Is this any more absurd than primitive peasant be-

Romanian peasant who lived near Castle Dracula and recounted tales about Vlad the Impaler. Photo taken by Raymond McNally in the autumn of 1969 while on an expedition seeking Dracula folklore in the castle area.

liefs? The vampire belongs to that common store of images which psychologists call symbols. Many people assume a symbol refers to an unreal event, but in fact most symbols are indications of actual occurrences, having universal application. Over time the historical connection is often forgotten and great effort must be made to retrieve its original meaning. As Jung put it, "It [symbol] implies something vague, unknown, hidden in us."

The vampire possesses powers which are similar to those belonging to certain twentieth-century comic book characters. During the day he is helpless and vulnerable like Clark Kent or Bruce Wayne. But just as the mild-mannered Clark Kent becomes Superman when called upon, and the effete Bruce Wayne becomes Batman when needed, so the vampire acquires great powers at night. The British author Clive Leatherdale has characterized Batman as "the count cleansed of his evil and endowed with a social consciousness."

Dracula the vampire-count is a kind of father figure of great potency. In many religions the opposite of God the Father, with his flowing white beard, is Satan, also a father figure, often portrayed with huge, dark, batlike wings.

The connection between Dracula, the devil, the bat, and the vampire becomes clear when one understands that in Romanian folklore the devil can change himself into an animal or a black bird. When he takes wing, he can fly like a bird or a bat. Satan seeks also to be nocturnal. During the day he remains in the quiet of Hell, like the bat in its refuge; when day is done, the night is his empire, just as it is the bat's.

The bat is the only mammal that fulfills one of man's oldest aspirations: it can fly, defying gravity not unlike Superman. Contrary to popular belief, the bat is not a flying rat. The wings of this small animal are actually elongated, webbed hands. The head of the bat is erect like a man's head. And, like man, the bat is one of the most versatile creatures in the world.

Why is the vampire image linked to that of the vampire bat in particular? Vampire bats do not exist anywhere in Europe, yet it is there that belief in the vampire as a night-flying creature that sucks the blood of the living has flourished.

When Cortés came to the New World, he found blood-sucking bats in Mexico. Remembering the mythical vampire, he called them vampire bats. The name stuck. So a word that signified a mythical creature in the Old World became attached to a species of bats particular to the New World. Vampire bats exist only in Central and South America.

The vampire bat, the *Desmodus rotundus,* is marvelously agile. It can fly, walk, dodge swiftly, and turn somersaults, all with swiftness and efficiency. Generally it attacks cattle rather than men. The victim is not awakened during the attack. The vampire bat walks very softly over the victim and, after licking a spot on the flesh, neatly inserts its incisor or canine teeth. As the blood surfaces, the bat licks it up. That the vampire bat subsists on blood alone is a scientific fact.

The once-human vampire's existence is a frightening tragedy, *sans* goodness or hope, repose or satisfaction. In order to survive, he must drink the blood of the living. The possibility of real death is closed to him. Thus he continues, wanting to live, wanting to die; not truly alive and not really dead. The folklore about him is not based on science, yet it is essentially true. As all vampire legends and customs attest, not only does man fear death, man fears some things even more than death. Stoker's notes, now housed at the Rosenbach Foundation in Philadelphia, indicate that he read *The Book of Werewolves* (1865), which had a section on the infamous "Blood Countess," Elizabeth Bathory, written by the Protestant minister and scholar Reverend Sabine Baring-Gould (best remembered for penning the words to the inspiring hymn "Onward, Christian Soldiers"). In fact, Stoker's description of Dracula's hands being squat with hair growing on the palms comes directly from Baring-Gould's book.

The Book of Werewolves recorded the basic legend of a Hungarian countess who killed her young female servants in order to bathe in their blood because she thought that such treatments kept her skin looking young and healthy. In all, she butchered some 650 girls for this purpose. Baring-Gould simply repeated the story popularized by the German scholar Michael Wagner during the late eighteenth century. Our recent investigation revealed hitherto unknown documentation from a court of inquiry which took place before Elizabeth Bathory's court trial in 1611. Testimony by hundreds of witnesses demonstrated that her supposed blood use for cosmetic purpose was a legend, but that she did indeed kill more than 650 girls (she recorded each separate atrocity in her diary). The countess evidently liked to bite and tear the flesh of her young servants. One of her nicknames was "the tiger of Cachtice." Cachtice, the town where her main castle was, once part of northwestern Hungary, is now located in Slovakia, north of Bratislava. Elizabeth Bathory was born in 1560 into one of the most powerful and illustrious Hungarian families of the time.

She tortured and murdered not only at Castle Cachtice but also in Vienna where she had a mansion on Augustinian Street at Lobkowitz Square, near the royal palace in the center of the city. During the trial of 1611 it was recorded that "In Vienna the monks there hurled their pots against the windows when they heard the cries [of the girls being tortured]." These monks must have been in the old Augustinian monastery across from the Bathory mansion. In the cellar, Bathory had a blacksmith construct a kind of iron maiden or cage in which to torture her victims.

Constant intermarriage among the Hungarian noble families, designed to keep the property in the family, led to genetic degeneration; Elizabeth herself was prone to epileptic fits. Also, one of her uncles was a noted Satanist, her aunt Klara an infamous sexual adventurer, her brother Stephen a drunkard and a lecher.

At age eleven Elizabeth was betrothed to the son of another aristocratic Hungarian family, Ferenc Nadasdy. She went to live with the Nadasdy family where, like a tomboy, she evidently enjoyed playing with the peasant boys on the Nadasdy estate. At thirteen she got pregnant by one of them. Her mother spirited her away to a remote Bathory castle where Elizabeth gave birth to a child who was secretly sent out of the country. Shortly before her fifteenth birthday, Elizabeth was married to Ferenc Nadasdy.

Ferenc, who later earned the nickname The Black Knight, was as cruel as his wife. He was off fighting in the wars against the Turks during most of their marriage. When home, he enjoyed torturing Turkish captives. He even taught some torture techniques to Elizabeth. One of them, star-kicking, was a variation of the hotfoot in which bits of oiled paper were put between the toes of lazy servants and set on fire, causing the victim to see stars from the pain and to kick to try to put out the fire. Meanwhile, Elizabeth stuck needles into servant girls' flesh and pins under their fingernails. She also put red-hot coins and keys into servants' hands, or she used an iron to scald the faces of lazy servants. She had other girls hurled out into the snow, where cold water was poured on them until they froze to death.

Ferenc showed Elizabeth how to discipline another of her servants. The girl was taken outside, undressed, and her body smeared with honey. She was then forced to stand outside for twenty-four hours, so as to be bitten by flies, bees, and other insects.

Ferenc died in 1604, leaving his widow free to indulge her morbid sexual fantasies. She set the pubic hair of one of her female servants on fire, according to testimony at the 1611 trial. Elizabeth also liked to have her female servants strip for her. She once pulled a serving girl's mouth until it split at the corners.

Bathory could get away with all this quite easily because she was a Hungarian aristocrat; the servants were Slovaks, to be treated like property or chattel, as cruelly as she wished, for they had no recourse. She lured servants to her castle with promises of wealth and prestige. When that method began to wane, she had her minions raid the surrounding villages and round up the victims.

Bathory finally tired of servant girls and began to entice aristocrats to her nightly games of sadism. That was her first mistake. Elizabeth carried out her atrocities in the company of a mysterious woman who dressed like a man.

Once when Bathory was sick in bed she commanded her elder fe-

The Blood Countess. *A late nineteenth-century painting of Elizabeth Bathory, by St. Csok.*

male servants to bring a young servant girl to her bedside. Bathory rose up "like a bulldog," bit the girl on the cheek, ripped out a piece of her shoulder with her teeth, and then bit the girl's breasts.

Disposing of the innumerable bodies became a growing technical problem: at one point Bathory even stuffed some of the bodies under beds in the castle. The stench became unbearable, and some of the older servants tossed some bodies, naturally drained of blood, in a field. The frightened local villagers believed that vampires were responsible for the blood-drained corpses.

Bathory was much wealthier than the Hungarian king Matthias II. In fact, he owed her a great deal of money. When news reached him that there was mounting evidence that Bathory was molesting girls of noble birth, he decided to act — out of economic reasons, not religious ones. Some scholars wrongly assumed that Matthias, a Catholic, attacked Bathory because she was Protestant. With the support of the nobles in the Hungarian Parliament, Matthias came to Bratislava and ordered Count Thurzo, the local governor, to investigate and ascertain the facts in the Bathory case. The king, who believed in witchcraft, as did most of his peers, was motivated mainly by financial considerations. If Bathory could be accused and found guilty of being a witch, then her vast property could be confiscated, and all of his debts to her nullified.

However, Count Thurzo was a close friend and relative of the Bathory family. Quickly, behind closed doors, the family, including Elizabeth's sons and daughters, agreed to make a deal with Thurzo: there would be a quick trial arranged by Thurzo before the king could act; Bathory would not take the stand, but her accomplices would be put on trial. In that way the property could remain in the Bathory family and not be taken over by the king.

The strategy worked. Thurzo planned his raid for Christmas, when the Hungarian parliament was not in session, so that he could have a free hand. On the night of December 29, 1610, Count Thurzo raided Castle Cachtice and found several mutilated bodies in full view.

Thurzo kept King Matthias II in the dark. The count controlled all the proceedings. The quickly arranged trial convened on January 2, 1611, in the Slovakian town of Bytca at Thurzo's castle north of Cachtice; a second trial took place on January 7. Only petty officials and peasants participated at the first trial, so Thurzo could manipulate everything. Bathory was not allowed to be present in court, even though she wanted to appear and protest her innocence. Her accomplices were formally tried and found guilty at the second trial, during which some twenty jurors and high-level judges heard the testimony. Church officials had been bribed to waive their right to interrogate the accused, even though there were questions of witchcraft. All attempts by the king's representative to place Bathory on the stand failed because of Thurzo's clever maneuvering. He argued that if the Court were to try Bathory it would be a blot on the honor of the Nadasdy and Bathory families and a trauma for the Hungarian nobility.

Bathory's accomplices had their fingers torn out with red-hot pincers by the executioner. They were then tossed alive on the fire. Elizabeth was placed under house arrest, condemned to be walled up in a room in her Castle Cachtice, never again to see the light of day. The property remained safely within the Bathory family's grasp.

Late in August 1614, one of Elizabeth's jailers wanted to get a look at her. Peeking through the small opening through which she received food, he saw the countess lying dead. Hungarian authorities tried to cover up all memory of the "Blood Countess," and they succeeded until her trial documents, kept in official secret archives, were discovered.

There are several links between the Bathory family and Dracula. The commander-in-chief of the expedition that put Dracula back on the throne in 1476 was Prince Stephen Bathory. In addition, a Dracula fiefdom became a Bathory possession during Elizabeth's time. Furthermore, the Hungarian side of Dracula's ancestors might have been related to the Bathory clan.

Accounts of living vampires like Elizabeth Bathory surfaced during the middle of the nineteenth century and were tied strongly to necrophilia. In 1849 at the famous Père Lachaise cemetery in Paris, where many famous artists and musicians were buried, reports circulated about a mysterious night creature who had disinterred and violated corpses there. The French newspapers named the culprit "the vampire of Paris." Traps were laid, and the authorities tracked down the perpetrator. He turned out to be a seemingly normal, handsome young blond sergeant named Victor Bertrand. At his trial on July 10, 1849, he testified that his obsession began in a village churchyard, where he witnessed a funeral and was seized with an overwhelming desire to dig up the corpse and rip it apart.

During the 1920s German newspapers were filled with stories about the "Hanover Vampire." His name was Fritz Haarmann; he had been in and out of prisons, madhouses, and the army, until he settled down to run a butcher shop in 1918. After World War I, Germany was filled with homeless boys and young men; Haarmann picked them up at the Hanover railroad station. He invited his victims home, where he pinned them down and murdered them by sinking his teeth in their throats. He killed at least twenty-four, and at his trial in 1925 he admitted to twenty-seven murders. Like the infamous Sweeney Todd, Haarman ground parts of his victims' bodies into sausage meat, some of which he ate and some of which he sold in his store.

An Englishman named George Haigh confessed to drinking the blood of nine victims and then dissolving their bodies in acid during the 1940s. English newspapers dubbed him the "Acid-Bath Vampire."

In the Wisconsin farmhouse of bachelor hermit Eddie Gein during the late 1950s investigators stumbled on a bizarre scene: heads, skins, and other parts of at least ten human bodies were discovered, and Gein had mummified several others. He admitted to two murders and said that he got the other bodies by robbing local graveyards. As a youth he had been fascinated with accounts of Nazi experiments on human flesh in the concentration camps. Gein's story inspired the films *Psycho, Deranged,* and *The Texas Chainsaw Massacre.*

As recently as 1981 a self-proclaimed living vampire named James Riva II was put on trial in Brockton, Massachusetts. His attorney told the jury that his client had "shot his grandmother twice and sucked the blood out of the bullet holes because he believed a vampire told him that was what he had to do." Despite the objection of the assistant district attorney to the defense's plea of "vampire," the judge overruled the objection and the defense continued their line of reasoning. This was undoubtedly the first time in history that vampirism was used in a *defense* plea! The defense's strategy was that if they could prove that Riva believed he was a vampire, there would be grounds for an insanity plea. During the trial, a doctor testified that Riva had killed a cat and drank its blood, and had once mixed horse's blood with crackers and drank it like soup. Riva was found guilty of the murder of his grandmother but was confined to a mental institution.

Medical doctors utilize the clinical classification "living vampire" in diagnosing cases of two types: those with a proven physical need for fresh healthy blood because their own blood is defective, such as in cases of severe anemia and other blood diseases; and those with a psychological need for blood because it provides a sexual or erotic thrill. These latter living vampires get their satisfaction by actually drinking blood.

One theory to explain the living vampire phenomenon is based on an erythropoietic disease, inherited porphyria. A relatively rare blood disorder, it is caused by a recessive gene that leads to the production of an excess of porphyrins, which are components of red blood cells.

The patient suffering from inherited porphyria becomes extremely sensitive to light. In addition, skin lesions may develop, and the teeth become brown or reddish brown because of the excess porphyrins.

This vampire disease may have been prevalent among the Eastern European nobility. Five hundred years ago physicians even recommended that some nobles replenish their blood by drinking the blood of their subjects. So when a peasant declared that there was a vampire living up in the castle, he wasn't referring to folklore but to an actual blood-drinker.

····CHAPTER 11····

BRAM STOKER

BOTH TERROR AND HORROR are responses to the frightful thing, person, deed, or circumstance. For the purposes of examining horror fiction, terror can be interpreted as the extreme *rational* fear of some form of reality, whereas horror can be interpreted as the extreme *irrational* fear of the unnatural or supernatural. Moreover, there is realistic horror — fear of the unnatural or supernatural presented in the guise of the normal. Terror is also dread of indiscriminate violence; horror the dread of something unpredictable, something that may have potential for violence.

When a mad bomber is on the loose in a city, the inhabitants become terrified; they are aware of the capabilities of a deranged person and understand the devastating effects of a bomb. The nature of the danger is clear, and any attendant mystery is susceptible to rational solution. But if a ghost is heard walking at night, the inhabitants of the house are horrified. What is a ghost? What might it do? What can it do? There is also realistic horror: perhaps there is a man in a tuxedo who looks and acts very natural at the country club, yet we are horrified when we see him flying over a bloodstained corpse on the seventh green. Horrible, mysterious, and yet somewhat comic. In short, it is some fundamental, forever inexplicable mystery that distinguishes horror from terror.

Bram Stoker's novel *Dracula* is one of the most horrifying books in English literature. Published in May 1897, it became a success after Stoker's death and has never been out of print. In America, where it has been available since 1899, it continues to be a bestseller.

In selecting a setting for Dracula, Stoker hit upon Transylvania because it was a faraway never-never land in the view of most Englishmen and Western Europeans, a "land beyond the forest" where anything could happen — the perfect home for a vampire. (Even in the musical *My Fair Lady*, the prince of Transylvania is regarded as coming from a wholly imaginary land.)

Most people are so overwhelmed by the movie version of *Dracula* that few remember the actual story line from Stoker's novel. Stoker chose to tell his story through the diaries of the English solicitor Jonathan Harker and his fiancée Mina Murray; the letters of Mina and her friend, Lucy Westenra; and the testimony of Dr. John Seward on a phonograph record — this last a rather novel touch for the time. The basic story line is simple, but most people recall the movie better than the novel.

Harker, a solicitor, travels to Transylvania in order to arrange for the purchase of Carfax Abbey, an English property, by a certain Count Dracula. Along the way Harker gets ominous warnings which he ignores, such as when one of his local traveling companions quotes from Gottfried Burger's popular ballad "Lenore": "For the dead travel fast." As a guest in the count's castle, Harker finds "doors, doors everywhere, and all bolted and locked," and rooms in which there is not a single mirror. He becomes gradually aware that Dracula is a vampire living with a harem of female vampires — and that he himself is a prisoner. He also learns that the count is planning to leave soon for Carfax Abbey, taking with him fifty coffins filled with Transylvanian soil. Dracula's ultimate intent: the conquest of England.

The count boards a Russian schooner, the *Demeter*, at the Bulgarian port of Varna on the Black Sea. En route to England, he kills the crew. After arriving in England, he attacks Lucy Westenra, who is on vacation with Harker's fiancée, Mina. Dracula gradually drains Lucy of her blood, and evidently infuses his own blood into her body. She then "dies" and becomes a vampire. Dr. Abraham Van Helsing, an expert from Amsterdam, tries to save her from vampirism but fails. The undead Lucy attacks children in Hampstead. When Van Helsing convinces her fiancé, Arthur Holmwood, to drive a stake through her heart, Lucy finds eternal repose. Dracula also dominates and victimizes Renfield, a patient in an insane asylum who has a taste for small animals.

Meanwhile, Harker has miraculously escaped to London, and Van

Top: Highgate Cemetery in London, the probable burial place of Stoker's Lucy.
Bottom: Hampstead, the London suburb where two places mentioned in Stoker's
novel, Jack Straw's Castle, an inn, and the Spaniards, a pub, can still be found.

Helsing persuades him and his young companions to help find Dracula's many coffins. Dracula preys on Mina and makes her drink his blood, apparently to antagonize the vampire hunters. When Harker learns of his wife's predicament, he records the following observation in his journal: "To one thing I have made up my mind: if we find out that Mina must be a vampire in the end, then she shall not go into that unknown and terrible land alone. I suppose it is thus that in old times one vampire meant many; just as their hideous bodies could only rest in sacred earth, so the holiest love was the recruiting sergeant for their ghastly ranks." Harker so loves Mina that he is willing to follow her to Hell. There is a thrilling search for Dracula, culminating in the arrival of the fearless vampire hunters at Castle Dracula in the Carpathian Mountains. Finally, Harker cuts off Drac-

A rare photographic portrait of Bram Stoker.

ula's head with a Kukri or Gurkha knife and Quincey Morris drives a bowie knife though Dracula's heart.

This fad for Dracula the vampire all began with Bram Stoker, but how did he get the idea? How did he come to create this classic of modern horror?

Stoker was born on a cold and wet November day in 1847 in a prim terraced house, 15 The Crescent, in the historic Dublin suburb of Clontarf, where Brian Baru had fought a famous, successful battle against the invading Danes. He was named Abraham after his father, an employee at the chief secretary's office in Dublin Castle, but he always preferred being called Bram. Bram was baptized by ministers from the Church of Ireland in the old Protestant Church on Castle Avenue.

As a child, Bram was so sick and feeble that he was not expected to live and was confined to his bed for the first eight years of his life. He later recalled that he never experienced standing up and walking before he was nine. He knew what it would be like for a vampire to be bound to his coffin and native soil. The exact nature of his disease was a mystery to him and to his doctors, as was his astonishingly complete recovery — it is no wonder that Bram retained a keen interest in mysterious diseases and diagnoses. During Bram's years of confinement, the Reverend William Woods, who had a private school in Dublin, was brought in to instruct him. He continued as his principal teacher until Bram entered college at age 16, but it was his strong-willed mother, Charlotte Thornley, daughter of Captain Thornley, who particularly influenced Bram's early childhood and his interest in horror and fantasy. Her warm love for her son harks back to Freud's dictum about the success assured to those sons who are especially loved by their mothers. Charlotte Stoker often declared that she loved her boys best and "did not care a tuppence" for her daughters. She told young Bram not only Irish fairy tales but also some true horror stories. An Irishwoman from Sligo, she had witnessed the cholera epidemic there in 1832; later Bram recalled her accounts of it, suggesting that the vampire pestilence in his novel owed much to the frightful stories told by his mother. When Bram was twelve years old a great deal of publicity followed the union of the two Romanian states, Moldavia and Wallachia — this was probably his initial introduction to that mysterious part of Europe.

Bram entered Trinity College, Dublin, in 1864, and had so overcome his mysterious childhood illness that he developed into a star
athlete. Popular among his fellow students, Bram was elected president of the Philosophical Society, the Trinity equivalent of the Oxford
Union, where he once gave a lecture on sensationalism in fiction and
society. But his interests lay more in drama than in his studies for a
civil service career. A theater habitué like his father, he regularly attended the Theatre Royal, Dublin's one large, regular theater. One
evening in August 1867 *The Rivals* was performed there, with Henry
Irving starring, and Stoker was enthralled by the famous actor. In
1868 Bram graduated from Trinity with honors in science, and following his father he became a civil servant at Dublin Castle. When his father and mother moved to Italy for financial reasons, Bram rented an
apartment at 30 Kildare Street, near the college (there is a commemorative plaque there now). He kept up his contacts at Trinity and returned to get his master's degree two years later.

Henry Irving returned to Dublin in a comedy entitled *Two Roses*,
and Stoker was again in the audience, along with another young Irish-
man — a fifteen-year-old clerk named George Bernard Shaw. Like

*Joseph Sheridan Le Fanu, the Irish
author of the short novel*
Carmilla, *one of the greatest
vampire stories of all time.*

Shaw, Stoker decided to become a drama critic. His first review appeared in the *Dublin Mail* in November 1871. It was unpaid for, as were his other reviews published in that newspaper. Stoker's interest in Sir Henry Irving was becoming joined with a curious interest in vampirism.

A Dublin author with the unlikely name of Joseph Sheridan Le Fanu had just written the short novel *Carmilla,* one of the greatest vampire stories of all time. Stoker read it and began thinking about writing his own vampire tale. In Le Fanu's work, the heroine Laura welcomes a strange girl named Carmilla into her father's castle and they become close companions. Laura senses, however, that she has seen Carmilla in her childhood nightmares. The author creates an aura of Romantic horror around the almost lesbian relationship between the blonde Laura and the beautiful, dark Carmilla, and achieves suspense so successfully that not until the story's end does one know whether Carmilla is a vampire or simply the victim of one. Finally, in the chapel of Karnstein, the grave of the Countess Mircalla is opened. Carmilla turns out to be the dead countess, whose "features, though a hundred and fifty years had passed since her funeral, were tinted with the warmth of life. Her eyes were open; no cadaverous smell exhaled from the coffin."

Le Fanu followed vampire mythology closely by asserting that her "limbs were perfectly flexible, the flesh elastic; and the leaden coffin floated with blood." To destroy the undead countess,

> The body . . . in accordance with the ancient practice, was raised, and a sharp stake driven through the heart of the vampire . . . the head was struck off . . . body and head were next placed on a pile of wood, and reduced to ashes.

Le Fanu's description of how a person becomes a vampire is also based upon folk belief in Eastern Europe:

> Assume, at starting, a territory perfectly free from that pest. How does it begin, and how does it multiply itself: I will tell you. A person, more or less wicked, puts an end to himself. A suicide, under certain circumstances, becomes a vampire. That spectre visits living people in their slumbers; they die and almost invariably, in the grave, develop into vampires.

Stoker found in *Carmilla* the basic literary ingredients for the vampire aspects of *Dracula*.

In 1872 Stoker was elected auditor of the Trinity College Historical Society. In that same year he published his fantasy story "The Crystal Cup" in the September issue of *The London Society*. His first horror story, "The Chain of Destiny," was published in four parts three years later in the Dublin magazine *The Shamrock*. It concerned an evil curse and a strange character called "the phantom of the Fiend." During the winter of the following year Henry Irving was in Dublin once again, and Stoker's praise of Irving's acting led to their meeting. Following a second meeting at a special social gathering, Irving gave a dramatic reading of the ghastly monologue *The Dream of Eugene Aram* in which the murderer succumbs finally to guilt and the fear of God. Stoker described him in the role of Eugene Aram with phrases that give a foretaste of Dracula: "The awful horror . . . of the Blood-avenging sprite — eyes as inflexible as Fate — eloquent hands, slowly moving, outspread, fanlike." Stoker tells us, in fact, that he broke down into uncontrollable hysterics at the reading. In a way he fell in love with Henry Irving and began working immediately in a part-time capacity that was to continue for the rest of Irving's life.

Meanwhile, a young beauty named Florence Balcombe, whom Stoker had known since childhood, turned down the marriage proposal of syphilitic Oscar Wilde and accepted Stoker's; Wilde was known to be unreliable, and Stoker had a steady, well-paying job. Stoker and Florence Anne Lemon Balcombe were married in 1878 at Saint Anne's Church in Dublin. Bram quit his civil service job and moved with his new wife to London to work for Henry Irving at a handsome salary. Irving had just taken over the Lyceum Theatre and needed his friend's help full-time. Bram arrived in London in June, the day before Irving was to appear in *Vanderdecken*, a weird play based on the legend of the Flying Dutchman. For the next six years, the Stokers lived in Chelsea, where their neighbors included Dante Gabriel Rossetti and James McNeill Whistler. There the Stokers had what was to be their only child; Stoker named the boy after his idol, Irving, but the boy apparently resented the connection and preferred to be called Noel.

In all, Stoker worked as Irving's private secretary and confidant for twenty-seven years, which are described in his *Personal Reminiscences of Henry Irving*. He called their friendship "as profound, as close, as lasting as can be between two men." But there was more to the relationship than that. Irving held such fascination for Stoker that he achieved an extraordinary dominance over him. Indeed, in life Irving was lord and master to Stoker as in fiction Dracula is to Renfield.

Although much of Stoker's time was taken up in arranging tours for Irving and his company, he continued to investigate vampirism and the gothic novel, both of which appealed to his fascination with the dark side of human experience. The gothic novel, a development in English literature which can be traced back to the late eighteenth century, was initially a tale of spooks with a medieval setting, highly charged with emotion. At the time, such stories were given rational endings: all of the mysteries turn out to have natural causes, the supernatural elements prove to be only illusions, and the horror is ex-

Sir Henry Irving in a portrait painted in 1880 by Jules Bastien Lepage. At this time Bram Stoker was Irving's private secretary, a working relationship that mirrored that of Dracula and Renfield in Stoker's Dracula.

plained away. But when Mary Shelley wrote *Frankenstein* in 1818, a new, *realistic* element was introduced into the gothic novel. Shelley achieved horror and mystery through the exploration of science. The agent of horror in her book was no spook, no supernatural being nor the illusion of such. It was a real monster manufactured by the technical expertise of a medical student.

Both the vampire and Frankenstein's creature were conceived at the same time — and at the same place. The coincidence occurred during the summer of 1816 in Geneva, Switzerland, where Mary Shelley, her stepsister Claire, Percy Bysshe Shelley, Lord Byron, and his personal physician, John Polidori, had gone on vacation. The group first stayed at the Hotel d'Angleterre, then rented adjacent villas along the shores of Lake Geneva. Mary later wrote that it was a "wet ungenial summer," and the rain "confined us for days." In order to amuse themselves, this gifted group decided to read German tales of horror. Then, one night in June, Byron said, "We will each write a ghost story."

Left: George Gordon, Lord Byron.
Right: John Polidori, Byron's personal physician and author of The Vampyre, *which, when first published in 1819, appeared under Byron's name.*

Before the end of the summer, the eighteen-year-old Mary, inspired by a philosophical discussion and a nightmare, had written a draft of *Frankenstein*. When it later appeared in print, some reviewers thought that her husband was really its author.

Mary Shelley wrote *Frankenstein* to show in a fairly sympathetic way the failure of a would-be scientific savior of mankind. The public turned it all upside down, and her creation inspired an endless run of stories about the mad scientist who tries to go beyond nature's laws, unlike ordinary, God-fearing mortals. In so doing he unwittingly creates a monster. Eventually, the unholy creature destroys its own creator.

Not to be outdone by any woman, Byron sketched out at Geneva a plan for a tale about a vampire, but he never finished it. Instead, twenty-year-old Polidori, an Englishman of Italian descent and a former student of medicine at the University of Edinburgh, took Byron's idea and used it as a basis for a story called "The Vampyre."

In April 1819 Polidori's tale appeared in the *New Monthly Magazine* under Byron's name, through a misunderstanding on the part of the editor. Goethe swallowed the story whole and declared it to be the best thing that Byron had ever written. Years before, Goethe himself had given substance to the vampire legend in his *Braut Von Korinth*.

In Polidori's "The Vampyre" a young libertine, Lord Ruthven, modeled loosely on Byron, is killed in Greece and becomes a vampire. He seduces the sister of his friend Aubrey and suffocates her on the night following their wedding. This story never caught on with the public, and two years after its publication Polidori, unsuccessful at both literature and medicine, took poison and died. The vampire myth, however, remained popular. Other writers tried their hand at creating a fascinating vampire figure, and Stoker profited from their attempts.

Alexandre Dumas *père* composed a drama entitled *Le Vampire* during the 1820s. In 1820 Nodier's *Le Vampire* was translated into English by J. R. Planche. Ten years later Planche's melodrama *The Vampire* was published in Baltimore. In *Melmoth the Wanderer* (1820), written by the eccentric Dublin clergyman Charles Robert Maturin, the hero is a meld of Wandering Jew and Byronic vampire. The character interrupts a wedding feast and terrifies everyone. Soon after the event the bride dies and the bridegroom goes mad. The vengeance of the vampire is complete.

Nearly a quarter-century after Polidori's "The Vampyre," James Malcolm Rymer published *Varney the Vampire or The Feast of Blood*, which

One of the orignal illustrations for James Malcolm Rymer's
Varney the Vampire or The Feast of Blood.

was well received. (The original edition, published in 1847, did not
name the author, and some experts, such as Devendra P. Varma and
Leonard Wolf, still believe that *Varney* was actually written by Thomas
Preskett Prest, but most others have agreed on Rymer.) Before writing
it, the author had studied the vampire legends in detail. His story is
set in the 1730s during the reign of George II. It concerns the
Bannesworth family and its persecution by Sir Francis Varney. Varney
sucks the blood of Flora Bannesworth, captures her lover, and insults
her family. Oddly, the author presents Varney as a basically good person who is driven to evil by circumstances. He often tries to save himself, but at the end of the story he is in utter despair and commits
suicide by jumping into the crater of Mount Vesuvius.

This solidly realistic horror-story tradition of Mary Shelley, Maturin,
and Rymer was the foundation upon which Stoker wrote his story.
Like them, he presented the vampire as an actual phenomenon. His
Dracula is, and remains, a vampire — quite different from some
gothic novels, in which what seems to be a bloody ghost turns out to

be only a wounded human being. Indeed, Stoker's novel made no attempt to explain away the vampire. Moreover, Stoker made Dracula contemporary, a vampire who lived in and walked the streets of Victorian England — a vast difference from the early gothic romances, which employed historic figures and ancient settings.

Even before Dracula the vampire became ink on paper, his shadow seems to have entered Stoker's life. In 1881 Stoker composed a book of horror stories for children entitled *Under the Sunset,* in which a character named the King of Death presages Dracula. The dreary, moody tale "The Invisible Giant" portrays an orphaned girl who envisions the plague spreading like an unimpeded vampire: "In the sky beyond the city she saw a vast shadowy form with its arms raised. It was shrouded in a great misty robe that covered it, fading away into air so that she could only see the face and the grim, spectral hands."

Stoker met Sir Richard Burton, the prominent adventurer and Orientalist. Burton had translated into English *The Arabian Nights,* in which there is a vampire tale, and in 1870 he translated and introduced some eleven Hindu vampire tales. It is fascinating to note that in his reminiscences, Stoker wrote how impressed he was not only by Burton's accounts, but also by his physical appearance — especially his prominent canine teeth.

Stoker organized the first American tour of Henry Irving's theater company, one of the first tours that included entire theatrical productions and equipment. Their big success was the French melodrama *The Bells,* based on the terror novel of Emile Erckmann; Irving played Mathias, a pillar of society with a murderous past. This brought Stoker to America several times, and he soon became one of the few British writers with pro-American sympathies. So strong was his enthusiasm that in December 1885 he delivered a lecture about the United States at the Birkbeck Institute in London, a talk that was revised and successfully published in book form as *A Glimpse of America.*

Stoker returned to America in 1887 to plan a tour of *Faust,* in which Irving later achieved a triumph in the role of Mephistopheles. Because of this role, Irving has been suggested as a model for Count Dracula. Stoker's dear friend, the author Thomas Hall Caine, to whom he dedicated *Dracula* with the words "To My Dear Friend HOMMY-BEG" (Caine's grandmother, from the Isle of Man, affectionately called him "Hommy-Beg," meaning "Little Tommy" in the Manx dialect), noted that the Flying Dutchman, Faust, the Wandering Jew, and the Demon Lover were all incorporated into the Dracula character. In addition, Stoker's imagination was also stimulated by the tales of Jack the Ripper, who terrorized London from August to November in 1888. Reporting the Ripper's murders, the *East London Advertiser* stated:

> It is so impossible to account, on any ordinary hypothesis, for these revolting acts of blood that the mind turns as it were instinctively to some theory of occult force, and myths of the Dark Ages arise before the imagination. Ghouls, vampires, blood-suckers . . . take form and seize control of the excited fancy.

Like Jonathan Harker, records show that Stoker was a well-known frequenter of the British Museum, and here he searched among the books and maps for information about Transylvania. The Lübeck pamphlet of 1485 describing Dracula's atrocities was one of the rare books placed on display in the exhibition on Eastern Europe at the British Museum during the early 1880s, so it is very likely Stoker would have known about it.

During 1889 Stoker wrote his first full length novel, *The Snake's Pass,* which gained widespread acclaim as a serial in several magazines before it was published as a book two years later. One critic favorably compared it to Le Fanu. The novel is set in western Ireland, where a young Englishman comes upon the legend of the Snake's Pass, where St. Patrick supposedly drove the snakes from Ireland and where French invaders were thought to have hid a treasure in the shifting bogs during the famous Irish uprising of 1789.

By spring of the next year Stoker was already hard at work on *Dracula,* which would eventually consume seven years of research and writing. Much is revealed in Stoker's diaries and journals from this period, now housed at the Rosenbach Foundation in Philadelphia. The most important of these documents is one dated March 8, 1890, in which he sketched out the main outline of his book; it was originally to be divided into three parts: London, Midsummer; Tragedy; and Discovery.

Throughout the novel allusions to Shakespeare's dramas — to *Hamlet* in particular — complement the story line. For example, early in the novel, in an entry dated 8 May, Midnight, Harker records in his diary that after a long talk with the count about his ancestry, from midnight to "close on morning," the count abruptly cuts off the con-

versation and flees, as if "everything has to break off at cock-crow . . .
like the ghost of Hamlet's father." Here Stoker provides one of the
first clues that the count acts like a ghost. On the morning of 16 May,
Harker notes that

> of all the foul things that lurk in this hateful place the Count is the
> least dreadful to me; that to him alone I can look for safety, even
> though this be only whilst I can serve his purpose. Great God! merci-
> ful God! . . . I begin to get new lights on certain things which have
> puzzled me. Up to now I never quite knew what Shakespeare meant
> when he made Hamlet say: "My tablets! quick, my tablets! 'Tis meet
> that I put it down."

Harker, feeling that his mind is becoming unhinged, regains his com-
posure and peace of mind by forcing himself to enter the bizarre
events in his diary. In her diary entry of 12 September Lucy notes,
"Well, here I am to-night, hoping for sleep, and lying like Ophelia in
the play, with 'virgin crants and maiden strewments.'" Later, on 1 October when Dr. Seward records in his diary his question to Renfield
whether he would like some sugar to attract flies, Renfield replies, "I
don't take any stock at all in such matters. 'Rats and mice and such
small deer,' as Shakespeare has it; 'chicken-feed of the larder' they
might be called. I'm past all that sort of nonsense." Stoker had probably absorbed this from seeing Irving perform *Hamlet* on so many
nights. The play opened on December 30, 1878, and ran for a hundred nights. It was the first time that Stoker had been involved in pro-
ducing a play. As he put it, "Now I began to understand *why*
everything was as it was. It was a liberal education." *Hamlet* evidently
remained on his mind when he wrote *Dracula*.

Van Helsing's name seems to be derived from the Danish name for
Hamlet's famed castle Elsinore — Helsingor, meaning "the island of
Helsing." Stoker appears to have identified strongly with the Van Helsing character in many ways, even giving Van Helsing his own first
name and that of his father, Abraham. Dr. Abraham Van Helsing is the
true hero of *Dracula*. Van Helsing has most of the advantages; he
knows that Dracula is relatively powerless during the day and can be
held off with garlic or the cross. Van Helsing the professor unites the
scientific with the occult; he is all-wise and all-powerful. His mind
pierces everyday reality to the reality beyond. Van Helsing is relentless

when confronting the ignorance of other scientists and unflinchingly resolute when up against the vampire himself.

Mina describes Van Helsing as

a man of medium height, strongly built, with his shoulders set back over a broad, deep chest and a neck well balanced on the trunk as the head is on the neck . . . the head is noble, well-sized, broad, and large behind the ears . . . big, bushy eyebrows. . . . The forehead is broad and fine, rising at first almost straight and then sloping back above two bumps or ridges wide apart; such a forehead that the red-dish hair cannot possibly tumble over it, but falls naturally back and to the sides. Big, dark blue eyes are set widely apart, and are quick and tender or stern with the man's moods.

This is a physical description of Bram Stoker. Van Helsing gets his gar-lic flowers from Haarlem, where his friend Vanderpool raises them in his glass-house all year long. The American, Quincey Morris, says that Van Helsing is Dutch, but that could refer to any German speaker, like the Pennsylvania Dutch who are, in fact, German. (Some literary ex-perts have called Van Helsing a Belgian without presenting any evi-dence.) Van Helsing administers three blood transfusions to Lucy Westenra; one from Harker, another from Holmwood, and the last from Quincey Morris, but Lucy dies unconscious after the final trans-fusion. Lucy is based upon Lucy Clifford, with whom Stoker was friendly. Lucy Clifford was Stoker's adopted niece and a popular au-thor of comic literature.

During the early 1890s Stoker was already working on the novel at his London home. While spending his summer holidays at the seaside resort of Whitby, which also figures in the novel, Stoker came across a book by William Wilkinson, self-styled British consul to Bucharest, which he checked out of the Whitby Public Lending Library. (Stoker even recorded the call numbers.) In it were important references to the historical Dracula, such as Vlad's war against the Turks, his res-oluteness and cruelty, and the treachery of his brother Radu. Stoker took copious notes for later inclusion verbatim in chapters 6 and 7 of *Dracula*.

In the meantime, Stoker discovered the Scottish seaside resort of Cruden Bay while on holiday in 1893. He was so enthralled with the solitary, isolated beauty of the place and the sound of the sea on the

Top: The Kilmarnock Arms, the small hotel at Cruden Bay, Scotland, where Bram Stoker stayed while writing Dracula.
Bottom: Slains Castle at Cruden Bay, the probable inspiration for Stoker's descriptions of Castle Dracula.

Scottish coast that he returned there for most of his subsequent summer vacations. That is where he wrote the initial chapters of *Dracula* — the first sixty pages which incorporate Jonathan Harker's experiences. Bram and Florence first rented rooms at the Kilmarnock Arms Hotel, but eventually bought a summer cottage at neighboring Whinnyfold across from the ruins of Slains Castle. Slains Castle probably inspired some of his descriptions of Castle Dracula. During the summers from 1893 through 1896 he worked particularly hard on his vampire at Cruden Bay.

As the idea of writing a vampire story increasingly preoccupied him, Stoker searched for a matrix that would give it an air of authenticity. Around 1890, he met with a Hungarian scholar. Professor Arminius Vambery, known for his travel talks, had become a lion of British society due to his work as a British spy. During the 1890s Vambery was famous in Eastern Europe for his *History of Hungary,* his autobiography, and his writings about his travels through Central Asia. The two men dined together, and during the course of their conversation Stoker became impressed by the professor's stories about his homeland. Unfortunately, no correspondence between Vambery and Stoker can be found today. Moreover, a search through all of the professor's published writings fails to reveal any comments on Vlad, Dracula, or vampires.

Stoker supplemented his knowledge about Dracula from old books in the British Museum Reading Room. There was, for instance, a book about Romania that stated, "In Wallachia, Vlad V, son of Vlad the Devil, cut his way to the throne, sabre in hand, and maintained it by the greatest terrorism and tyranny," and "Vlad was created for the part he played; he hated foreigners, he hated the *boyars!* He hated the people! He massacred, impaled, killed without distinction for his own pleasure and security." Seeking material on Transylvania, Stoker gathered all the guidebooks and survey maps he could find, as evidenced in his notes.

A very important source in his years of preparation was Madame Emily de Laszkowska Gerard's *Land Beyond the Forest* (1888), which included a discussion of Romanian superstitions. Stoker's amendments to his own notes indicate the change of the setting from Styria (the setting of Le Fanu's *Carmilla*) to Transylvania was due to Mme. Gerard. She was a regular contributor to the London Magazine *The Nineteenth Century* in which Stoker published some of his own work. In her article entitled "Transylvanian Superstitions," published first in the

July 1885 issue and later incorporated into her book, she recorded: Transylvania might well be termed the land of superstitions, for nowhere else does this curious crooked plant of delusion flourish as persistently and in such bewildering variety.

She gave the following reasons for her assertion: first of all, Transylvanian scenery "is peculiarly adapted to serve as background to all sorts of supernatural beings and monsters," since it has "innumerable caverns" and "solitary lakes," and "Rumanians are by nature imaginative and poetically inclined. . . . Secondly there is here the imported superstition . . . old German customs and beliefs . . . preserved here in greater perfection than in the original country. . . . Thirdly, there is the wandering superstition of the Gypsy tribes . . . whose ambulatory caravans cover the country." Hence Transylvanians "believe themselves to be surrounded on all sides by a whole legion of evil spirits." As she put it in the book:

> Even a flawless pedigree will not ensure one against the intrusion of a vampire into their family vault, since every person killed by a Nosferatu (a vampire) becomes likewise a vampire after death, and will continue to suck the blood of other innocent persons 'till the spirit has been exorcised by opening the grave of the suspected person and either driving a stake through the corpse or else firing a pistol shot into the coffin.

Mme. Gerard certainly provided Stoker with authentic Transylvanian folklore about vampires, as well as the setting for his story.

Stoker's masterpiece was initially entitled *The Un-Dead*. In fact, when Stoker signed his book contract on March 20, 1897, with the London publishers Archibald Constable and Company, the title was still *The Un-Dead*. It was only when the book was in galleys that he changed the title to *Dracula*.

Dracula begins with the entry in Jonathan Harker's journal: "3 May, Bistritz." In the entry that follows, Jonathan Harker records, "I found that Bistritz, the post town named by Count Dracula, is a fairly well-known place . . . a very interesting old place." The town marks the beginning of the Borgo Pass, which leads into Moldavia — a true description of a real location. Indeed, after *Dracula* was published, Stoker was complimented for his accurate, seemingly firsthand descriptions of a country which he had never actually seen.

The link between Stoker's *Dracula* and the region of Bistrita is not

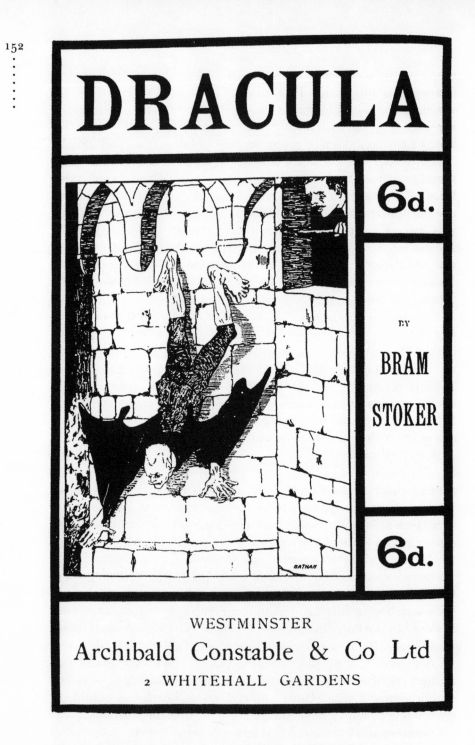

The rare dustjacket for Stoker's 1901 abridgment of his novel.

wholly imaginary. There was an old Szekely family in this region. The family was called Ordog, which is a Hungarian translation of the word *dracul,* or devil. In the novel, the people of the Bistrita region speak the word *ordog* before Jonathan Harker takes off in the carriage to the Borgo Pass.

The major elements of Stoker's ritual acts against vampires correspond with Eastern European folk beliefs. According to James G. Frazer: "Among the Romanians in Transylvania . . . in very obstinate cases of vampirism it is recommended to cut off the head and replace it in the coffin with the mouth filled with garlic; or to extract the heart and burn it, strewing the ashes over the grave." In *Dracula,* as in Romanian folklore, garlic has the power to protect men against vampires and a vampire can be killed by decapitation and a stake driven through the heart.

In Stoker's novel, Dracula appears in the form of mist or phosphorescent specks; the vampire of Romanian folklore also sometimes appears as points of light shimmering in the air. Stoker's vampire can turn into a wolf or a bat, particularly the latter. The Transylvanian Szekely, self-supposed descendants of an East Asian race older than the Magyars, link the bat with vampirism in their folklore. Following Slavic folklore, Stoker's vampire moves only at night, casts no reflection in a mirror, and is repelled by the sign of the cross.

These and many other details reveal the range and accuracy of Stoker's research. The persistence with which Stoker worked is expressed via Van Helsing's remark, "I have studied, over and over again since they came into my hands, all the papers relating to this monster." The 1984 appearance of the authentic typewritten text of the novel showing the author's corrections and amendments has proved that Stoker worked very diligently on the story.

The story is susceptible to many interpretations. Some see it as a Christian allegory or a parody — Count Dracula as an evil inversion of Jesus Christ, offering eternal life if one drinks his blood; others detect an occult subtext; others interpret it as a feminist or antifeminist tract; and still others see it as a racist or antiracist exercise.

That delightfully crazy character Renfield provides the main clues in the novel, though his comments are often ignored by both the other characters and by most readers, since he has been branded insane. Renfield understands what the count is all about; Dracula is a parasite who takes the life force from the living in order to prolong his own unnatural life. Renfield yearns to do the same, but he is on a lower level of existence. He thinks that he can increase his own life by ingesting living things, so he begins by catching flies. He eats some of them but feeds the others to spiders in order to fatten up the spiders for eating. But he soon tires of what he calls "puny things." He begs Dr. Seward to get him a cat, or at least a kitten, but his request is denied. Resolute to the end, Renfield finds a way of luring birds to the window of his cell. One day the birds have mysteriously vanished, though feathers are found suspiciously strewn around Renfield's cell. Renfield then disgorges a lot of feathers. He is gradually making his way up the evolutionary ladder, but he never graduates because he gets an attack of guilt and betrays his mentor, the count, who promptly breaks Renfield's back.

Stoker knew what his contemporary Sigmund Freud was just beginning to discover in Vienna — that things are rarely what they seem to be. Count Dracula appears to be a gentleman, but he is a predator. Renfield seems to be insane but often is not. Stoker was fascinated by masks and masquerades. In one of his last books, entitled *Famous Imposters* (1910), he probed into histories of women who took on the outward appearance of men and vice versa. In a hitherto unpublished preface to that book, now housed in the Trinity College Archives in Dublin, Stoker revealed his fascination: "The subject of imposture is ever new. It is based on principles of human nature, and so long as social life works within the broad lines of demarcation, it can never have an end." Stoker ends the preface with one of the keys to his *Dracula:* "To the author of this book the great lesson which it inculcates is that the basic works of nature, as well as the noble, have their utility in the furtherance of good. And as the greatest work is the diffusion of truth so it, too, must be tested by the most exhaustive means."

As every street urchin who has stood up for himself knows, every bully is basically a coward. So Dracula threatens the human vampire hunters, "You think to baffle me, you — with your pale faces all in a row, like sheep in a butcher's. You shall be sorry yet, each one of you! You think you have left me without a place to rest; but I have more. My revenge is just begun! I spread it over centuries, and time is on my side." But Van Helsing, while admiring Dracula's *sang-froid* in the face of death, correctly senses that "he fears us; he fears time, he fears want! For if not, why does he hurry so? His very tone betrays, or my eyes deceive."

When trapped, Dracula does not stand his ground. He flees alone, as he did when he lost to the Turks and "when he was beaten, came again and again though he had to come alone from the bloody field where his troops were being slaughtered, since he knew that he alone could ultimately triumph." Dracula is a loner. The others succeed against him only so long as they work together. The message is clear: seek the strength of community and good will win the everlasting battle against evil.

Stoker's *Dracula* is based on the notion that certain beings do not die but instead undergo a transformation into another form of life. This seems close to the Oriental concept of eternal return. As the author himself noted in *The Jewel of Seven Stars,* "it is in the arcana of dreams that existences merge and renew themselves, change and yet keep the same — like the soul of a musician in a fugue."

In Stoker's *The Lady of the Shroud* (1909), in which the lady of the title is forced to pose as a vampire in order to ward off unwanted prowlers, there is a passage explaining Stoker's view that most humans desire physical immortality:

Surely the old myths were not absolute inventions; they must have had a basis somewhere in fact. May not the world-old story of Orpheus and Euridyce have been based on some deep-lying principle or power of human nature? There is not one of us that has not wished at some time to bring back the dead.

Sixty-four-year-old Bram Stoker, creator of Count Dracula, recreator of the devilish and heroic Prince Dracula, died in near poverty on April 20, 1912, at his home in Saint George's Square, London. He did not live to see the remarkable success of his novel. He wrote eighteen books in all, but none achieved the eventual fame of *Dracula.* Sir Henry Irving had predeceased him by seven years. The death certificate lists the official cause of Stoker's death as "exhaustion." Since, like many of his Victorian colleagues, Stoker harbored doubts about any traditional Christian resurrection of the body, his body was cremated.

· · · · CHAPTER 12 · · · ·

ON STAGE, IN FICTION,
AND ON FILM

THOUGH STOKER'S NOVEL would go on to achieve the coveted status of bestseller in the twentieth century and would be translated into most major languages, Dracula's first appearance was on stage, second in fiction, but it was on film that the count finally achieved his true immortality. But his road to becoming a household word was a long and tortuous one.

Just a few days before Stoker's vampire novel was published, Dracula appeared on stage for the first time in a play entitled *Dracula, or The Un-Dead*, written for the stage by Stoker himself. It was solidly based on the book, but unfortunately its playing time was something more than four hours, much too long for any ordinary stage production aside from a Wagnerian opera. It was no hit. The first and only performance at the Lyceum Theatre in London on May 17, 1897, was also the only stage version of *Dracula* that Stoker ever witnessed. Sir Henry Irving, who drifted in to watch the performance, characterized the play as "dreadful."

A fellow Irish actor-manager, Hamilton Deane, who had read *Dracula* in 1899, felt that a money-making stage play could be made from the novel. He secured copyright permission from Stoker's widow, Florence, and tried for many years to interest various playwrights into adapting a script. Finally, bedridden with a severe cold, Deane himself took on the task in 1923. He cut out the opening in Transylvania, as well as the chase scene set there at the end of the novel, and made the Texan, Quincey Morris, into a woman. His play was performed in June 1924 at the Grant Theatre in Derby. It was an immediate and lasting success. On February 14, 1927, the Deane play opened in London, where it enjoyed one of the longest runs in English theatrical history. In fact, the play went on to become a staple for theatrical companies in need of financial success. Deane once admitted that whenever his company was in financial straits they would mount the Dracula play on the boards and it would always make money.

Most people do not realize how much the popular Count Dracula image owes to Hamilton Deane's wardrobe. It was Deane who came up with the idea of having the count wear a tuxedo and cape with stand-up collar. Deane's reasoning was actually a matter of practicality: the tuxedo could be used on-stage for Dracula and then by the leading actor at dinner parties before and after the play, thus saving on wardrobe costs. The stand-up collar on the cape was used on-stage for the scenes in which Dracula had to disappear; it hid the actor's head when he turned his back to the audience and thus enabled him to slip out of the cape through a trapdoor in the floor, leaving the impression that he had disappeared when the cape fell suddenly in a heap. It was Deane who also arranged to have a uniformed nurse available at performances, ready to administer smelling salts to those members of the audience who might faint from fright during the play. He saw this ploy as a fine publicity stunt, which was imitated when the American version of the play opened on Broadway.

For the New York stage, the noted American playwright John L. Balderston was commissioned to revise the Deane script, technically in collaboration with Deane, but in fact his revision amounted to a complete rewrite (Balderston and Deane did not get along, so collaboration was out of the question). Actually, Balderston's changes enhanced the dramatic pacing for American audiences. This wholly revised American version, known as the Balderston-Deane version (the one most often produced today), opened at the Fulton Theater in October 1927 and starred the then-unknown Hungarian actor Bela Lugosi in the title role. Lugosi was so proud of being Hungarian that he never bothered to learn English, a serious mistake that would hamper his career in the United States. He learned his lines phonetically and often did not know the meaning of what he was saying. In fact, he could not understand why other foreign-born actors ever bothered to learn English rather than follow his example. The show ran for a year on Broadway, and for two years on tour, breaking all previous records for any play ever put on tour in the United States.

Over forty years passed before a wholly new Dracula play was writ-

*Bela Lugosi
in his most famous role.*

ten and produced. During the early 1970s the Cherry Lane Theater (off-Broadway) presented a play entitled *The Passion of Dracula,* a vampire love story by Bob Hall and David Richmond, based on Stoker's novel and starring Christopher Bernau. The play showed how far the genre had gone; neck-biting, which had been merely suggested in the 1927 version, came to occupy center stage. The early seventies were the heyday of nudity on the American stage, so most of the actors proceeded to strip with little or no motivation for doing so. Other naked actors writhed and twisted around them throughout the performance. There was one fine moment when the reporter-suitor, who had fallen in love with a female Nordic minion of Dracula, felt compelled to destroy her off-stage and exclaimed in stiff-upper-lip British fashion, "You could have had me, my darling, but you *cannot* have England!"

In 1977 the Balderston-Deane play was successfully revived on Broadway with marvelous, suitably weird sets by the artistic genius of the macabre, Edward Gorey. Frank Langella starred and obviously played it for laughs. The play was a success. Other modern rewrites, including a popularly performed college version by actor/writer Ted Tiller, encounter a perennial problem: it is almost impossible for a contemporary audience to take the dialogue seriously.

A significant off-Broadway theatrical presentation, amusingly called *Vampire Lesbians of Sodom,* opened in 1984 at the Limbo Lounge and enjoyed a long, successful run; a fuller version was presented at the Provincetown Playhouse the next year. The play has as its central character a campy two-thousand-year-old Hollywood lesbian movie star–columnist who is also a vampire; she is accompanied by deliberately bizarre characters, plot, and dialogue. The vampire theme seems to have reached the apex of self-parody.

Though Stoker's novel remained popular and was never out of print in either England or the United States, it was almost seventy-five years after its publication that the Dracula character was evidently so ingrained in American folklore that it was used in comic fashion by Woody Allen in his book *Getting Even* (1971) in a short story entitled simply "Count Dracula." Fooled by a solar eclipse into thinking that night had fallen, Count Dracula arrives early at a dinner party. When Dracula finally realizes his dangerous mistake, he makes several unsuccessful attempts to leave. Eventually he hides out in a dark closet until the ignorant mayor opens the door and Dracula promptly disintegrates into ashes as the sunlight streams in on him.

It was the first edition of *In Search of Dracula* (1972) that inspired new approaches to the Dracula story by combining history with fiction. This was the first book to prove conclusively that the vampire Count Dracula could be traced back to a real human being, the flesh-and-blood, fifteenth-century Romanian prince, Vlad Dracula.

One of the cleverest tales to combine the vampire theme with this new information about a historical Dracula was "The Dracula File" (1978) by the talented British writer Tim Stout. The story is presented through a series of newspaper reports and radio broadcasts announcing that a new comedy film called "It's Fun to Be Dead" about Count Dracula is being planned. But Bram Stoker comes back from the dead; the producer is decapitated; the screenwriter is bitten in the throat and smothered in a sealed coffin. The supposed murderer is finally captured, and he claims that he is Bram Stoker risen from the grave to punish those who would tamper with his creation. However,

Stoker is himself a vampire, and he too is mysteriously killed by a wooden stake while in his prison cell. A news release details a new production entitled "The Great Impaler" based on the life of the historical Dracula which will present Vlad Tepes in a favorable light "stressing his courage, patriotism, military genius and compassion." A strange Eastern European nobleman, who has only recently come to London and whose name and identity remain a mystery, cast in the title role, declares to the press: "Your author Bram Stoker did a great disservice to my country by blackening the name of our national hero. I am pleased to see that the people of England now hold the name in honour and affection, and I myself anticipate a long and fruitful stay in your pleasant land." The reader, of course, realizes that the mysterious aristocrat is none other than Vlad the Impaler himself, who as King Vampire has returned to London and destroyed Bram Stoker.

During the 1970s and 1980s vampire stories and novels enjoyed a modest renaissance. The way was opened already in the 1961 story "Some of Your Blood" by Theodore Sturgeon, in which a young sol-

Christopher Lee as Vlad Tepes in the documentary film In Search of Dracula.

dier named George Smith is a habitually taciturn patient in a military hospital mental ward. He has had a nervous breakdown. His medical file serves as the basis for the unfolding of the story — along with the patient's autobiography, transcripts of his therapy sessions, and off-the-cuff letters between two psychiatrists. They finally succeed in getting the patient to reveal his secret past, which was filled with murder, blood-drinking, and mutilation. George, it turns out, is a living vampire.

Other modern vampire stories and novels began to flourish during the seventies, especially with Douglas Drake's "Something Had to Be Done," Suzy McKee Charnas's *The Vampire Tapestry,* George R. R. Martin's *Fevre Dream,* Marc Behm's *The Ice Maiden,* John Skipp and Craig Spector's *The Light at the End,* and Robert Lory's *The Dracula Horror Series,* portraying humans as more evil than Count Dracula. The surge in contemporary vampire literature culminated with Stephen King's *Salem's Lot* and the separate series of vampire novels by Fred Saberhagen, Peter Tremayne, Chelsea Quinn Yarbro, Les Daniels, and, most especially, Anne Rice.

The 1976 Douglas Drake story "Something Had to Be Done" updated the vampire genre to the Vietnam War. A vampire named Stefan Lunowski kills five men in his outfit before his superior officer, Sergeant Morezek, realizing that Lunowski is a vampire, destroys him with a grenade. Colin Wilson added a touch of sci-fi to the vampire tale in his novel *Space Vampires* (1976), in which a spaceship is discovered with a crew of apparently dead humanoids. Once brought to earth, these humanoids emerge as alien outer-space vampires who suck the life force out of humans during sex.

One of the major trends in this new vampire literature is to present the vampire as an objective observer of humankind. He or she becomes a critic of the basic violence in human behavior. The writer Fred Saberhagen initially chartered the most significant changes in the genre, which subsequent authors imitated. For example, Saberhagen chose to tell his story from the viewpoint of Count Dracula rather than from that of the humans as Stoker had done, and to correct Stoker's supposed mistakes. In *The Dracula Tapes,* Saberhagen has Dracula argue that it was the stupidity and incompetence of Dr. Van Helsing that was responsible for Lucy's death. Saberhagen's Dracula says, "Lucy I did not kill. It was not I who hammered the great stake through her heart. My hands did not cut off her lovely head, or stuff her breathless mouth — that mouth — with garlic, as if she were a dead pig. . . . Only reluctantly had I made her a vampire, nor would she ever have become a vampire were it not for the imbecile Van Helsing and his work." Specifically, Saberhagen's Dracula blames Van Helsing for performing the dangerous blood transfusions on Lucy because, although medical doctors in the 1890s did not know all there was to know about blood types, they knew enough to avoid doing such transfusions, as they often resulted in death. Van Helsing just happened to be lucky that the first two transfusions worked, but the transfusion of Quincey's blood to Lucy ended with her body's rejection of it and her death. As Saberhagen points out, the careful reader will have noted that Lucy was sickly and anemic long before Dracula attacked her. Van Helsing misdiagnosed her illness as blood loss, but it was a biochemical disorder causing her lethargy, evident before Dracula ever touched her. It was only out of pity for Lucy that Dracula turned her into a vampire. Van Helsing is a racist, a sadist, and a blasphemer. Van Helsing's use of the sacred host is sacrilegious, as Dracula correctly points out. After Dracula attacks Mina, the reason she declares herself "Unclean, unclean!" is not simply because, a good Victorian, she is frightened of being discovered as passionate. Mina and Dracula eventually fall in love but Mina conceals her true feelings because she is afraid that if the others find out, they will drive a stake through her heart. At the conclusion of *The Dracula Tapes* Dracula only appears to be destroyed in order to protect Mina. Two months after his assumed death, he visits Mina in England. She is pregnant, and he leaves her in peace.

Saberhagen followed the *The Dracula Tapes* with *The Holmes-Dracula File* (1978), in which Sherlock Holmes's mother supposedly had an affair with Dracula's vampire-brother Radu the Handsome. We find out that vampires can have children, provided the woman in question is already pregnant by a mortal man; the vampire feeds her his blood which then mixes with that of the fetus in her womb. (In authentic Transylvanian folklore, the male vampire can impregnate a woman, but the children are born without bones.) In Saberhagen's fiction, twins are born; Sherlock Holmes's twin brother turns out to be a vampire. Seward is the villain of the piece, which is narrated by Dr. Watson for the Sherlock Holmes section, and by Vlad Dracula himself for the part involving him. Eventually the two strands of the novel come together; Dracula returns to London under the pseudonym Emil

Cordery and joins with Sherlock Holmes to solve a crime. Saberhagen next placed Dracula in Chicago in *An Old Friend of the Family* (1979), and alternated both geographically and historically between Renaissance Italy and contemporary Phoenix, Arizona, in *Thorn* (1980). Saberhagen's latest effort in the series, entitled *A Question of Time*, places Dracula in the Grand Canyon.

Simultaneously with Saberhagen, Peter Tremayne was also pursuing an image of the vampire as an attractive, positive figure in his series: *Dracula Unborn* (1977), which was retitled in the U.S. *Bloodright: Memoirs of Mircea — Son to Dracula* (1979), *The Revenge of Dracula* (1979), and *Dracula, My Love* (1980), the last being a *Jane Eyre*–type gothic tale.

Also during the late seventies and into the eighties, Chelsea Quinn Yarbro in *Hotel Transylvania* (1978), *The Palace* (1978), *Blood Games* (1978), *Path of the Eclipse* (1981), *Tempting Fate* (1982) and *The Saint-Germain Chronicles* (1983), describes the experiences of the vampire Saint-Germain from ancient Egypt through the Roman Empire, Renaissance Italy, and eighteenth-century France to twentieth-century England in the style of historical novels. The multiple horrors perpetrated by humans over the centuries make the vampire appear much less terrifying than Stoker's archvampire Dracula — or at a minimum certainly less cruel than humans. The vampire Saint-German actually delights in sexual contact with human beings. He eventually turns up in Russia during the 1917 Revolution, where he adopts a little girl and journeys to pre-Nazi Germany in the company of a Russian noblewoman .

Les Daniels's vampire series, beginning with *The Black Castle* (1978), *The Silver Skull* (1979), and *Citizen Vampire* (1981), traces the exploits of the vampire Don Sebastian de Villanueva across the ages, from the Spanish Inquisition to the Spanish conquest of America to the French Revolution. Don Sebastian is repelled by the true horrors of the Inquisition, the atrocities of the Spanish conquistadors, and finally by the excesses of the Reign of Terror. Daniels has Don Sebastian turn up in London during the nineteenth century, but under an Anglicization of his name, Sebastian Newcastle, in his novel *Yellow Fog*. This was followed by *No Blood Spilled* (1991), in which the vampire protagonist appears in India. Sebastian Newcastle wants to revive the cult of the Thuggee, only recently wiped out by the British. The title, *No Blood Spilled*, comes from the Thuggee practice of strangling their victims and not spilling their blood, in honor of their patroness, Kali. Naturally the Thugs are incensed to witness Newcastle rip a victim's throat and drink the spurting blood, but he presents himself as a messenger from Kali herself, in the hope that they will lead him to the goddess of death. Throughout the Daniels series the vampire is upset by horrors which would not have bothered Stoker's evil count.

Another turning point in the modern vampire genre comes with Suzy McKee Charnas's *The Vampire Tapestry* (1980), which presents a psychotic living vampire as the focus of the story. A cultural anthropologist, tall, handsome Dr. Edward Lewis Weyland avers, "I seem to have fallen victim to a delusion of being a vampire." A woman he attacks shoots and wounds him, and in order to keep his college teaching job, Dr. Weyland is forced to undergo psychiatric therapy. His therapist, Floria, at first calls her patient Dracula in jest. He initially resists the analysis but finally yields to reveal his absolute growing conviction that he is a vampire. Patient and therapist then interact with terrifying results, exposing a strange, deep bond as much between doctor and patient as between monster and victim.

Unlike the many series that appeared in the 1970s Stephen King's vampire novel *Salem's Lot* was actually based on Stoker's *Dracula*. In this early King novel the evil Marsten House is Castle Dracula; Barlow, the king vampire, is Count Dracula; and Straker, his minion, is a bit like Renfield. The tale transfers the setting to contemporary Maine, and makes children the agents of the spread of vampirism to the adults. Young Mark Petrie, who knows all about vampires and werewolves because he collects horror magazines and figurines, is the adolescent hero who courageously defies and destroys the vampires together with the writer Ben Mears. King's important contributions to the genre were placing the vampire in a contemporary American setting and making the reader see the events through the eyes of a child.

In Whitley Strieber's novel *The Hunger* (1981), Miriam, the vampiress, is seen existing from ancient times to the present. Each segment of the novel is a kind of short historical vignette in which Miriam appears against a rich background of authentic historical detail. She can cry and even have nightmares, but she is unable to keep her lovers alive for very long, so she pathetically hides their remains in boxes in her attic. A slick movie extravaganza, which looked more like an ad from *Cosmopolitan* than a horror film, was loosely based on Strieber's novel. New this time was an emphasis on the female vampire's seductive side and her bisexuality.

Michael Talbot's novel *The Delicate Dependency* (1982) portrays vampires for the first time as an advanced race of erotic beings who honor and conserve the artistic and scientific achievements of the human race. This is the story of Dr. Gladstone's savant daughter who has been captured by the vampires while she and her father are living in a luxurious Paris mansion. The vampires are in effect *illuminati*, benevolent preservers of the best in human history, out to save the humans from themselves.

Jody Scott, in her story "I, Vampire," presents her vampire character — with the charming, *double-entendre* name Sterling O'Blivion — confessing, "To remain young and adorable, I must drink six ounces of human arterial blood once a month. This is not an ethical choice. I was born this way. If society wants to kill or cure me, that's not up to me." Scott transforms the vampire from a creature cursed with blood lust into a sympathetic person who just happens to have a peculiar physical need.

John Skipp and Craig Spector's splatter-punk *The Light at the End of the Tunnel* (1986) is set in contemporary New York, where a spiky-haired artist named Rudy is growing fangs and becoming gradually more dangerous. This is one vampire who doesn't suffer isolation, for within the stinking metropolis filled with everyone else's garbage, a small group of vampire people form a loyal community. They are considered oddballs by other New Yorkers as they travel the filthy subways and dirty streets in their attempt to purge the sick New York scene of disease.

In *The Empire of Fear: An Epic Vampire Novel* (1988), Brian Stableford attempts to blend vampirism, history, folklore, and fiction in a story that spans three centuries of a world dominated by aristocratic vampires. The story begins in the seventeenth century with Edmund Cordery (courtier to Richard the Lionheart), shifts for an African interlude, and then moves on to a contemporary American climax. Partway into the first chapter appears "Voivode Vlad the Fifth — whose scribes signed him Dragulya and who was known to the world as Vlad Tepes, the Impaler." Vlad is supposedly out to ruin Cordery's base in Malta.

Brian Lumley penned *Vamphyri* (1988), in the *Necroscope* series, in which a scientific, biological theory for the vampire phenomenon is presented as fact, accompanied by such strange terminology as "jugular teeth," and the author's evident inability to distinguish between incisors and canine teeth. The child of a businessman and a lawyer, the young male hero yearns to be a musician, but his family forces him into their mold. He turns to drugs, messes up his life, and wants to kill himself until he meets Tatiana Romanov, a vampiress who saves him. Here the theme of the female vampire savior rather than destroyer is depicted by Lumley in rather humorous prose. More recently, C. S. Friedman's novel *The Madness Season* (1990) attempted to fuse the vampire theme with hardcore sci-fi. In some excellent writing that eschews the usual flashbacks, Friedman places the vampire five hundred years in the future and has him look and act like a human. In the plot, aliens have long ago taken over Earth. A teacher in the United States takes pills to try to suppress his vampire tendencies. Captured by the aliens and deprived of his medicine, he becomes a vampire and must save the humans from the aliens. In a similar vein, noted sci-fi writer Brian Aldiss sets his story *Dracula Unbound* (1991) in the Utah desert in the future, where an archaeological dig turns up two human skeletons. A ghost train passes the site each night. The hero, Joe Bodenland, hitches a ride and finds himself as Bram Stoker's guest in 1896 London; Van Helsing turns up, and they plan to go into the far future and then into the far past to slay the vampires.

The genre has also been adapted to appeal to the young adult market by Caroline Cooney in her successful novel *The Cheerleader* (1991), in which a vampire promises that he can make the friendless Althea popular, and sees to it that she even makes the cheerleading squad. Cooney's vampire novel was so unusual and popular with the younger readers that she produced a quick sequel called *The Return of the Vampire* (1991). L. J. Smith also wrote for young adult readers in her three-volume work *The Vampire Diaries* (1991), wherein a teenage girl's infatuation with a vampire turns into a romantic triangle and results in another variation of the small town versus the vampire.

Eric Garber expanded the limits of the genre with his book *Embracing the Dark* (1991), vampire stories aimed directly at gay and lesbian readers. Nancy Collins's successful erotic vampire story *Sunglasses after Dark* spawned a sequel called *In the Blood* (1992). Robert McCammon produced one of the best recent vampire novels, entitled *They Thirst*, presenting vampires who emerge from the desert to take over Los Angeles during a sandstorm. Lee Weathersby's *Kiss of the Vampire* (1992) centers on the vampire Simon Tepes Drake who is engaged in a vampire hunt of his own.

In *The Vampire Odyssey* (1992), the first in a series of vampire novels by Scott Ciencin, a reticent young orphan, Dani, meets rich, young Madison, but her eyes are really on Japanese-American Bill Yoshino. An unusual attempt is made to explain the origin of the first vampire, a problem which has haunted the genre for years. According to Ciencin, the first vampire was actually a Roman centurion who kept Christ's blood, drank it, died, and rose to immortal life three days later. His descendants must drink human blood to survive.

The themes of alienation and love of the macabre are combined with an underground punk culture to present mutated vampires in New Orleans's low-culture bars and herbal shops in Poppy Z. Brite's *Lost Souls* (1992). Her vampires prefer blood laced with liquor. They are suburban youths yearning to avoid mediocrity. They are also so obsessed with death that they foster a uniform vampiric look in order to recognize their soul mates. Since their traditional families are fashionably dysfunctional, the young are trying to form new kinds of communities, which shock their elders. Here the traditional black clothes and cape represent the generation gap and the youngsters' break with the values of their parents. Just as the Victorians sought a sense of community in Stoker's novel, so do the contemporary young people in Brite's tale.

The anthology *Mammoth Book of Vampires* (1992), edited by Stephen Jones, includes new and old vampire tales, like Robert Bloch's "Hungarian Rhapsody" in which Mafia types compete with vampires, and Les Daniels's "Yellow Fog," set in England during the time of the publication of *Varney the Vampire,* as well as an interesting new story called "Blood Gothic." Byron Preiss edited another anthology called *The Ultimate Dracula* (1992), containing nineteen stories by such famous authors as Anne Rice and Karen Robards, and including Dan Simmons's tale "All Dracula's Children," combining for the first time a Romanian setting with the horrors of AIDS and Ceausescu. This later became the first chapter of his novel *Children of the Night,* in which American hematologist Kate Neuman adopts a Romanian infant named Joshua who miraculously metabolizes blood that restores his immune system. Neuman thinks that this might be a breakthrough in AIDS research, but Joshua turns out to be Dracula's successor, heir to his vampire heritage.

In the anthology *Dracula: Prince of Darkness* (1992) there is a fine story called "Voivode" by Douglas Barron which also combines an authentic Romanian setting with references to the historical Dracula, vampire lore, and Ceausescu. It is somewhat like the Dan Simmons story except that this tale is told as the journal of a screenwriter named Eric Payne who begins on May 3 in Bucharest in a style reminiscent of Stoker. He bribes a taxi driver to take him to the Snagov Monastery. Payne writes: "Officially the count is said to be buried there; but, according to the Florescu-McNally book, excavation of the purported grave in 1931 revealed only an open hole." He then goes to Castle Bran and then on to Castle Dracula, where he supposedly finds the tomb of Ceausescu zealously guarded by a devoted Romanian. We find out that the vampire Dracula has actually been inhabiting Ceausescu's body since 1944. Suddenly the vampire rises from its coffin to attack Payne, who flees. But Dracula-Ceausescu pursues Payne and tears out his throat. The police are baffled by the murder and cannot figure out the meaning of a mysterious note left by Payne, with an actual quotation from Ceausescu: "A man like me comes along only every five hundred years!"

But among all the contemporary books, Anne Rice's series is undoubtedly the most important vampire fiction produced since Stoker's *Dracula*. She has revolutionized the genre. Her vampire world is much like our own. Garlic, crucifixes, mirrors, and stakes do not frighten them any more. Some vampires are good and trustworthy; they even join together to protect humans from other bad vampires. The good vampires are the heroes; men are the villains. The vampires are also bisexual.

In Rice's first novel in the Vampire Chronicles, *Interview with the Vampire*, a young reporter interviews Louis, a Louisiana plantation owner who was turned into a vampire by the powerful Lestat during the late eighteenth century. Louis and Lestat once formed the core of a vampire family. They attacked a five-year-old girl to create their "child," Claudia, a lovely but ruthless vampire. Lestat so loves Claudia that he becomes jealous of Louis's hold on the child. Claudia so detests Lestat that she contrives to destroy him by offering him boys whose blood she has contaminated. Claudia and Louis erroneously believe that Lestat has been eliminated, and they travel leisurely around Europe until Louis has a dire encounter with a more ancient and powerful vampire named Armand. The mood of the novel is morbid and erotic, set mostly in a lushly imagined New Orleans.

In *The Vampire Lestat*, Rice's second in the series, Lestat has become a rock superstar. *Queen of the Damned*, the third, traces the origins of the vampire to ancient Egypt. By the fourth volume, *The Tale of the Body Thief* (1992), Lestat returns to tell his story again. Lestat used to enjoy the company of other vampires, but no more; he is "grieving for other mortals." In New Orleans Lestat meets Louis again and explains the main theme of the novel: humans want to be eternally young and vampires yearn to feel the way humans do. The body thief, James Raglan, proposes to trade bodies with Lestat, and Lestat is so eager to feel like a human that he agrees. But Lestat becomes sick with a severe case of pneumonia and soon wants his vampire body back. With the help of his human lover, David, Lestat tracks down Raglan and resumes his former incarnation.

Anne Rice's Lestat got it right when he stated, "Try to see the evil that I am. I stalk the world in mortal dress, the worst of fiends, the monster who looks exactly like everyone else." Rice's vampires are recognizable — they are ourselves with extraordinary powers.

It was neither stage nor literature but film that gave Dracula mass appeal. In some place, somewhere, at this moment, in a movie theater or on television, audiences are thrilling to the bloodthirsty count. In our opinion, there are six great films based — more or less — on Stoker's story: *Nosferatu* (1922), *Dracula* (1931), *Horror of Dracula* (1958), *Love at First Bite* (1979), *Dracula* (1979), and *Bram Stoker's Dracula* (1992). Our comments here are largely restricted to those movies. (An annotated filmography of the entire genre of vampire and Dracula films covering the period 1896–1992 may be found in the appendixes.)

F. W. Murnau was a gifted young film director known to the popular press as "the German genius." He had been born Friedrich Plumpe in Westphalia in 1888 and had taken the name Murnau from a German village near Garmisch-Parteinkirchen. After being schooled as an art historian, Murnau decided to create a film based on Dracula. That same year, the Danish screenwriter Henrik Galeen adapted Stoker's novel for the German cinema. Though Murnau gave full credit to Stoker, he failed to obtain copyright permission. This required that he change the names of the main characters, shift the setting from Transylvania to the Baltic, and add his own erotic ending. His silent film, entitled *Nosferatu*, was released by Prana Films in 1922. Stoker was dead, but his widow, Florence, brought suit against Murnau and won a settlement, causing Prana Films to go bankrupt. Although the courts had ordered the negative and all prints of *Nosferatu* destroyed, this for-

Left: Count Orlok (Dracula), portrayed by Max Schreck in the greatest Dracula film ever made: Nosferatu, *directed by F. W. Murnau in 1922.*

Below: This frame from Nosferatu *shows the count on board a ship arriving in Bremen with a cargo of coffins.*

tunately did not happen. The film opened on a limited basis in London in 1928 and in the United States in 1929. *Nosferatu* continues to be shown in art cinemas and on television.

The central locale of *Nosferatu* is the port of Bremen in northern Germany. The Dracula character, called Graf Orlok (played by Max Schreck), has a Renfield-like real estate agent, Knock (Alexander Granach), in Bremen who sends young Hutter (Gustav Von Wangenheim) to Transylvania so that he can discuss with Orlok the rental of a home in Bremen. During Hutter's stay with him, Orlok sees a photograph of Hutter's beloved wife, Ellen (Greta Schroeder-Matray), and becomes attracted to her "lovely throat." Orlok eventually attacks Hutter, loads his coffins on a wagon, and leaves to board a ship for Bremen.

During the voyage, Orlok kills the entire crew. Upon his debarkation, fear arises that the plague has arrived in the city. The vampire installs himself in a house across the road from Ellen and Jonathan

Death of Count Orlok in Nosferatu.

Hutter's home while local inhabitants begin dying of a plaguelike disease. Meanwhile Hutter, who has recovered from the vampire's attack, has also returned home. He warns Ellen about the stranger from Transylvania, but she reads in *The Book of Vampires* that the vampire can be destroyed only if a virtuous woman allows him to stay with her until cockcrow. At the movie's end, Ellen realizes that she must spend the night with Orlok and keep him by her side until daylight in order to save her husband and her fellow humans. As the morning sunlight falls upon Orlok, he disintegrates. Jonathan enters the room and Ellen expires in his arms. This bizarre ending was invented by Murnau, and shows a strange, perhaps Teutonic attitude toward the femme fatale — it takes real guts to go to bed with such a disgusting creature, even if it's in order to save mankind.

While stage versions were becoming huge successes in England and the United States, film director Tod Browning decided to make his own Dracula movie. Accordingly, in 1930 Universal Pictures bought the motion picture rights to the Balderston-Deane version, resulting in the studio's biggest money-maker in 1931.

Browning's film presents the existence of Dracula the vampire as an accepted fact. Bela Lugosi, the stage Dracula, played the lead in this, his most famous American film. The actor was born Bela Blasko in the town of Lugoj, which is located in the Banat region of Transylvania. His thick accent and slow manner of speaking, his aquiline nose, high cheekbones, and six-foot frame all were perfect for the part. The eerie effect of his almond-shaped, crystal blue eyes was heightened in the film by focusing light on them through two small holes in a piece of cardboard.

The film's story line differs from both the novel and the stageplay. In Browning's film, Renfield, not Jonathan Harker, is the London firm's agent, sent to Transylvania to obtain the signature on the lease for Carfax Abbey. On the way, the peasants warn Renfield about Dracula. He meets Dracula at his castle, and is attacked by him there.

Dracula travels by boat to London, accompanied by Renfield, who is now his slave. Dracula kills all the sailors on board. In London, Renfield is placed in an insane asylum. At the opera Dracula meets Lucy and Mina. Lucy is fascinated by him, and Dracula later makes her into one of his entourage of female vampires. He also begins the process of converting Mina into one, while he kills other Londoners.

Then Professor Van Helsing, an expert on vampires, arrives on the scene. He declares, "Gentlemen, we are dealing with the undead, Nosferatu, the vampire." He notes that Count Dracula throws no reflection in a mirror. He repels him with a cross. In the course of this film, the character Van Helsing becomes the archetype of the fearless vampire killer. He convinces Mina's father and Jonathan that they must find Dracula in his coffin during the day and kill him in order to save Mina from his control. Together they discover Dracula's coffin at Carfax Abbey, and off-screen Van Helsing drives the stake into Dracula's heart. The vampire seems to be destroyed forever. Halfway through the end title of the movie, Van Helsing appears to deliver the verbatim epilogue from the stage version: "Just a moment, ladies and gentlemen! Just a word before you go. We hope the memories of Dracula and Renfield won't give you bad dreams, so just a word of reassurance. When you get home tonight and the lights have been turned down and you are afraid to look behind the curtains and you dread to see a face appear at the window — why, just pull yourself together and remember that after all *there are such things.*"

Bela Lugosi.

The American version became even more popular because of the almost simultaneous release of *Frankenstein* in 1932. It is interesting to speculate on whether there is any correlation between the popularity of these creatures and the period in which they were released — the Great Depression. The optimistic Dr. Frankenstein created a monster that ultimately destroyed him, just as many optimistic investors created a market that in 1929 destroyed them. Dracula drained away the life of his victims, an effect comparable to that of the economic depression.

Lugosi's only rival as the horror king was Boris Karloff, who played Dr. Frankenstein's monster, a role that Lugosi had refused. By now Lugosi was hopelessly typecast. Seven years after Dracula was released it was reissued, and there followed a long line of horror films in which Lugosi participated: *The Return of the Vampire, House of Dracula,* and so on. Lugosi also toured in the role of Dracula both in America and in England. He was addicted to drugs, and by 1955 was institutionalized. He said he had taken morphine during filming in 1931 to relieve the pain in his legs, but he had been a long-time drug user. In August 1956, Bela Lugosi, the vampire king, the living embodiment of Drac-

Christopher Lee, the screen Dracula of the 1950s and 1960s.

ula, died at seventy-two years of age. Although Dracula and other horror roles had netted him more than $600,000, he had only $2,900 left at the time of his death. In accordance with his request, Lugosi was buried wearing his tuxedo, medallion, and black Dracula cloak lined in red satin.

During the 1950s classic horror films were revived on TV, and the Dracula movie became popular again, to a whole new generation of viewers. In 1958 the British screenwriter Jimmy Sangster wrote a new Dracula script that was somewhat based on Stoker's story line for Hammer Films. In *Horror of Dracula* he made Dracula into a realistic monster in technicolor. The director was Terence Fisher. The erotic element predominated: women are attracted to Dracula, they eagerly await his kisses and bites — and he kisses and bites them in full view. Christopher Lee, six-foot-four, thin, macabre, played Dracula. At the end of the film Van Helsing, portrayed by veteran actor Peter Cushing, traps Dracula as he is rushing to get back to his coffin at break of day. In a desperate leap Van Helsing rips the drapes to let in the light, fashions a cross from two huge gold candelabras, and forces Dracula into the sunlight, where the vampire disintegrates into dust. The new Dracula movie opened in May 1958 in both London and New York, and in less than two years it had made eight times its original cost. Several variations on the vampire theme were then made by Hammer Studios of London, including *The Brides of Dracula* (1960), *Kiss of the Vampire* (1963), *Dracula — Prince of Darkness* (1965), *Dracula Has Risen from the Grave* ("You just can't keep a good man down!" screamed the publicity) (1968), *Lust for a Vampire* (1970), *The Vampire Lovers* (1970), *Countess Dracula* (1970), *Scars of Dracula* (1970), *Dracula, A.D.* (1972), *Dracula and the Legend of the Seven Gold Vampires* (1974), and *The Satanic Rites of Dracula* (1978). Queen Elizabeth knighted the head of Hammer Films, Michael Carreras, for reinvigorating the British film industry with his lush horror films.

In the meantime, attempts were being made to make vampire comedies. Roman Polanski directed the stylish *Dance of the Vampires,* retitled *The Fearless Vampire Killers, or Pardon Me, Your Teeth Are in My Neck* (1967) in its American release; however, it was *Love at First Bite* (1979), starring George Hamilton — doing a Bela Lugosi imitation — which achieved vast commercial success. The movie opens in the count's old castle in Transylvania, where the wolves are howling outside and Dracula comments, "Children of the night, shut up!" When the Communist authorities arrive to throw Dracula out of his castle, and the peasant mob turns up with the usual pitchforks, he warns them, "Vat vould Transylvania be without Dracula? It vould be like Bucharest on a Monday night." Dracula takes an airplane to contemporary New York, but there is a mixup with the coffins and he ends up in Harlem. Dressed in the traditional tuxedo and cape, strolling down the streets, he is accosted by some black youths who taunt him, "Hey, superdude! Hey, honkey! Why you all decked out like that?" Dracula solemnly declares, "I am not hunkie, I am Romanian!" Cindy Sonheim, played by Susan St. James, meets Dracula in a disco, invites him back to her cluttered, clothes-on-the-floor messy apartment, and asks him in typical American fashion, "Is there anything I can get for you?" To which Dracula replies, "A broom, perhaps." The Freudian psychiatrist, Dr. Rosenberg, portrayed by Richard Benjamin, who thinks he may be in love with Cindy, tries unsuccessfully to ward off the vampire with a Star of David medallion. In the end, Cindy succumbs to Dracula's charms, and the two fly off in bat form to Transylvania.

In that same year Universal Studios revived its horror tradition from the thirties by releasing a new version of the vampire story called *Dracula,* the same title as their 1931 classic but this time with Frank Langella in the title role. The film carried on the erotic element begun by *Horror of Dracula* twenty years before. The vampire is a sensual, soft-spoken seducer, and the women love him. In the end, Lucy tries to flee with Dracula, but they are discovered onboard a ship leaving England. After a scuffle, Dracula is caught on the hook of a masthead cable and tries to escape, but to no avail; he is hoisted above deck and the sun scorches him. He appears to have been destroyed, except that a batlike cape floats off in the wind as Lucy smiles ambiguously.

Francis Ford Coppola's *Bram Stoker's Dracula* is our final choice because it introduces new approaches to the vampire story. The film opens with the historical prince Vlad Dracula coming home from the crusades, having defeated the Turks in June 1462, only to discover to his horror that his beloved wife, falsely informed that he had died, has drowned herself. Dracula goes into a rage and curses God. He stabs the crucifix, scoops up the blood from the floor, drinks it, and vows vengeance on God. He has lost his faith. The scenario then returns to Stoker's basic story line, except that Mina in the film is the reincarnation of Dracula's wife. This twist probably occurred to Coppola because he was familiar with the 1930 movie *The Mummy,* in which the

Above: Jonathan Harker (Keanu Reeves) is confronted by Dracula (Gary Oldman) in the 1992 film Bram Stoker's Dracula *directed by Francis Ford Coppola. Below: Quincey Morris (Bill Campbell), Arthur Holmwood (Cary Elwes), Abraham Van Helsing (Anthony Hopkins) and Dr. Seward (Richard E. Grant) watch for signs of life as Lucy (Sadie Frost) is laid to rest.*

ancient, lost beloved is reincarnated in a contemporary woman. Another major change from the Stoker story is that Mina, rather than developing into a relentless vampire hunter, turns her gun on her husband and the other vampire killers because she has fallen deeply in love with Dracula. The emphasis is on the love story rather than the horror tale.

···· CHAPTER 13 ····

CONCLUSION

His right hand gripped her by the back of the neck, forcing her face down on his bosom. Her white nightdress was smeared with blood, and a thin stream trickled down the man's bare breast, which was shown by his torn-open dress. The attitude of the two had a terrible resemblance to a child forcing a kitten's nose into a saucer of milk to compel it to drink.

This is the climax of Stoker's novel. Dracula cuts into a vein in his own breast and forces Mina to drink his blood. He has previously drunk her blood, so turnabout is fair play. At last Dracula's sexual secret is out in the open: it is not traditional genital sex that Dracula craves but oral sex. In Coppola's film Gary Oldman, who plays the count, heavily intones these words as Winona Ryder's Mina drinks his blood, "Blood of my blood . . . Drink and join me in eternal life." It is the supreme act of unholy communion, which the Freudian critic Leslie Fiedler has called, "an adulterous union more intimate than mere copulation." Through the mutual drinking of precious bodily fluids, the two lovers become one in mind and heart; a triumph of oral over genital sex.

Changing attitudes toward sex account for the modifications in the vampire theme from the days of Bram Stoker and F. W. Murnau to the contemporary era of Francis Ford Coppola and Anne Rice. Though, obviously, human hostility has existed independent of sexuality, many psychiatrists doubt whether there can ever be sexuality without hostility. One person must take on the role of aggressor in any sexual encounter, and the other must submit. No lover without a beloved. No vampire without a donor. But not to worry — as the contemporary literary critic Lloyd Worley has pointed out, the vampire practices the love techniques of a *castrato,* with no danger of pregnancy. And just as in the Ottoman harem where women often preferred sex with eunuchs since there was no chance of impregnation, so today some women find the contemporary vampire attractive for similar reasons.

The AIDS epidemic is also alluded to in both Coppola's movie, with shots of blood under a microscope, and in Rice's most recent novel, in which the vampire Lestat puts on a condom when he engages in genital sex. The ultimate fascination is with the erotic reality of blood disease and death. Many people may be ambivalent in the face of death, but all fear loss of blood and infections such as AIDS. Just as in *Nosferatu* Murnau presented a powerful parallel between the bubonic plague and the spread of the vampire disease, so both Coppola and Rice emphasize the similarities between the prolonged effects of vampire attacks and AIDS. The element of danger, mystery, and even death associated with sex is thus recreated and preserved in an intelligible contemporary context.

Created during the fifteenth century, the sanguinary villain of the German tales was transformed into a vampire by Stoker and became a permanent myth transcending the limitations of time, geography, and human frailty. But part of mankind's current love affair with Dracula lies in the fact that he was a real historical figure. That is why this book covers both the fictional and the historical aspects of the Dracula image, since our historical research has exerted such a special impact upon so many of the Gothic novels, plays, and films created since 1972. It seems fitting that this work should come on the eve of the centenary celebration of the publication of Stoker's novel.

The mystery of Dracula endures. It lives on in contemporary transformations in vampire fiction and movies, which someday may inspire yet another Harker to journey to Transylvania and the Borgo Pass, or impel a zoologist to study the incidence of large bats in the Carpathian Mountains. It may stimulate a scientist to investigate strange blood diseases like porphyria or AIDS in Eastern Europe, or encourage other historians to carry on the research of this vast topic. The mystery continues at the foot of Castle Dracula, where the Romanian peasants still warn one not to trespass at night, and where local villagers tell frightening tales about still hearing the plaintive voice of Dracula's wife, drowned in the Arges River. Hence, Professor Van Helsing proves to be an expert on human experience and a prophet when he warns: "My friends . . . it is a terrible task we undertake, and there may be consequence to make the brave shudder. For if we fail in this our fight he must surely win: and then where end we? . . . to fail here is not mere life or death. It is that we become as him."

Dracula re-teaches us to deal with what we know from experience but do not like to admit, that things are rarely what they seem to be. Today, the sanitized, comical count appears to be just an amusing teacher of counting for children on *Sesame Street*. An amusing Dracula has even turned up on TV commercials for batteries and home insurance, and on the box of a breakfast cereal called Count Chocula. There is a role-playing game called Vampire, the Masquerade, and a candy with the enticing name Drac Snax.

But behind these seemingly innocent, nonthreatening, often comic portrayals, we all know deep down that Dracula represents what Freud called the uncanny, that which should have remained hidden but does not. There is something both familiar and alien about Dracula the vampire which we try not to recognize, because such recognition is too frightening to face. Hence we invariably see only our own images in the mirror and mysteriously cannot discern those of the vampire. That is why, after all our research, we are more confident than ever that, so long as humans have not discovered the secret to both physical immortality and eternal youth, the mystery of Dracula will live on.

Our book, which began as an intuition some thirty-five years ago, has thus seen the Dracula fad reach its apogee in our day. The memory of Prince Vlad Dracula, which might have been consigned to the dustbin of history along with the lives of so many even more famous Eastern European warlords, had once been kept alive by horror pamphlets and the invention of the printing press. His name had fallen into oblivion by the sixteenth century but was resurrected in the late nineteenth century by Bram Stoker. Similarly in our day, the vampire, which had existed for thousands of years mostly in oral traditions, and which had enjoyed a temporary revival of interest in scholarly circles during the eighteenth century's so-called age of reason, has been given a new lease on life. Both Coppola's Dracula and Rice's Lestat are more like fallen angels than the predatory, evil animal-like Dracula of Stoker.

Above: The counting count of Sesame Street, just one of the ubiquitous incarnations of Stoker's most famous creation.

Left: Cereal killer. Since 1971 the count has been featured on his own breakfast cereal.

It is our fondest wish that this, our latest book on Dracula, may help him at least temporarily rest in peace. But we realize that as long as science has failed to solve the mystery of how to live forever, or how to have absolutely safe sex without the danger of AIDS or some other form of lingering death, Dracula will be back. Hence the warnings of the peasants about the perils of seeking the great undead and about the curse that haunts Dracula's castle may derive from more than a pedestrian sense of caution. They may be warnings from the spirit of Dracula himself. For us, a signal finally came through as we were reaching the last few yards separating us from the castle. A senior member of our expedition slipped, fell down the mountainside, and broke his hip. In horror, the rest of us hurried down to the village and secured a stretcher from the peasants. We transported the victim to a Bucharest hospital, where he attempted to recuperate for six months, but in the end he died of complications from the fall. Was it Dracula's way of saying that he still rules in some other, unearthly domain?

MAPS

CHRONOLOGIES

GENEALOGY

APPENDIXES

ANNOTATED BIBLIOGRAPHY

FILMOGRAPHY

TRAVEL GUIDE

EUROPE
circa 1500 A.D.

NORTH SEA · BALTIC SEA · DENMARK · COPENHAGEN · TEUTONIC ORDER · MOSCOW · HOLY ROMAN EMPIRE · LUXEMBURG · MAINZ · BOHEMIA · PRAGUE · POLAND · CRACOW · LITHUANIA · PARIS · FRANCE · BAVARIA · VIENNA · HUNGARY · BUDAPEST · TRANSYLVANIA · MOLDAVIA · WALLACHIA · VENICE · SERBIA · DANUBE · BULGARIA · BLACK SEA · TREBIZOND · PAPAL STATES · ROME · ADRIATIC SEA · ALBANIA · OTTOMAN EMPIRE · CONSTANTINOPLE · MEDITERRANEAN SEA · ATHENS

DRACULA'S ROMANIA

60 miles
100 km

Budapest · Hungary · BUKOVINA · Dniester R. · STOKER CASTLE · Suceava · Prut R. · BORGO PASS · BISTRITZA · Cluj · TRANSYL-VANIA · Bistritza R. · Siret R. · MOLDAVIA · Mures R. · AMLAS · SIGHISOARA · TARA BIRSEI · BRASOV · KING'S ROCK · CASTLE DRACULA · CHILIA · Black Sea · HUNEDOARA · SIBIU · FAGARAS · BANAT OF SEVERIN · TURNU ROSU · Tirgoviste · BRAILA · Belgrade · COZIA · Arges R. · NIGHT ATTACK · Buzau · DOBRUJA · TISMANA · SEVERIN · Dimbovita R. · SNAGOV · Bucharest · SMEDEREVO · WALLACHIA · GLAVACIOC · Olt R. · SILISTRIA · Turkish Serbia · Danube R. · TURNU · GIURGIU · NICOPOLIS · VARNA · Turkish Bulgaria

Legend:
- ♜ : Castles
- ★ : Battles
- ● : Capitals
- ▬ ▬ : present frontier of Romania
- ⛪ : Monastery
- ▒ : Wallachian possessions in Transylvania
- R. : Rivers

CHRONOLOGIES

PRINCES OF WALLACHIA

Basarab I 1310–52
Nicolae Alexandru 1352–64
Vladislav I 1364–77
Radu I 1377–83
Dan I 1383–86
Mircea the Great/the Old 1386–1418
Mihail 1418–20
Dan II 1420–31
Alexandru Aldea 1431–36
Vlad Dracul (the Devil) 1436–42
Basarab II 1442–43
Vlad Dracul 1443–47
Vladislav II 1447–48
Vlad the Impaler (Dracula) October–November 1448
Vladislav II 1448–56
Vlad the Impaler (Dracula) 1456–62
Radu the Handsome 1462–73
Basarab Laiota (the Old) 1473–74
Radu the Handsome 1475
Basarab Laiota (the Old) 1475
Vlad the Impaler (Dracula) November–December 1476

KINGS OF HUNGARY

Sigismund of Luxembourg 1387–1437 (Holy Roman Emperor,
   1411–33; King of Bohemia, 1420)
Albert II 1438–39
Interregnum 1444–46
Governor: John Hunyadi 1446–53
Ladislas V (the Posthumous) 1440–57 (King of Bohemia, 1453)
Matthias Corvinus 1458–90 (crowned 1464; King of Bohemia, 1469)
Pretender: Frederick III 1440–93 (Holy Roman Emperor; crowned King
   of Hungary, 1459)

SULTANS OF THE OTTOMAN EMPIRE

Murad II 1421–51
   (gave power to his son Mehmed II for a brief period)
Mehmed II 1444–46; 1451–81

Constantine XI Palaeologus 1448–53 (last of the emperors of the Eastern Roman Empire; killed by Turks when they captured Constantinople)

EVENTS

1422	Unsuccessful siege of Constantinople by the Turks.
1427	Turkish domination in Serbia.
1431	Birth of Dracula. His father, Vlad II, invested with the Order of the Dragon, an organization dedicated to fighting the Turks.
1440	Unsuccessful siege of Belgrade by the Turks.
1442–43	Victories of John Hunyadi over the Turks in Transylvania and Wallachia.
1443	Dracula and his brother Radu the Handsome are taken hostage in the Ottoman Empire.
1443–44	The "long campaign" of Hunyadi in the Ottoman Empire.
1444	The Crusade of Varna. Dracula and Radu in danger of death.
1445	The campaign of the Burgundian fleet on the Danube.
1446	Sultan Murad II invades Greece. Mistra becomes a vassal state of the Turks.
1447	Assassinations of Dracula's father, Dracul, and of Dracula's brother Mircea.
1448	Turkish victory over Hunyadi at Kosovo. First reign of Dracula in Wallachia. Turkish domination in the Balkans, except Albania.
1453	Fall of Constantinople to the Turks. Death of Constantine XI, last of the emperors of the Eastern Christian Empire.
1456	Unsuccessful siege of Belgrade by the Turks. Death of John Hunyadi. Moldavia pays tribute to the Turks. Dracula begins his second and major reign in Wallachia.
1457	Dracula's cousin Stephen the Great becomes prince of Moldavia. Victories of Scanderbeg over the Turks in Albania.
1458	The Turks conquer Athens. Matthias Corvinus becomes king of Hungary.
1460	The Turks conquer Mistra and Thebes.
1461	Fall of Trebizond to the Turks.
1462	Turkish campaign against Wallachia. Dracula taken prisoner by King Matthias.
1463–65	The Turks invade Bosnia and Hertzegovina.
1468	Death of Scanderbeg.
1474	Dracula granted freedom by King Matthias.
1475	The Tartar Khan of Crimea becomes a vassal of the Turks. Hungarian campaign in Bosnia. Dracula given a military command by Matthias.
1476	Dracula's third reign in Wallachia begins in November; ends in December when he is killed in battle near Bucharest.

GENEALOGY

Mircea the Great/the Old
(?–1418)
Prince of Wallachia 1386–1418
|
Vlad II, Dracul
(?–1447)
Prince of Wallachia 1436–1442; 1443–1447

Mircea (?–1447)	Vlad the Impaler, Dracula (1431–76) *Prince of Wallachia* *1448; 1456–62; 1476* m. (1) Transylvanian noblewoman	Radu III, the Handsome (1438/9–1500) *Prince of Wallachia* *1462–75*	Vlad (Mircea) the Monk (?–1496) *Prince of Wallach* *1482–95*

Mihnea the Bad
Prince of Wallachia 1508–09
m. (1) Smaranda
m. (2) Voica

Milos	Mircea II *ruled 1509–10* *coregent with father 1509* m. Maria Despina

Alexandru II Mircea *ruled 1574–77* m. Catherine Salvarezi	Peter the Lame *Prince of Moldavia 1574–77* m. (1) Maria Amirali m. (2) Irina the Gypsy
Mihnea II, the Islamized *ruled 1577–83* m. (1) Neaga m. (2) Voica	Stefanita

Radu Mihnea
ruled intermittently 1611–23 in
Wallachia and Moldavia
m. Arghira Minetti
|
Alexandru the Cocoon
ruled 1623–27
died 1632 without known heirs
m. Ruxandra Beglitzi

SECOND MARRIAGE OF VLAD THE IMPALER
(the Hungarian line)

m. (2) relative of Matthias Corvinus, King of Hungary,
probably Ilona Szilagy

Vlad Dracula
m. (?)
claimant to Wallachian throne

Ladislas Dracula
m. member of Vass de Czege family
(land in Banat)

son (name unknown)
died c. 1482
lived with Bishop of Oradea
(no heirs)

Ladislas Dracula de Sintesti
(patent of nobility 1535)
m. Anna Vass de Czege

John Dracula de Band
(land in Szekler region)
m. Anna
(no heirs)

John Dracula
m. (?)
(patent of nobility 1535)

George Dracula
(land in Szekler region)

daughter (name unknown)
m. Getzi family, which kept
Dracula name
(land in Borgo Pass)

Line dies out in
seventeenth century

GERMAN STORIES

Translation by Raymond T. McNally of Manuscript No. 806
at the library of St. Gall Monastery, Switzerland.

1. Once the old governor had the old Dracul killed, Dracula and his brother, having renounced their own faith, promised and swore to protect and uphold the Christian faith. [Reference is to the assassination of Dracula's father and the rumor that Vlad and Radu had converted to Islam during their Turkish captivity.]

2. During these same years Dracula was put on the throne and became lord of Wallachia; he immediately had Ladislaus Waboda [Vladislav II], who had been ruler of that region, killed. [The killing of Vladislav II occurred in 1456.]

3. After that Dracula immediately had villages and castles burned in Transylvania near Hermannstadt [Sibiu], and he had fortifications in Transylvania and villages by the name of the monastery Holtznuwdorff and Holtznetya [Hosmanul] completely burned to ashes.

4. He had Berkendorf [Benesti] in Wuetzerland [Tara Birsei] burned; those men, women, and children, large and small, whom he had not burned at the time, he took with him and put them in chains and had them all impaled.

5. Dracula imprisoned merchants and carriage-drivers from Wuetzerland on a holiday and on that same holiday he had many impaled. [Confirmed by Romanian sources.]

6. Young boys and others from many lands were sent to Wallachia, in order to learn the language and other things. He brought them together and betrayed them. He let them all come together in a room and had them burned. There were four hundred in the room. [Confirmed by Romanian sources.]

7. He had a big family uprooted, from the smallest to the largest,

children, friends, brothers, sisters, and he had them all impaled. [Execution of the Wallachian *boyar* family named Albu is confirmed elsewhere.]

8. He also had his men bury a man naked up to the navel, then he had them shoot at him. He also had some others roasted and some skinned alive.

9. He also captured the young Darin [Dan]. Later on he allowed him to go through his priestly function, and when he had completed it all, then he had him make a grave according to the custom of Christians, and he had his body slaughtered by the grave. [Dan's execution is a historical fact confirmed elsewhere.]

10. Ambassadors, numbering fifty-five, were sent to Wallachia to Dracula from the king of Hungary and from the Saxons in Transylvania. There Dracula had the lords held captive for five weeks and had stakes made for their hostel. And they thought that they would all be impaled. Oh, how greatly troubled they were! He held them so long so that they might betray him. And he set off with all his army and went to Wuetzerland. Early one morning he came to the villages, castles, and towns. All those whom he overcame he also destroyed and had all the grain and wheat burned. And he led away all those whom he had captured outside the city called Kranstatt [Kronstadt; Brasov] near the chapel called St. Jacob [Tampa Hill]. And at that time Dracula rested there and had the entire suburb burned. Also as the day came, early in the morning, all those whom he had taken captive, men and women, young and old, he had impaled on the hill by the chapel and all around the hill, and under them he proceeded to eat at table and get his joy in this way. [Undoubtedly these ambassadors were men sent by King Matthias to learn Dracula's precise relationship with the Turks.]

11. Once he had St. Bartholomew's Church [in Brasov] burned, then he also stole and took away the vestments and chalices. Once he sent one of his captains to a great village called Zeyding [Codlea] to burn it, but that same captain could not burn it, because the villagers resisted. Then he went to his lord and said: "Lord, I was not able to bring myself to do what you ordered me to do." Then he took him and hoisted him up on a stake. [Attack on this church and execution of the Wallachian captain who was unable to capture the fortress of Codlea are historical facts appearing in other sources.]

12. Once he impaled all the merchants and other men with merchandise, the entire merchant class from Wuetzerland near to Thunow and to Pregel, six hundred of them with all their goods and he took the goods for himself.

13. Once he had a great pot made with two handles and over it a staging device with planks and through it he had holes made, so that men's heads would fall through them. Then he had a great fire made underneath it and had water poured into the pot and had men boiled in this way. He had many men and women, young and old, impaled.

14. Also he came again to Siebenburgen [the seven fortresses of Transylvania] to attack Talmetz [Talmetch, near Sibiu]. There he had men hacked up like cabbage and he had those whom he took back to Wallachey [Wallachia] as captives cruelly and in various ways impaled.

15. Once he had thought up terrifying and frightening and unspeakable tortures, so he had mothers impaled and nursing children, and he had one- and two-year-old children impaled. He had children taken from their mothers' breasts, the mothers separated from the children. He also had the mothers' breasts cut out and their children's heads pushed through the holes in their mothers' bodies and then he impaled them. And he caused many other sufferings and such great pain and tortures as all the bloodthirsty persecutors of Christendom, such as Herod, Nero, Diocletian, and other pagans, had never thought up or made such martyrs as did this bloodthirsty berserker.

16. He had people impaled, usually indiscriminately, young and old, women and men. People also tried to defend themselves with hands and feet and they twisted around and twitched like frogs. After that he had them impaled and spoke often in this language: "Oh, what great gracefulness they exhibit!" And they were pagans, Jews, Christians, heretics, and Wallachians.

17. He caught a Gypsy who had stolen. Then the other gypsies came to him and begged Dracula to release him to them. Dracula said: "He should hang, and you must hang him." They said: "That is not our custom." Dracula had the Gypsy boiled in a pot, and when he was cooked, he forced them to eat him, flesh and bone.

18. A nobleman was sent to him, who came to him among the people whom he had impaled. Dracula walked under them and gazed upon them, and there were as many as a great forest. And he

asked Dracula why he walked around under the stench. Dracula asked: "Do you mind the stink?" The other man said: "Yes." So Dracula immediately had him impaled and hoisted him up high in the air, so that he would not smell the stench.

19. A priest had preached that sins could not be forgiven until one made good the injustice done. Then Dracula had that same priest invited to his house and set him at his table. Then the lord had simmel bread put into his food. The priest took the broken bread up with his tablespoon. Then the lord spoke about how the priest had preached about sins, etc. The priest said: "Lord, it is true." He said: "Why then do you take from me my bread, which I have unjustly broken into the food?" And Dracula immediately had the priest impaled.

20. He invited all the landlords and noblemen in his land to his house, and when the meal was over, he turned to the noblest men and asked them how many voevods or lords they remembered who had ruled that same land. One answered him as many as he could think of. So did the other lords, both young and old, and each among them asked how many lords they could recall. One answered fifty; another, thirty; one, twenty; twelve answered similarly, so that none was so young as to remember seven. So he had all those same lords impaled, and there were five hundred of them.

21. He had a mistress who announced that she was pregnant, so he had her looked at by another woman, who could not comprehend how she could be pregnant. So he took the mistress and cut her up from under to her breast and said: "Let the world see where I have been and where my fruit lay." He also had similar things cut or pierced and did other inhuman things which are said about him.

22. In the year 1460, on the morning of St. Bartholomew's Day, Dracula came out of the forest with his servants and had all the Wallachians of both sexes tracked down. Outside the village of Humilasch [Amlas] it is said that he was able to bring so many together that he let them get all piled up in a bunch, and then he cut them up like cabbage with swords, sabers, and knives; as for their chaplain and the others whom he did not kill there, he led them back home and had them impaled. And he had the village completely burned up with their goods and it is said that there were more than 30,000 men killed.

23. In the year of Our Lord 1462 once Dracula came to the large city

of Schylta [Nicopolis], where he had more than 25,000 people of all kinds of ethnic groups killed, Christians, pagans, etc. Among them were the most beautiful women and maidens, who had been taken captive by his courtiers. The courtiers begged Dracula to give the women to them as honorable wives. Dracula did not want to do this and ordered all of them, together with the courtiers, to be cut up like cabbage, because he was angry that he had become obliged to pay tribute to the Turkish sultan, who had demanded the tribute from him. Immediately Dracula let the sultan's people know that he wished to give over the tribute personally to the sultan. The people there were overjoyed, so he let his people come to him in large groups one after the other and he let the remaining courtiers ride with him. And then he had these people all killed. Also he had the same region called Pallgarey [Wulgerey] completely burned. He also had others nailed down by their hair and in all there were 25,000 killed not counting those whom he had burned.

24. Messengers from Hermannstadt saw the dead and impaled in Wallachia like a huge forest, aside from those whom he had roasted, boiled, and skinned.

25. He rounded up an entire region called Fugrash [Fagaras], women, men, and children, and led them to Wallachia where he had them impaled. Similarly, he had the heads cut off his men who had helped him to bury his treasure.

26. He had several lords beheaded and took their bodies and had food cooked up from them. After that he had their friends invited to his house and he gave them something to eat from that food and said to them: "Now you are eating the bodies of your friends." After that he impaled them.

27. He had seen a worker in a short shirt and said to him: "Have you a wife at home?" He said: "Yes." Dracula said: "Bring her here to me." Then he said to her: "What do you do?" She said: "I wash, cook, spin, etc." He immediately had her impaled because she had not made her man a long shirt, so that one could not see the seam. Dracula at once gave him another wife and ordered that she should make a long shirt for her man, or he would also have her impaled.

28. He had a donkey impaled and on the earth above it a Franciscan monk whom he had met.

29. Some three hundred gypsies came into his land; he thereupon

took the best three out and had them roasted and made the other gypsies eat, and said to them: "Thus each of you must eat the others until there are none left," or he sent them against the Turks and fought with them. They were very willing to go there, where he wanted them to go. Then he did something: he clothed them all in cowhide, and similarly their horses as well. And as they came upon one another, the Turkish horses shied away and fled because of the cowhide clothing which their horses did not like and the Turks fled to some water and the gypsies after them, with the result that they all drowned.

30. He also had the poor people who were in his land invited to his house; after they had eaten there, he had them all burned in a small building. There were two hundred of them.

31. He had young children roasted and forced their mothers to eat them. He cut the breasts off women and forced their husbands to eat them; after that he had the men impaled.

32. Several Wahlen [Western ambassadors] were sent to him. When they came to him, they bowed and took off their hats and under them they had brown and red berets or caps, which they did not take off. So he asked them why they had not taken off their caps or berets. They said: "Lord, it is not our custom." And as they thanked his grace, he had them take good strong nails and had them nailed around the caps into the head, so that they could not take them off. In this way he strengthened them in their custom. [In most versions, including the Romanian, the victims are Turkish ambassadors.]

RUSSIAN STORIES

Translation by Raymond T. McNally of the oldest Russian manuscript about Dracula: MS 11/1088 in the Kirillov-Belozersky Monastery Collection at the Saltykov-Schredin Public Library, Leningrad. First translation of this document into a Western language.

Among the very few authentic, signed documents which have been preserved from the late fifteenth century is the Russian "Story about

Dracula." Copies of it were made from the fifteenth to the eighteenth century in Russia. It is one of the first instances of belletristic writing in Russian literature, and the historian Nicholas Karamzin has called it his country's first historical novel.

This manuscript was written by the monk Efrosin from the Kirillov-Belozersky Monastery in northern Russia in the year 1490. In it the monk states that he copied the story from another manuscript penned in 1486. No one knows who the author of that earlier manuscript was. Most scholarly opinion has focused upon a Russian diplomat who was at the Hungarian court in the 1480s, Fedor Kurytsin; he could have picked up the tale there since Dracula had been a captive of the Hungarian king from 1462 to 1474. Moreover, the monk states that the earlier author had seen one of the sons of Dracula.

Whoever the original author was, he was more disturbed by the prince's abandonment of Orthodoxy than by his cruelties. While in prison Dracula "forsook the light" of the Orthodox Church and accepted the "darkness" of the Roman Church because he was too attracted to the "sweetness" of this earthly life and not motivated enough by concern for the next one. Thus, the story has a marked religious tone.

The manuscript supports the notion of a "cruel but just" autocrat in its presentation of Dracula. However cruel his actions may have appeared they were necessary for the good of the state. In order to ward off not only the Turkish invaders but also the continual threat of opposition from the aristocratic *boyars,* Dracula had to take harsh measures. Obviously, the manuscript was written to indicate support of the autocratic ruler in Russia at the time, Ivan III, known as Ivan the Great. Here is the text:

1. There lived in the Wallachian lands a Christian prince of the Greek faith who was called Dracula in the Wallachian language, which means devil in our language, for he was as cruelly clever as was his name and so was his life.

   Once some ambassadors from the Turkish sultan came to him. When they entered his palace and bowed to him, as was their custom, they did not take their caps from their heads and Dracula asked them: "Why have you acted so? You ambassadors have come to a great sovereign and you have shamed me." The ambassadors answered, "Such is the custom of our land and our sovereign."

And Dracula told them, "Well, I want to strengthen you in your custom. Behave bravely." And he ordered that their caps be nailed to their heads with small iron nails. And then he allowed them to go and said, "Go relate this to your sovereign, for he is accustomed to accepting such shame from you, but we are not accustomed to it. Let him not impose his customs upon other sovereigns who do not want them, but let him keep his customs to himself." [This episode confirmed in Romanian and German sources.]

2. The Turkish sultan was very angered because of that, and he set out with an army against Dracula and invaded with overwhelming force. But Dracula assembled all the soldiers he had and attacked the Turks during the night, and he killed a great many of them. But he could not conquer them with his few men against an army so much greater than his, so he retreated.

He personally examined those who had fought with him against the Turks and who had returned. Those wounded in the front he honored and armed them as knights. But those who were wounded in the back he ordered to be impaled from the bottom up and said: "You are not a man but a woman." And when he marched against the Turks once again, he spoke to his entire army in this way, "Whoever wants to think of death, let him not come with me but let him remain here." And the Turkish sultan, hearing of this, retreated with great shame. He lost an immense army and never dared again to set out against Dracula. [The night attack is confirmed by an eyewitness report.]

3. The sultan sent an ambassador once to Dracula, in order that he be given the yearly tribute. Dracula greatly honored this ambassador, and showing him all that he had, he said, "I not only wish to give the sultan the tribute, but I also wish to place myself at his service with my whole army and with my whole treasury. I shall do as he commands, and you shall announce this to your emperor, so that when I shall come to place myself at his disposal, he will give orders throughout his whole land that no harm should come to me or to my men. And, as for me, I shall come to the emperor after your departure and I shall bring him the tribute, and I shall come in person."

When the sultan heard from his ambassador that Dracula wished to submit his service, the emperor honored this man, gave him gifts and was elated because at that time he was at war with the emperors and lands of the East. Immediately the sultan sent to all his fortified cities and throughout his land the message that when Dracula comes, not only should no one do him any harm but, on the contrary, they should honor Dracula when he comes. Dracula set out with his whole army and with him were officers of the emperor who greatly honored him. And he traveled throughout the Turkish empire for about five days. But then suddenly he turned around and began to rob and attack the cities and the towns. And he captured many prisoners whom he cut into pieces. He impaled some Turks, others he cut in two, and then he burned them. The whole country which he penetrated was laid to waste. He allowed no one to remain alive, not even the babes in arms. But others, those who were Christian, he displaced and installed them in his own lands. After taking much booty, he returned home. And, after having honored the officers, he said, "Go and tell your emperor what you have seen. I served him as much as I could. If my service has been pleasing to him, I am again going to serve him with all my might." And the emperor could do nothing against him but was shamefully vanquished. [This episode confirmed by historical documents.]

4. Dracula so hated evil in his land that if someone committed a misdeed such as theft, robbery, lying, or some injustice, he had no chance of staying alive. Whether he was a nobleman or a priest or a monk or a common man, or even if he had great wealth, he could not escape death. And he was so feared that in a certain place he had a source of water and a fountain where many travelers came from many lands, and many of these people came to drink at the fountain and the source, because the water was cool and sweet. Dracula had put near this fountain in a deserted place a great cup wonderfully wrought in gold; and whoever wished to drink the water could use this cup and put it back in its place. And as long as this cup was there, no one dared steal it. [Romanian folklore stresses Dracula's maintenance of law and order.]

5. Once Dracula ordered throughout the land that whoever was old or sick or poor should come to him. And there gathered at the palace a huge multitude of poor and vagabonds, who expected some great act of charity. And he ordered that all these miserable people be gathered together in a large house which was prepared

with this idea in mind. And he ordered that they be given food and drink in accordance with their wishes. Then, after having eaten, they began to amuse themselves. Then Dracula personally came to see them and spoke to them in the following way: "What else do you need?" And they answered him in unison, "Lord, only God and your Highness knows, as God will let you hear." He then said to them, "Do you want me to make you without any further cares, so that you have no other wants in this world?" And, as they all expected some great gift, they answered, "We wish it, Lord." At that point he ordered that the house be locked and set on fire, and all of them perished in the fire within it. During this time he told his nobles, "Know that I have done this first of all so that these unfortunate people will no longer be a burden on others, and so that there should be no more poor in my land but only rich people, and in the second place, I freed these people, so that none of them suffers any longer in this world either because of poverty, or because of some sickness." [Dracula's killing of the sick and poor is a favorite theme in Romanian folklore. One critic has suggested that the prince's motive was control of the plague.]

6. Once there came from Hungary two Roman Catholic monks looking for alms. Dracula ordered them to be housed separately. And he first of all invited one of these monks and showed him in the court countless people on stakes and spokes of wheels. And he asked the monk, "Have I done well? How do you judge those on the stakes?" And the monk answered, "No, lord, you have done badly. You punish without mercy. It is fitting that a master be merciful, and all these unfortunate people whom you have impaled are martyrs." Dracula then called the second monk and posed the same question. The second monk answered, "You have been assigned by God as sovereign to punish those who do evil and to reward those who do good. Certainly they have done evil and have received what they deserved." Dracula then recalled the first monk and told him, "Why have you left your monastery and your cell, to walk and travel at the courts of great sovereigns, as you know nothing? Just now you told me that these people are martyrs. I also want to make a martyr out of you so that you will be together with these other martyrs." And he ordered that he be impaled from the bottom up. But to the other monk, he ordered that he be given fifty ducats of gold and told him, "You are a wise

man." And he ordered that a carriage be prepared for him in order that he be driven with honor to the Hungarian border. [Note different ending in Romanian story no. 6. Note, too, that the Russian version seems designed to support one-man rule, however cruel.]

7. Once a merchant, a foreign guest from Hungary, came to Dracula's capital city. Following his command, the merchant left his carriage on the street of the city before the palace and his wares in the carriage, and he himself slept in the house. Someone came and stole 160 golden ducats from the carriage. The merchant went to Dracula and told him about the loss of the gold. And Dracula told him, "You may go in peace; this night your gold will be returned." And he issued orders to look for the thief throughout the entire city and said, "If you do not find the thief, I will destroy the entire city." And he ordered that the gold be placed in the carriage during the night, but he added one additional gold coin. The merchant got up in the morning and found his gold and he counted the pieces once, twice, and found the one additional gold coin. He went to Dracula and told him, "Sire, I have found the gold, but look, there is one additional gold coin which does not belong to me." At that moment they brought in the thief who had the original gold with him. And Dracula told the merchant, "Go in peace. If you had not told me about the additional gold coin, I was ready to impale you, together with this thief." [This tale recurs in Romanian folklore. Russian version is obviously meant to stress Dracula's sense of justice.]

8. If a married woman committed adultery Dracula ordered that her shameful parts be cut and she be skinned alive. Then he ordered that her skin be hung on a pole in the middle of the city at the marketplace. He did the same thing with young girls who had not preserved their virginity and also widows [who fornicated]. In some cases he cut the nipples off their breasts. In other cases he took the skins from their vagina and he rammed an iron poker, reddened by fire, up their vaginas so far upwards that the iron bar emerged from their mouths. They remained naked, tied to a pole until the flesh and bones detached themselves or served as food for the birds. [A favorite theme in the German pamphlets is Dracula's austere standards for women.]

9. Once when he was traveling, Dracula saw a poor man with a shirt

torn and in bad shape. And he asked that man, "Have you a wife?" And he answered, "I have, sire." Then Dracula said, "Take me to your house, so that I can see her." And in the house of the man he saw a young and healthy wife. Then he asked her husband, "Did you sow grain?" And the husband answered, "Lord, I have much grain." And he showed much grain to him. Then Dracula said to his wife, "Why are you lazy toward your husband? It is his duty to sow and to work and to feed you, but it is your duty to make nice clean clothes for your husband. Only you do not even wish to clean his shirt, though you are quite healthy. You are the guilty one, not your husband. If your husband had not sown the grain, then your husband would be guilty." And Dracula ordered that both her hands be cut off and that she be impaled.

10. Once Dracula was feasting amid the corpses of many men who had been impaled around his table. There amid them he liked to eat and have fun. There was a servant who stood up right in front of him and could not stand the smell of the corpses any longer. He plugged his nose and drew his head to one side. Dracula asked him, "Why are you doing that?" The servant answered, "Sire, I can no longer endure this stench." Dracula immediately ordered that he be impaled, saying, "You must reside way up there, where the stench does not reach you." [Dracula's macabre sense of humor is highlighted in German pamphlets.]

11. On another occasion, Dracula received the visit of an emissary from Matthias the Hungarian king. The ambassador was a great noble of Polish origin. Dracula invited him to stay at his royal table in the midst of the corpses. And set up in front of the table was a very high, completely gilded stake. And Dracula asked the ambassador, "Tell me, why did I set up this stake?" The ambassador was very afraid and said, "Sire, it seems that some nobleman has committed a crime against you and you want to reserve a more honorable death for him than the others." And Dracula said, "You spoke fairly. You are indeed a royal ambassador of a great sovereign. I have made this stake for you." The ambassador answered, "Sire, if I have committed some crime worthy of death, do what you wish because you are a fair ruler and you would not be guilty of my death but I alone would be." Dracula broke out laughing and said, "If you had not answered me thus, you would really be on that very stake yourself." And he honored him greatly

and gave him gifts and allowed him to go, saying, "You truly can go as an envoy from great sovereigns to great sovereigns, because you are well versed in knowing how to talk with great sovereigns. But others let them not dare talk with me, before learning how to speak to great sovereigns."

12. Dracula had the following custom: whenever an ambassador came to him from the sultan or from the king and he was not dressed in a distinguished way or did not know how to answer twisted questions, he impaled them, saying, "I am not guilty of your death but your own sovereign, or you yourself. Don't say anything bad about me. If your sovereign knows that you are slow-witted and that you are not properly versed and has sent you to my court, to me a wise sovereign, then your own sovereign has killed you. And if somehow you dare to come without being properly instructed to my court, then you yourself have committed suicide." For such an ambassador he made a high and wholly gilded stake, and he impaled him in front of all, and to the sovereign of such a foolish ambassador he wrote the following words: "No longer send as an ambassador to a wise sovereign a man with such a weak and ignorant mind."

13. Once artisans made him some iron barrels. He filled the barrels with gold and put them at the bottom of a river. Then he ordered that the artisans be killed, so that no one would know the crime committed by Dracula except for the devil whose name he bore. [The story of the persons who killed the workmen who hid Dracula's treasure occurs the world over, thus this episode can be considered as a mythical one.]

14. On one occasion the Hungarian king Matthias set out with an army to war against Dracula. Dracula met him, they fought, and in the battle they captured Dracula alive, because Dracula was betrayed by his own men. And Dracula was brought to the Hungarian king, who ordered him thrown in jail. And he remained in jail at Visegrad on the Danube up from Buda for twelve years. And in Wallachia the Hungarian king ordered another prince. [Dracula's presence in Hungary is confirmed by Hungarian sources, reports by papal representatives in Buda, and the memoirs of Pius II.]

15. After the death of this prince, the Hungarian king sent a messenger to Dracula, who was in jail, to ask him whether he would like

to become prince in Wallachia again. If so, he must accept the Latin faith, and if he refuses, he must die in jail. But Dracula was more attached to the sweetness of this passing world than life eternal. That is why he abandoned orthodoxy and forsook the truth; he abandoned the light and received the darkness. He could not endure the temporary sufferings of prison, and he was prepared for the eternal sufferings; he abandoned our Orthodox faith and accepted the Latin heresy. The king not only gave him the princedom of Wallachia but even gave him his own sister as a wife. From her he had two sons, he lived for another ten years, and he ended his life in this heresy. [Sources given above confirm Dracula's restoration in 1476, and his heresy in eyes of the Orthodox Church.]

16. It was said about him that even when he was in jail, he could not abandon his bad habits. He caught mice and bought birds in the market. And he tortured them in this way: some he impaled, others he cut their heads off, and others he plucked their feathers out and let them go. And he taught himself to sew, and he fed himself. [This incident is not recorded in any other known sources.]

17. When the king freed him from jail he brought him to Buda where he gave him a house located in Pest across from Buda. At a time before Dracula had seen the king, it so happened that a criminal sought refuge in Dracula's house. And those chasing the criminal came into Dracula's courtyard, began looking for him, and found the criminal. Dracula rose up, took his sword, and cut off the head of the prefect who was holding the criminal and then Dracula liberated the criminal. The other guards fled to the municipal judge and told him what had happened. The judge and his men went to the Hungarian king to complain against Dracula. The king sent a messenger to ask him: "Why have you committed this misdeed?" But Dracula answered in this way: "I did not commit a crime. He committed suicide. Anyone will perish in this way should he thievingly invade the house of a great sovereign. If this judge had come to me and had explained the situation to me, and if I had found the criminal in my own home, I myself would have delivered the criminal to him or would have pardoned him of death." When the king was told about this, he began to laugh and marvel at his courage. [Not found elsewhere.]

18. The end of Dracula came in the following way: while he was ruling Wallachia, the Turks invaded and began to conquer it. Dracula attacked the Turks and put them to flight. Dracula's army began killing the Turks without mercy. Out of sheer joy Dracula ascended a hill in order to see better his men massacring the Turks. Thus, detached from his army and his men, some took him for a Turk, and one of them struck him with a lance. But Dracula, seeing that he was being attacked by his own men, immediately killed five of his would-be assassins with his own sword; however, he was pierced by many lances and thus he died. [That Dracula died in 1476 is certain; whether he died in the circumstances related here is not known.]

19. The king took his sister with the two sons of Dracula to Buda in Hungary. One of these sons still lives with the king's son, whereas the other who was with the bishop of Oradea has died in our presence. I saw the third son, the eldest, whose name was Mikhail, in Buda. He fled from the Turkish emperor to the king of Hungary. Dracula had him by a certain woman when he was not yet married. Stephen of Moldavia, in accord with the wish of the king, helped establish in Wallachia the prince's son called Vlad. This same Vlad was in his youth a monk, later a priest, and subsequently the abbot of a monastery. He was then defrocked and was set up as prince and married. He married the widow of a prince who ruled a little later after Dracula [Basarab III the Young, 1477–1482], and who was killed by Steven the Vlakh. He took the former's wife and now rules Wallachia — the same Vlad who previously had been a monk and abbot. This was first written on February 13, 1486; later, on January 28, 1490, I have transcribed [the text] a second time, I, the sinner Efrosin. [The historical references here are fairly accurate, Dracula's son here called Mikhail was also known as Mihnea. Specific mention of Vlad, "a former monk" as "the present ruler" points to Vlad the Monk (1482–1495) and supports authenticity of the date of the manuscript.]

ROMANIAN STORIES

Translations by Radu Florescu of folktales handed down by word of mouth.
First rendering of this material into another language.

One of the central points made in this book is that the general themes
in the oral Romanian folktales concur with those in the printed German pamphlet and the Russian manuscript sources dating from the
fifteenth and sixteenth centuries. Since the Romanian narratives are
longer, often containing a moral, only a few examples are presented
here.

1. THE FOREIGN MERCHANT. [In Romanian folklore there
   are three variants of this story. Variant A is closest to Russian story
   no. 7. Variant B is very Romanianized and probably developed
   later; for instance, lei, the Romanian currency, are cited instead
   of ducats. Variant C takes a new form altogether; thus it, too, is
   probably a more recent development. It should be noted that
   Variant C shows that in Romania itself the name Dracula was associated with "the Impaler."]

   Variant A: When Dracula ruled Wallachia, an important Florentine merchant traveled throughout the land, and he had a great
   deal of merchandise and money.
      As he reached Tirgoviste, the capital of the country at the time,
   the merchant immediately went to the princely palace and asked
   Dracula for servants who might watch over him, his merchandise,
   and his money.
      Dracula ordered him to leave the merchandise and the money
   in the public square and to come to sleep in the palace.
      The merchant, having no alternative, submitted to the princely
   command. However, during the night, someone passing by his
   carriage stole 160 golden ducats.
      On the next day, early in the morning, the merchant went to
   his carriage, found his merchandise intact, but 160 golden ducats
   were missing. He immediately went to Dracula and told him
   about the missing money. Dracula told him not to worry and
   promised that both the thief and the gold would be found. Se-

cretly he ordered his servants to replace the gold ducats from his own treasury, but to add an extra ducat.

He ordered the citizens of Tirgoviste to immediately seek out the thief, and if the thief were not found, he would destroy his capital.

In the meantime, the merchant went back to his carriage, counted the money once, counted it a second time, and yet again a third time, and was amazed to find all his money there with an extra ducat. He then returned to Dracula and told him: "Lord, I have found all my money, only with an extra ducat."

The thief was brought to the palace at that very moment. Dracula told the merchant: "Go in peace. Had you not admitted to the extra ducat, I would have ordered you to be impaled together with this thief."

This is the way that Dracula conducted himself with his subjects, both believers and heretics. [Mihail Popescu, ed. *Legende istorice ale romanilor din cronicari*, Bucuresti, 1937, pp. 16–18.]

Variant B: In times gone by when Prince Vlad the Impaler was reigning, a merchant, who was traveling throughout our land, yelled at all the crossroads that he had lost a moneybag full of one thousand lei. He promised a hundred lei to whoever would find it and bring it to him. Not long after that, a God-fearing man, as were the Romanians at the time of Prince Vlad the Impaler, came up to the merchant and said to him: "Master merchant, I found this moneybag on my way at the turn in the crossroad at the back of the fish market. I figured that it must be yours, since I heard that you had lost a moneybag." The merchant replied: "Yes, it is really mine, and I thank you for bringing it to me."

As the merchant began to count the money, he was at wits' end to find a way of not giving the promised one-hundred-lei reward. After he had counted the coins, to the amazement of the other man, he put them back in the moneybag and said to the man who had brought it: "I have counted the money, dear sir, and I noticed that you have taken your promised reward. Instead of a thousand leis, I found only nine hundred. You did well, since it was your right. I thank you once again that you saved me from the tight spot in which I was to fall. God keep you in his grace." The Christian answered: "Master merchant, you erroneously and without cause tell me that you are missing one hundred lei. I did not even untie the moneybag to look inside, and I did not even know how much money it contains. I took it to you as I found it." "I told you," replied the merchant cuttingly and with a double meaning, "I had lost a moneybag with one thousand lei. You brought it to me with nine hundred. That's how it is. Even if I should wish it, I cannot give you more. In the last resort, make out a petition and put me on trial."

The merchant blushed to his ears for shame when he realized that the peasant suspected him. The peasant did not say a word but left bidding him farewell, and he went straight to the prince to complain. "Your Highness," he said, "I bring this charge, not because of the promised one hundred lei, but because of the fact that he suspects that I am not an honest man when I know that I was as honest as pure gold, and when it did not even cross my mind to deceive him." The prince recognized the trickery of the merchant, since the prince himself was a clever fellow, and he ordered that the merchant be brought to him. Both the plaintiff and the accused were present. The prince listened to both, and when placing both versions in the balance of justice, the prince realized on which side it weighed. Looking the merchant straight in the eye, he said, "Master merchant, at my court people do not know what a lie is. It is strongly suppressed. You have lost a moneybag containing one thousand lei and you have found it proper to proclaim this at all the crossroads. The moneybag that this Christian brought you contained nine hundred lei. It seems quite obvious that this was not the moneybag that you lost. On the basis of what right did you accept it? Now, give the moneybag back to the man who found it and wait until the moneybag which you lost is found. While you, fellow Christian," added the prince, turning to the accused, "keep the moneybag until the man who lost it shows up." And so it was done, since there was no way of doing otherwise. [Petre Ispirescu, ed., *Povesti despre Vlad Voda Tepes opera postuma* Cernauti, story 4, 1935, pp. 83 and 160.]

Variant C: Once there reigned in Wallachia a Prince Dracula, also known as the Impaler. This prince was very severe, but also just. He would not tolerate thieves, liars, and lazy people. He did all in his power to extirpate such men from his land. Had he reigned longer he would probably have succeeded in freeing his land from such parasites and perhaps even prevented that others of that kind be born. But no such luck today!

At that time a merchant from the city of Florence in Italy was returning to his native land with inestimable wares and a large sum of money. He had to pass through Tirgoviste for there was the seat of the prince at that time. Since he had heard the Turks relate that half had perished at Dracula's hand, he thought that the Romanians were dishonest — as bad as forest thieves. As he reached Tirgoviste, the merchant went straight to Dracula with a great gift and told him: "Your Highness, fate has compelled me to pass through the land that you rule, with all my fortune which I have accumulated through the sweat of many years of hard work in Eastern countries. This land of yours is supposedly Christian. I don't want to have to relate in the West where I am going that a Christian was robbed by Christians, particularly when he was able to escape the sword of the pagan. On my knees I beg Your Highness to lend me a few guards to look after my goods until such time as I leave."

Dracula who was as quick as fire frowned with his eyebrows when he heard that request and said: "Keep your gifts, you Christian. I order you to leave all your possessions in any square or any street, in any part of the city which will appear to you most isolated. Leave your fortune there unguarded until morning. If some theft should occur, I shall be responsible."

This was no joking matter. Dracula's command had to be obeyed — otherwise he would have lost his temper. The Florentine, heart frozen with fright, submitted to the order. He did not sleep a wink because of worry and doubt.

In the morning the merchant returned only to find his possessions intact, as he had left them. He looked at them and could hardly believe his eyes. He went to Dracula, told him that all his possessions were found untouched, and praised his land. He had never seen such a thing in any of the other countries that he had visited and he had been traveling since childhood. "What is the worth of the gift you intended to give me?" asked Dracula. The merchant was somewhat hesitant to reveal it. Dracula insisted on finding out the amount of the gift the merchant had intended to pay. Dracula then told him: "Tell whomever you meet what you have seen in my country." [Ispirescu, story no. 4, 1935, pp. 83–84.]

2. DRACULA AND THE TURKISH AMBASSADORS. [Compare with Russian story no. 1 and German story no. 32.]
It is said that during the reign of Dracula in Wallachia, Sultan Mehmed II sent some ambassadors.

Having entered the reception hall of the prince, the ambassadors paid homage in accordance with their custom of not taking their caps off. Dracula then asked: "Why do you behave in this way? You introduce yourselves to me and then do me dishonor." The Turkish representatives answered in unison: "This is the custom with the rulers of our country." Dracula then spoke to them in this way: "I, too, would like to strengthen your customs, so that you may adhere to them even more rigidly."

He then immediately ordered his retainers to bring him some nails in order to secure the caps on the heads of the Turkish ambassadors.

Having done this, he allowed the envoys to leave and told them: "Go and tell your master that he may be accustomed to suffer such indignity from his own people. We, however, are not so accustomed. Let him not send either to this country or elsewhere abroad, ambassadors exporting his new customs, for we shall not receive them." [Popescu, pp. 15–16.]

3. THE BOYAR WITH A KEEN SENSE OF SMELL. [Compare with Russian story no. 10 and German story no. 18.]
There were times when for whatever crime, whether judged or not judged, a man would lose his life. It is well that those times are now remote; may they never come back. It is well that we can now afford to relate these methods and not be victims anymore.

Some unruly *boyars* had been ordered impaled by Dracula. After some time Dracula, being reminded of the victims, invited yet other *boyars* to watch the spectacle with their own eyes and see how he could punish — seeing is believing. Perhaps Dracula simply wished to find out whether he could recognize some of the *boyars* — for within his retinue were many of the other faction [Danesti]. One of these *boyars,* either because he had been involved in the intrigues of the impaled victims or perhaps because he had been friendly to some of them, and fearing not to admit that he was overcome by pity, dared to tell Dracula: "Your Highness, you have descended to this spot from the palace. Over there the air is pure, whereas here it is impure. The bad smell might affect your health." "Do you mean to say it stinks?" asked Dracula, quickly leaning toward him and looking at him intently. "This is so, Your Highness, and you would do well to leave a place which might be detrimental to the health of a prince who has the good of his subjects at heart."

Perhaps because Dracula had finally penetrated into the depths of the mind of the *boyar*, or perhaps in order to shut up the remarks of other *boyars*, he shouted: "Servants, bring me a stake three times as long as those that you see yonder. Make it up for me immediately in order that you impale the *boyar*, so that he may no longer be able to smell the stench from below."

The unfortunate *boyar* begged on his knees. He wanted to kiss Dracula's hands on both sides, all in vain. After a short time he was struggling on a stake much higher than all the others and he moaned and groaned so vehemently that you heaved a sigh. [Ispirescu, story no. 6, 1935, pp. 25–27.]

4. THE LAZY WOMAN. [Compare with Russian story no. 9 and German story no. 27.]
Dracula was a clever man who insisted on good order in his state. Woe to any soldier whom he saw improperly attired — he rarely escaped with his life. He liked to see his citizens cleanly attired and looking smart. Around him, he could not tolerate anyone who floundered or was slow in his work. Whenever he noticed a libertine or a rake he lost his temper.

One day he met a peasant who was wearing too short a shirt. One could also notice his homespun peasant trousers which were glued to his legs and one could make out the side of his thighs when he saw him [dressed] in this manner. Dracula immediately ordered him to be brought to court. "Are you married?" he inquired. "Yes, I am, Your Highness." "Your wife is assuredly of the kind who remains idle. How is it possible that your shirt does not cover the calf of your leg? She is not worthy of living in my realm. May she perish!" "Beg forgiveness, My Lord, but I am satisfied with her. She never leaves home and she is honest." "You will be more satisfied with another since you are a decent and hard-working man."

Two of Dracula's men had in the meantime brought the

wretched woman to him and she was immediately impaled. Then bringing another woman, he gave her away to be married to the peasant widower. Dracula, however, was careful to show the new wife what had happened to her predecessor and explained to her the reasons why she had incurred the princely wrath.

Consequently, the new wife worked so hard she had no time to eat. She placed the bread on one shoulder, the salt on another and worked in this fashion. She tried hard to give greater satisfaction to her new husband than the first wife and not to incur the curse of Dracula. Did she succeed?

It is just as well that Dracula does not rule our country today, for he would have had to expend many stakes, which might have eliminated from our land the innumerable drones who wither the very grass on which they sit. [Ispirescu, story no. 5, 1935, pp. 21–25.]

5. THE BURNING OF THE POOR. [This tale has a particularly moral bent to it. Compare with Russian story no. 5 and German story no. 30.]

The tale relates that there were a great number of people out of work at the time of Prince Vlad the Impaler. In order to live they had to eat, since the unmerciful stomach demanded food. So, in order to eat they wandered aimlessly and begged for food and they subsisted by begging without working. If a man, as I say, were to ask one of these beggars why they didn't work a little, too, some would answer: "Don't I wander around all day long? If I cannot find work, am I to blame?" One of that kind an onlooker could set straight with the proverb: "I am looking for a master but God grant that I don't find one." The others also always found a pretext for not working, such as: "The furrier strains his legs day and night, but does not get anything out of it; the tailor works all his life and his reward is like the shadow of a needle; the shoemaker bends and stoops until he gets old and when he dies he is buried with an empty collection plate." And in this way they found something wrong with all the trades.

When the prince heard of this and saw with his own eyes the large number of beggars who were really fit for work, he began to reflect. The Gospel says that man shall earn his daily bread only through the sweat of his brow. Prince Vlad thought: "These men live off the sweat of others, so they are useless to humanity. It is a form of thievery. In fact, the masked robber in the forest demands your purse, but if you are quicker with your hand and more vigorous than he you can escape from him. However, these others take your belongings gradually by begging — but they still take them. They are worse than robbers. May such men be eradicated from my land!" And after due reflection, he ordered that the announcement be made throughout the land that on a certain day all beggars should assemble, since the prince was going to distribute a batch of clothes and to treat them to a copious meal.

On the appointed day, Tirgoviste groaned under the weight of the large number of beggars who had come. The prince's servants passed out a batch of clothes to each one, then they led the beggars to some large house where tables had been set. The beggars marveled at the prince's generosity, and they spoke among themselves: "Truly it is a prince's kind of grace — even this charity is at the expense of the people. Couldn't the prince give us something out of his own pocket for a change?" "Hey, the prince has changed. He is no longer the way you knew him." "A wolf can change his fur, but not his bad habits."

Then they started eating. And what do you think they saw before them: a meal such as one would find on the prince's own table, wines and all the best things to eat which weigh you down. The beggars had a feast which became legendary. They ate and drank greedily. Most of them got dead drunk. As they became incoherent, they were suddenly faced with fire on all sides. The prince had ordered his servants to set the house on fire. They rushed to the doors to get out, but the doors were locked. The fire progressed. The blaze rose high like inflamed dragons. Shouts, shrieks, and moans arose from the lips of all the poor enclosed there. But why should a fire be moved by the entreaties of men? They fell upon each other. They embraced each other. They sought help, but there was no human ear left to listen to them. They began to twist in the torments of the fire that was destroying them. The fire stifled some, the embers reduced others to ashes, the flames grilled most of them. When the fire finally abated, there was no trace of any living soul.

And do you believe that the breed of poor was wiped out? Far

. . . . . .

from it — don't believe such nonsense. Look around you and ascertain the truth. Even today times are not better than they were then. Beggars will cease to exist only with the end of the world. [Ispirescu, story no. 8, 1936, pp. 1–6.]

6. THE TWO MONKS. [Compare with Russian story no. 6 and with German story no. 19.]

A crafty Greek monk who, like many others, was beginning to travel throughout the land, happened to meet a poor Romanian priest, an honest God-fearing man. Every time they met, the two clerics argued and between them there arose a fiery dispute. The Greek monk was constantly belittling the priest and criticizing Romanians. The native answered: "If you find Romanians stupid and uncouth, why don't you return to your land among your subtle and wily Greek compatriots? Who has brought you hither and who has called you like a plague on our heads?"

News about the two clerics reached Dracula's ears. He wished to see them and ordered that on a certain day they both be brought to the palace.

They came on the appointed day. He received them in separate rooms. The Greek monk was proud to have been received by the prince, but he did not know that the native cleric had also been invited. The latter was astonished and could not understand how Dracula had found out about him, but he determined that should he find him well disposed he would place a good word for his parishioners. Dracula, however, wished to probe their innermost thoughts, for His Highness was crafty in this respect. When the Greek monk entered the chamber, Dracula asked him: "Reverend priest, you have traveled through my country in the service of the church. You had occasion to speak to good and bad people, with the rich and the poor. Tell me, what do the people say about me?"

To such an obvious question the priest thought that he had the obvious retort. With a craftiness of which only a Greek is capable, he answered in a honeyed and false way: "Your Highness, from one end of the land to the other everyone praises your name. Everyone is pleased with your reign. They say that such a just ruler has never reigned in Wallachia. To which compliment I shall add that you need to do one more thing: be kinder to those of your subjects who come from the holy places [Greeks] and give them financial aid, so that they may bring consolation for the misfortunes suffered by their monks at these holy places. Then your name will be blessed of the angels with undying praise." "You are lying, you unworthy priest, like the villain that you are," shouted Dracula, angered and frowning with his brows. It was obvious that he had been informed about the priest. The proverb states that even the sun cannot give heat to everyone. Opening the door he ordered his retainers who were on guard: "Soldiers, this wicked, unworthy being must be executed." The order was immediately obeyed and the monk was impaled. Then going to the Romanian priest who was ignorant of all that had happened, Dracula asked him the same question: "Tell me, what do people say about me?" "What should they say, Your Highness? People have not spoken with one voice. Recently, however, they are beginning to castigate you everywhere and say that you no longer lessen their burdens, which were small in the days of your predecessor." "You dare to speak fairly," said Dracula in a gleeful tone of voice. "I will think about that. Be the court confessor from this point onward and go in peace." [Ispirescu, story no. 7, 1935, pp. 27–32.]

7. DRACULA'S MISTRESS. [Compare with German story no. 21 and Russian story no. 8.]
Dracula had a mistress. Her house was located in a dark and isolated suburb of Tirgoviste. When Dracula went to see her he was oblivious of everything, for this woman unfortunately happened to be to his taste. For her he had mere physical attraction, nothing else. The unfortunate woman tried in every way to be pleasing to Dracula. And he reciprocated all the outward manifestations of love which she showed him. One might almost say that Dracula expressed a certain gaiety when he was by her side.

One day when she saw his expression somewhat gloomier, she wished in some way to cheer him up and she dared tell him a lie. "Your Highness, you will be glad to hear my tidings." "What news can you give me?" answered Dracula. "The little mouse," she answered allegorically, "has entered the milk churn." "What does this mean?" questioned Dracula, grinning. "It means, Your Highness, that I am with child." "Don't you dare prattle such tales."

The woman knew Dracula's method of punishing lies and wished to justify her statement. "It is, Your Highness, as I have said." "This will not be," said Dracula, frowning with his eyebrows. "But if it were possible I reckon that Your Highness would be glad," dared she continue. "I told you this will not be," retorted Dracula, rudely stamping his foot, "and I will show you it will not happen." Unsheathing his sword, he opened her entrails in order to see for himself whether she had spoken the truth or had lied.

As the woman lay dying, Dracula told her: "You see that it cannot be." He left while she agonized in great pain. She was punished because, hoping to cheer up her lover, she had told a lie. [Ispirescu, story no. 3, 1935, pp. 14–16.]

8. VLAD THE IMPALER. [In their characterization of the tyrant prince, the following accounts concur with the Russian and German sources.]

Variant A: And the old folks said that this village of ours, Vladaia, including its property, takes its name from a prince of the land called Vlad the Impaler. This prince had here, where the town hall now stands, a big house in which he sentenced the guilty and impaled them. Even today one may find in the soil the remains of those who had been impaled on the hill near the fountain. And perhaps if so many cruel battles had not taken place at Vladaia during the time of Vlad the Impaler and in more recent days, one would find even today the house where the judgments were made, as well as the dreadful impalement stake. [Told by Dinu Dimitriu, age sixty, of Vladaia, Mehedinti district.]

Variant B: Good God, times were bad because of the Turks at the time of Vlad the Impaler! The tax collectors came and took men either as hostages or to enroll them as their soldiers. They even took from our herds one out of every tenth one and what was better and more plentiful than sheep at that time? The poor sheep — "Come summer, they sweeten you, come winter, they warm you." Milk was so plentiful that at that time our ancestors made mamaliga with milk instead of water, as the milk was cheap. And all that was the reason why Prince Vlad hated the Turks. He pursued them to the last man and when he caught them, he had them impaled.

Prince Vlad also punished the *boyars* who were often conniving with the Turks or did not behave honestly with people such as we. On one occasion, in order to trip them up more easily, he gave a great feast and also summoned those *boyars* against whom he bore a grudge. But when they came, he impaled them. [Told by Ghita a lui Dinu Radului of Almajel, Mehedinti district.]

Variant C: Mother! It is said that Vlad the Impaler was a terribly harsh ruler. He impaled whoever he caught lying or behaving badly toward the elderly or oppressing the poor. He also impaled the Turks who came, from time to time, to rob our country. It is said that this prince had a house in some bigger village where he sat in judgment and where he also had stakes and gallows.

The house where justice was administered was in our village, Albutele, near Beleti. Whoever he caught red-handed was sentenced and hanged there. And after he had taken their life, he impaled them. [Told by Marga Bodea Matusa, age seventy-six, of Muscel district; recorded in "Legende, traditii si amintire istorice adrurate din Oltenia si din Muscel," *Ac. Rom. din viata poporului Roman Culegeri si Studii,* Bucuresti, 1910.]

ANNOTATED
BIBLIOGRAPHY
· · · · · · · · · · · · · · · ·

BOOKS BY BRAM STOKER

The Duties of Clerks of Petty Sessions in Ireland, by Bram Stoker, Inspector of Petty Sessions (The Authority, Dublin, printed for the author by John Falconer, 53 Upper Sackville Street, Dublin, 1879). A standard reference book for clerks in the Irish civil service.

Under the Sunset, with illustrations by W. Fitzgerald and W. V. Cockburn (Sampson & Low, London, 1881). A collection of horror stories for children. *See also* Douglas Oliver Street, "Bram Stoker's *Under the Sunset.* An Edition with Introductory Biographical and Critical Materials" (Newcastle Publishers, North Hollywood, 1978).

A Glimpse of America: A Lecture Given at the London Institution 28 December 1885 (Sampson & Low, London, 1886).

The Snake's Pass (Sampson & Low, London, 1890; American edition, Harper & Brothers, N.Y., 1890). A romantic novel set in western Ireland, where an Englishman on vacation encounters the legend of "Shleenanaher" or "Snake's Pass," an opening leading to the sea in the mountain of Knockcalltecrore, where French invaders were thought to have buried a great treasure in the shifting bog. The story introduced the *gombeen* man, a ruthless moneylender preying on the poor, and used Irish dialect. The tale was praised by critics, one of whom compared it favorably to Sheridan LeFanu's "Carmilla."

The Watter's Mou (Theo. L. De Vinne & Co., N.Y., 1894). A romantic story of smuggling and love set in Cruden Bay, Scotland. "The Watter's Mou" meant "The Water's Mouth" in Scottish dialect, referring to the water of Cruden Bay, which runs to the sea between the village and Slains Castle.

Crooken Sands (Theo. L. De Vinne & Co., N.Y., 1894). A thriller set in Cruden Bay, where a London merchant on vacation dresses up as a Highland chieftain, only to be shocked when he sees his own image get sucked into the quicksand.

The Shoulder of Shasta (A. Constable & Co., Westminster, 1895; Macmillan & Co., London, N.Y., 1895). A romantic novel set in northern California on the shoulder of Mount Shasta, where a weak young girl temporarily succumbs to a case of puppy love for rough mountain man, Grizzly Dick.

Dracula (A. Constable, Westminster, 1897; Doubleday & McClure, N.Y., 1899). Stoker's mother hit the mark when she wrote to Bram about it, "No book since Mrs. Shelley's *Frankenstein* or indeed any other at all has come near yours in originality, or terror."

Miss Betty (C. A. Pearson Limited, London, 1898). Rich Miss Betty Pole falls in love with poor Rafe Otwell, who undergoes some trials before the happy ending. The only novel Stoker ever dedicated to his wife, and the only one with a frontispiece portrait of him. *Miss Betty*, a play in four acts by Stoker, was performed at the Lyceum Theatre that same year.

The Mystery of the Sea (W. Heinemann, London, 1901; Doubleday, Page, N.Y., 1902). A rousing romantic novel again set in Cruden Bay. Rich adventurer Archie Hunter discovers sixteenth-century Spanish writing in code which he deciphers with great difficulty; it pinpoints the location of a treasure from one of the ships of the Spanish Armada, which wrecked off Cruden Bay. Together with an American heiress, Archie sets out to solve the mystery of the sea and must battle foreign agents also after the treasure.

The Jewel of Seven Stars (W. Heinemann, London, 1903; Harper & Brothers, N.Y., 1904). Like *Dracula,* this story was based on a real historical character and on extensive research into Egyptian folklore. In Notting Hill, London, attempts are being made on the life of a man who has devoted his life to gathering mummies and relics associated with the Egyptian queen Thera, who practiced witchcraft to defend herself against her own priests. The jewel of seven stars contains the secret of the queen's intention to come back from the dead by transferring her soul into that of a living woman five thousand years after her own death. In the conclusion, the final experiment is conducted in a cave by the sea in Cornwall to see if Thera can succeed in coming back. The publishers found the original ending to be so frightening that Stoker was asked to rewrite a somewhat less scary *dénouement,* which he did. The 1903 Heinemann and the 1904 Harper editions contain the original horrific ending. Two movies were based on *The Jewel of Seven Stars, Blood from the Mummy's Tomb* (1971) and *The Awakening* (1980). Most critics agreed that this was Stoker's best horror story since *Dracula.*

The Man (W. Heinemann, London, 1905; an abridged edition, *The Gates of Life,* was published by Cupples & Leon Co., N.Y.). The strong-willed Stephen Norman is a young woman who proposes marriage to a male scoundrel and is rejected. She spurns her real lover, but it all leads eventually to their happy reunion in the end. In it Stoker demonstrated his uncanny ability to deal sympathetically with both feminine and masculine characteristics in the young heroine.

Personal Reminiscences of Sir Henry Irving (W. Heinemann, London, 1906; Macmillan Co., N.Y., 1906).

Lady Athlyne (W. Heinemann, London, 1908; Paul R. Reynolds, N.Y., 1908). An Anglo-American romance in which a Kentucky colonel's daughter named Joy Ogilvie (who has adopted the name Lady Athlyne for fun) journeys to Britain and, after several harrowing Scottish adventures, finds love.

Snowbound: The Record of a Theatrical Touring Party (Collier & Co., London, 1908). A collection of fifteen stories, some of which appeared in the British *Collier's Magazine.*

The Lady of the Shroud (W. Heinemann, London, 1909).

Famous Imposters (Sidgwick & Jackson, London, 1910; Sturgis & Walton, N.Y., 1910). A collection of infamous impersonators across the ages, including Cagliostro, Mesmer, and "The Bisley Boy," a legend that Queen Elizabeth I was actually a man.

The Lair of the White Worm (W. Rider, London, 1911; abridged and rewritten edition, Foulsham, London, 1925; first American edition, published as *The Garden of Evil,* N.Y. Paperback Library, 1966; contains the complete unabridged text of all forty chapters of the original British edition). The story is based on the folklore of the giant serpents or worms which once lived in England. A snake woman, Lady Arabella, secrets herself in a deep mud hole and projects herself in the form of a woman, but the hero unmasks her and dynamites her lair. Stoker's last novel and one of his weirdest.

Dracula's Guest and Other Weird Stories (G. Rutledge, London, 1914;

reprint by Hillman-Curl, N.Y., 1937). Published two years after Stoker's death; originally titled *Walpurgis Night*.

The Bram Stoker Bedtime Companion, edited by Charles Osborne (Victor Gollancz, London, 1973, and Taplinger, N.Y., 1973). Contains ten stories by Stoker.

Midnight Tales, edited by Peter Haining (Peter Owen, London, 1990). An anthology of Stoker's short stories.

PRIMARY SOURCES

At the Philip H. and A. S. W. Rosenbach Foundation, Philadelphia, Pa.: anonymous German printed pamphlet, *Die Geschicht Dracole Waide*. Nürnberg: Wagner, 1488. Available in English translation in a pamphlet edited by Beverly Eddy entitled *Dracula: A Translation of the 1488 Nürnberg Edition*, Philadelphia, Pa.: Rosenbach Museum and Library Publication, 1985.

Also at the Rosenbach Foundation: seventy-eight pages of the unpublished Stoker notes, outlines, time sequences, plans for characters and chapters, and diagrams for his novel *Dracula*, plus his lists and quotations from the books that he used while composing his novel. Put on auction in 1913 by Sotheby's, London. Sold by Philadelphia book dealer Charles Sessler to the Rosenbach Foundation in 1970.

At the British Museum Library, London: Ms. 24315, 138–143. Fifteenth-century Dracula manuscript. Anonymous German pamphlet *Ein wünderliche und erschröliche Hystorie*. Bamberg: Hans Spörer, 1491.

NONFICTION

Books

Barber, Paul. *Vampires, Burial and Death: Folklore and Reality*. New Haven, Ct.: Yale University Press, 1988. Scholarly study of the connections between vampire tales and burial practices.

Baring-Gould, Sabine. *The Book of Werewolves*. London: Smith, Elder, 1865; New York: Causeway, 1973. From this book Stoker took his physical description of Count Dracula's strange hands, information about the life and legend of the Blood Countess, Elizabeth Bathory, and the notion of the vampire using blood to restore and retain youthful appearance.

Brokaw, Kurt. *A Night in Transylvania: The Dracula Scrapbook.* New York: Grosset and Dunlap, 1976. Large format with illustrations and photos: intro., "The Dracula Phenomenon" by Raymond McNally and Radu Florescu; a good general introduction to the novel's actual setting and a useful travel guide.

Bunson, Matthew. *The Vampire Encyclopedia.* New York: Crown, 1993. Tidbits of information about vampire-related topics.

Carter, Margaret. *Shadow of a Shade: A Survey of Vampirism in Literature.* New York: Gordon Press, 1975. Excellent study of the vampire theme in literature.

————, ed. *Dracula: The Vampire and the Critics.* Ann Arbor, Mich.: UMI Research Press, 1988. Superb analysis of the tortured path of Stoker's novel on its way toward begrudging acceptance as a classic by most literary critics.

————. *The Vampire in Literature: A Critical Bibliography.* Ann Arbor/London: UMI Research Press, 1989. Useful guide to vampire fiction.

Copper, Basil. *The Vampire in Legend, Fact, and Art.* Secaucus, N.J.: The Citadel Press, 1974. Competent investigation into vampire bats, literature, and cases of living vampires.

Cox, Greg. *The Transylvanian Library. A Consumer's Guide to Vampire Fiction.* San Bernardino, Calif.: Borgo, 1993. An up-to-date, fairly comprehensive review of vampire fiction with valuable commentaries.

Farson, Daniel. *The Man Who Wrote Dracula: A Biography of Bram Stoker.* London: M. Joseph, 1975; New York: St. Martin's, 1976. A controversial book which highlights Romanian touristic exploitation of the historical Dracula and advances but does not prove the theory that Stoker may have died of syphilis.

Florescu, Radu R., and Raymond T. McNally. *Dracula: A Biography of Vlad the Impaler.* New York: Hawthorn, 1973. A preliminary study of the historical Dracula within the Romanian context.

————. *Dracula, Prince of Many Faces.* Boston: Little, Brown, 1989. Biography placing Vlad the Impaler in his European historical setting.

————. *The Complete Dracula.* Acton, Mass.: Copley, 1992; reprint of *In Search of Dracula* and *Dracula: A Biography of Vlad the Impaler* in one volume.

Gerard, Emily de Laszowska. *The Land Beyond the Forest.* London: W. Blackwood and Sons, 1888. One of Stoker's main sources for Romanian vampire folklore, especially Gerard's chapter entitled "Transylvanian Superstitions."

Leatherdale, Clive. *Dracula, the Novel and the Legend: A Study of Bram Stoker's Gothic Masterpiece.* Wellingborough Northamptonshire, U.K.: Aquarian, 1985. Revised edition, Brighton, U.K.: Desert Island, 1993. Excellent analysis of the main factors behind the creation of Stoker's novel and its appeal.

———. *The Origins of Dracula: The Background to Bram Stoker's Gothic Masterpiece.* London: William Kimber, 1987. Well-written probe into the literary creation of Count Dracula but leaves the important mystery unsolved as to exactly how and why Stoker succeeded in writing a classic horror novel.

Ludlam, Harry. *A Biography of Dracula: The Life Story of Bram Stoker.* New York: Foulsham, 1962. Although largely restricted to his activity in the theater, it remains the most complete Stoker biography to date.

Mackenzie, Andrew. *Dracula Country: Travels and Folk Beliefs in Romania.* London: Arthur Barker, 1977. A competent travelogue with short sections on Stoker, the historical Dracula, and Romanian folklore.

McNally, Raymond T., and Radu R. Florescu. *In Search of Dracula: A True History of Dracula and Vampire Legends.* Greenwich, Ct.: New York Graphic Society, 1972; New York: Warner, 1973. A pioneer work that traced the links between the Dracula of fiction and film and the historical Vlad Dracula, the Impaler.

McNally, Raymond T. *Dracula Was a Woman.* New York: McGraw-Hill, 1983. A study of the life and legend of the infamous Blood Countess, Elizabeth Bathory, and her influence upon Stoker's vampire count.

Riccardo, Martin. *Vampires Unearthed.* New York: Garland, 1983. A comprehensive bibliography of vampire themes in fiction, theater, movies, nonfiction, and magazines.

Ronay, Gabriel. *The Truth about Dracula.* New York: Stein & Day, 1972; also published as *The Dracula Myth.* London: W. H. Allen, 1972. The first part traces the history of vampires; the second part deals with Stoker; the third part is essentially the history of Countess Elizabeth Bathory.

Roth, Phyllis A. *Bram Stoker.* Boston: Twayne, 1982. An excellent short biography of Bram Stoker.

Summers, Montague. *The Vampire: His Kith and Kin.* London: Routledge and Kegan Paul, 1928; reprint, New Hyde Park, N.Y.: University Books, 1960. A pioneering work by an avid vampire researcher.

———. *The Vampire in Europe.* London: Routledge and Kegan Paul, 1929; reprint, New Hyde Park, N.Y.: University Books, 1962. An original contribution to the field.

Treptow, Kurt, ed. *Dracula. Essays on the Life and Times of Vlad Tepes.* East European Monographs, no. 323, New York: Columbia University Press, 1991. Includes research by Raymond McNally on Romanian folklore about Dracula and by Radu Florescu on Dracula's military exploits.

Wilkinson, William. *An Account of the Principalities of Wallachia and Moldavia, with Various Political Observations Relative to Them.* London: Longmans, 1820; reprint, New York: Arno Press, 1971. Stoker obtained most of his information about the historical Dracula from this book.

Articles

Barber, Paul. "Forensic Pathology and the European Vampire." *Journal of Folklore Research,* vol. 24, no. 1 (1987).

———. "The Real Vampire." *Natural History,* October 1990.

Bentley, C. F. "The Monster in the Bedroom: Sexual Symbolism in Bram Stoker's *Dracula.*" *Literature and Psychology,* vol. 22, no. 1 (1972).

Bierman, Joseph S. "Dracula: Prolonged Childhood Illness and the Oral Triad." *American Imago,* vol. 29 (summer 1972).

———. "Genesis and Dating of Dracula from Bram Stoker's Working Notes." *Notes and Queries,* 222 (new series 24, January–February 1977).

Blinderman, Charles S. "Vampurella: Darwin and Count Dracula." *Massachusetts Review,* vol. 21 (1980).

Byers, Thomas B. "Good Men and Monsters: The Defenses of *Dracula.*" *Literature and Psychology,* vol. 31, no. 4 (1981).

Craft, Christopher. " 'Kiss Me with Those Red Lips': Gender and Inversion in Bram Stoker's *Dracula.*" *Representations,* no. 8 (fall 1984).

Czabai, Stephen. "The Real Dracula." *Hungarian Quarterly,* Autumn 1941.

Demetrakopoulos, Stephanie. "Feminism, Sex Role Exchanges, and

Other Subliminal Fantasies in Bram Stoker's *Dracula.*" *Frontiers: A Journal of Women's Studies,* vol 2, no. 3 (1977).

Dukes, Paul. "Dracula: Fact, Legend and Fiction." *History Today,* vol. 32 (July 1982).

Florescu, Radu R. "Dracula as Hero: Apology for a Part-Time Monster." *International History Magazine,* vol. I, no. 8 (August 1973); reprinted in Haining. *The Dracula Scrapbook.* London: New English Library; New York: Bramhall House, 1976.

Fontana, Ernest. "Lombroso's Criminal Man and Stoker's Dracula." *Victorian Newsletter,* no. 66 (fall 1984).

Fry, Carrol L. "Fictional Conventions and Sexuality in *Dracula.*" *Victorian Newsletter,* no. 42 (fall 1972).

Griffin, Gail B. " 'Your Girls That You All Love Are Mine': *Dracula* and the Victorian Male Sexual Imagination." *International Journal of Women's Studies,* vol. 3, no. 5 (1980).

Hatlen, Burton. "The Return of the Repressed/Oppressed in Bram Stoker's *Dracula.*" *Minnesota Review,* no. 15 (fall 1980).

Heick, Alex. "Prince Dracula, Rabies, and the Vampire Legend." *Annals of Internal Medicine,* vol. 117, no. 2 (July 15, 1992).

Hennelly, Mark M. "Dracula: The Gnostic Quest and Victorian Wasteland." *English Literature in Transition: 1880–1920,* vol. 20, no. 1 (1977).

Johnson, Alan P. " 'Dual Life': The Status of Women in Stoker's *Dracula.*" In *Sexuality and Victorian Literature,* no. 27, *Tennessee Studies in Literature,* edited by Dan Richard Cox. Knoxville: University of Tennessee Press, 1984.

Kayton, Lawrence. "The Relation of the Vampire Legend to Schizophrenia." *Journal of Youth and Adolesence,* vol. 1, no. 4 (1972).

Kinder, Nancy. "The Vampires of Rhode Island." *Mysterious New England,* edited by Austin N. Stevens. Dublin, N.H.: Yankee Inc. (1971).

Kirtley, Bacil F. "Dracula, the Monastic Chronicles and Slavic Folklore." *Midwest Folklore,* vol. 6, no. 3 (fall 1956).

MacGillivray, Royce. "*Dracula:* Bram Stoker's Spoiled Masterpiece." *Queen's Quarterly,* vol. 79, no. 4 (winter 1972).

McCully, Robert S. "Vampirism: Historical Perspective and Underlying Process in Relation to a Case of Auto-Vampirism." *Journal of Nervous and Mental Disease,* vol. 139, no. 5 (November 1964).

McNally, Raymond T. "The Fifteenth Century Manuscript of Kritiboulos of Imbros as an Historical Source for the History of Dracula." *East European Quarterly*, vol. 21, no. 1 (March 1987).

———. "Origins of the Slavic Narrative about the Historical Dracula." In *Romania between East and West*, edited by S. Fischer-Galati, Radu R. Florescu, and G. R. Ursul. East European Monographs; New York: Columbia University Press, 1982.

———. "Blood Myth" and "Terror." In *The Oxford Companion to the Mind*, edited by Richard L. Gregory, with O. L. Zangwill. New York: Oxford University Press, 1987.

———. "In Search of the Real Dracula." *Dracula, the Complete Vampire*, *Starlog Magazine*, no. 6 (1992).

McNally, Raymond T., and Stefan Andreescu. "Exactly Where Was Dracula Captured in 1462?" *East European Quarterly*, vol. 23, no. 3 (September 1989).

Nandris, Grigore. "A Philological Analysis of *Dracula* and Rumanian Place-names and Masculine Personal Names in -a/-ea." *The Slavonic and East European Review*, vol. 37 (June 1959).

———. "The Dracula Theme in European Literature of the West and of the East." In *Literary History and Literary Criticism*, edited by Leon Edel. New York: New York University Press, 1965.

———. "The Historical Dracula." In *Comparative Literature: Matter and Method*, edited by A. Owen Aldridge. Urbana: University of Illinois Press, 1969.

Oinas, Felix. "East European Vampires & Dracula." *Journal of Popular Culture*, vol. 16, no. 1 (summer 1982).

Prins, Herschel. "Vampirism — Legendary or Clinical Phenomenon?" *Medicine, Science, Law*, vol. 24, no. 4 (1984).

Ramsland, Katherine. "Hunger for the Marvelous: The Vampire Craze in the Computer Age." *Psychology Today* (November 1989).

Roth, Phyllis A. "Suddenly Sexual Women in Bram Stoker's *Dracula*." *Literature and Psychology*, vol. 27, no. 3 (1977).

Senf, Carol A. "*Dracula:* The Unseen Face in the Mirror." *Journal of Narrative Technique*, vol. 9, no. 3 (1979).

Stetson, George R. "The Animistic Vampire in New England." *American Anthropologist*, vol. 9, no. 1 (January 1896).

Twitchell, James B. "The Vampire Myth." *American Imago*, vol. 37, no. 1 (spring 1980).

Vanden Bergh, Richard L., and John F. Kelly. "Vampirism." *Archives of General Psychiatry*, vol. 11, no. 5 (November 1964).

Wall, Geoffrey. " 'Different from Writing': *Dracula* in 1897." *Literature and History*, vol. 10, no. 1 (spring 1984).

Weissmann, Judith. "Women and Vampires: *Dracula* as a Victorian Novel." *Midwest Quarterly*, vol. 18, no. 4 (summer 1977).

Winkler, Louis and Carol. "A Reappraisal of the Vampire." *New York Folklore Quarterly*, vol. 29, no. 3 (September 1973).

WORKS OF PSYCHOLOGY, ANTHROPOLOGY, AND LITERATURE

Bhalla, Alok. *Politics of Atrocity and Lust: The Vampire Tale as a Nightmare History of England in the Nineteenth Century.* New Delhi, India: Sterling Publishers, 1990.

Bonewits, Wanda. "Dracula, the Black Christ." *Gnostica*, vol. 4, no. 7 (March 1975).

Burton, Sir Richard, trans. *Vikram the Vampire.* London: Longmans, Green & Co., 1870; New York: Dover, 1969.

Calmet, Dom Augustin. *Traité sur les Apparitions des Esprits et sur les Vampyres.* Paris, 1751; published as *The Phantom World,* trans. Henry Christmas, London: R. Bentley, 1850 (2 vols.); Philadelphia: A. Hart, 1850 (2 vols. in 1).

Carroll, Noel. *The Philosophy of Horror, or Paradoxes of the Heart.* New York: Routledge, 1990.

Dalby, Richard. *Bram Stoker: A Bibliography of First Editions.* London: Dracula Press, 1983.

Dresser, Norine. *American Vampires.* New York: Norton, 1989.

Farrant, David. *Beyond the Highgate Vampire: A True Case of Supernatural Occurrences and Vampirism.* London: British Psychic and Occult Society, 1991.

Frazer, James G. *The Fear of the Dead in Primitive Religions.* London: Macmillan, 1934; reprint, New York: Arno Press, 1977.

Frost, Brian J. *The Monster with a Thousand Faces: Guises of the Vampire in Myth and Literature.* Bowling Green, Ohio: Bowling Green State University Popular Press, 1989.

Gladwell, Adele Olivia, and James Havoc, eds. *Blood and Roses: The Vampire in Nineteenth-Century Literature.* London: Creation Press, 1992.

Glut, Donald. *True Vampires of History.* New York: HC Publishers, 1971; Methuen, N.J.: Scarecrow, 1975.

Grixti, Joseph. *Terrors of Uncertainty: The Cultural Contexts of Horror Fiction.* New York: Routledge, 1989.

Grudin, Peter D. *The Demon-Lover: The Theme of Demonality in English and Continental Fiction of the Late Eighteenth and Early Nineteenth Centuries.* New York: Garland, 1987.

Guiley, Rosemary. *Vampires among Us.* New York: Pocket, 1991.

———. *The Complete Vampire's Companion.* New York: Prentice Hall, 1994.

Haining, Peter, ed. *The Dracula Scrapbook.* London: New English Library; New York: Bramhall House, 1976; Stamford, Conn.: Longmeadow, 1992.

———. *The Dracula Centenary Book.* London: Souvenir Press, 1987.

Halliwell, Leslie. *The Dead That Walk.* London: Grafton, 1986.

Haworth-Maden, Clare. *The Essential Dracula.* New York: Crescent, 1992.

Hill, Douglas. *Return from the Dead.* London: Macdonald, 1970; as *The History of Ghosts, Vampires and Werewolves.* New York: Harrow, 1973.

Howe, Marjorie. "The Mediation of the Feminine, Bisexuality, Homoerotic Desire, and Self-Expression in Bram Stoker's *Dracula.*" *Texas Studies in Literature and Language* (spring 1989).

Holt, Olga. *Lust for Blood: The Consuming Story of Vampires.* New York: Stein & Day, 1984; Chelsea, Mich.: Scarborough House, 1990.

Hurwood, Bernhardt, J. *Terror by Night.* New York: Lancer, 1963; as *The Monstrous Undead.* New York: Lancer, 1969; as *The Vampire Papers.* New York: Pinnacle, 1976.

———. *Monsters and Nightmares.* New York: Belmont, 1967.

———. *Vampires, Werewolves and Ghouls.* New York: Ace, 1968; London: Target, 1975.

———. *Passport to the Supernatural.* New York: Taplinger, 1972. Pinnacle, 1976.

———. *Vampires.* New York: Quick Fox, 1981.

Jann, Rosemary. "Saved by Science? The Mixed Message of Stoker's *Dracula.*" *Texas Studies in Literature and Language,* vol. 31, no. 2 (summer 1989).

Jones, Ernest. *On the Nightmare.* New York: Liveright Publishing Corp., 1951.

Karp, Walter. "Dracula Returns; or Vampirism as an Antidote to the Blues." *Horizon,* vol. 18, no. 4 (autumn 1976).

Kayton, Lawrence. "The Relationship of the Vampire Legend to Schizophrenia." *Journal of Youth and Adolescence,* vol. 1, no. 4 (1972).

Kendrick, Walter. *The Thrill of Fear: 250 Years of Scary Entertainment.* New York: Grove Weidenfeld, 1991.

King, Stephen. *Danse Macabre.* New York: Everest House, 1981.

Lefebure, Charles. *The Blood Cults.* New York: Ace, 1969.

McNally, Raymond T., and Radu Florescu. *The Essential Dracula.* New York: Mayflower, 1979.

Manchester, Sean. *The Highgate Vampire: The Infernal World of the Undead Unearthed at London's Famous Highgate Cemetery and Environs.* London: British Occult Society, 1985; revised edition published by London: Gothic, 1991.

Marcus, Steven. *The Other Victorians: A Study of Sexuality and Pornography in Mid-Nineteenth-Century England.* New York: Basic Books, 1966, 1975.

Mascetti, Manuela Dunn. *Vampire: The Complete Guide to the World of the Undead.* New York: Viking Penguin, 1992.

Masters, Anthony. *The Natural History of the Vampire.* New York: Putnam, 1972; New York: Berkeley, 1976.

Murgoci, Agnesa. "The Vampire in Roumania." *Folk-lore,* vol. 37, no. 4 (December 1926).

Noll, Richard. *Vampires, Werewolves and Demons: Twentieth Century Reports in the Psychiatric Literature.* New York: Brunner/Mazel, 1992.

Page, Carol. *Bloodlust: Conversations with Real Vampires.* New York: HarperCollins, 1991; New York: Dell, 1992.

Perkowski, Jan L., ed. *Vampires of the Slavs.* Cambridge, Mass.: Slavica, 1976.

———. *The Darkling: A Treatise on Slavic Vampirism.* Columbus, Ohio: Slavica, 1989.

Raible, Christopher Gist. "Dracula: Christian Heretic." *The Christian Century,* vol. 96, no. 4 (January 31, 1979).

Ramsland, Katherine M. *Prism of the Night: A Biography of Anne Rice.* New York: Dutton 1991; New York: Plume, 1992.

Senf, Carol A. *The Vampire in Nineteenth-Century English Literature.* Bowling Green, Ohio: Bowling State University Popular Press, 1988.

Senn, Harry A. *Were-wolf and Vampire in Romania.* East European Monographs no. 99. New York: Columbia University Press, 1982.

Twitchell, James B. *The Living Dead: A Study of the Vampire in Romantic Literature.* Durham, N.C.: Duke University Press, 1981.

Van Over, Raymond. "Vampire and Demon Lover," in *The Satan Trap: Dangers of the Occult,* edited by Martin Ebon. Garden City, N.Y.: Doubleday, 1976.

Varma, Devendra P. *The Gothic Flame.* London: A. Barker, 1957; reprint, Metuchen, N.J.: n.p., 1987.

Volta, Ornella. *The Vampire.* London: Tandem, 1965; New York: Award Books, 1970.

Wallace, Bruce. "Vampires Revamped." *Omni,* vol. 1, no. 9 (June 1979).

Wolf, Leonard. *A Dream of Dracula.* Boston: Little, Brown, 1972; New York: Popular Library, 1972.

———. *The Essential Dracula.* New York: Plume Books, 1993.

Wright, Dudley. *Vampires and Vampirism.* London: W. Rider, 1914 (2d rev. ed. 1924); New York: Gordon, 1970; New York: Dorset, 1987; as *The Book of Vampires.* New York: Causeway, 1973; Detroit, Mich.: Omnigraphics, 1989.

Zink, K. Charles and Myrna. *Psychological Studies on the Increase of Lycanthropy and Vampirism in America, 1930–1941.* New Orleans: Zachary Ken, 1952.

BOOKS ON MOVIES, THEATER, AND TELEVISION

Beck, Calvin. *Heroes of the Horrors.* New York: Collier-Macmillan, 1975.

Brunas, Michael. *Universal Horrors.* Jefferson, N.C.: McFarland, 1990.

Butler, Ivan. *Horror in the Cinema.* (International Film Guide Series). New York, 1971 (originally published in 1967 as *The Horror Film*); second revised edition, 1970; third revised edition, New York: A. S. Barnes, 1979.

Clarens, Carlos. *An Illustrated History of the Horror Film.* New York: Putnam, 1979; first published as *Horror Movies,* Canada: Longmans, 1967.

Coppola, Francis Ford, and James V. Hart. *Bram Stoker's* Dracula: *The Film and the Legend.* New York: Newmarket Press, 1992.

Coppola, Francis Ford, and Ishioka Eiko. *Coppola and Eiko on Bram Stoker's Dracula,* edited by Susan Dworkin. San Francisco: Collins, 1992.

Daniels, Les. *A History of Horror in the Mass Media.* New York: Scribner's, 1975.

Douglas, Drake. *Horror!* New York: Macmillan, 1966; revised edition, Woodstock, N.Y.: The Overlook Press, 1989.

Dracula: The Complete Vampire (Starlog Movie Magazine no. 6). New York: Starlog Communications International, 1992.

Eisner, Lotte H. *The Haunted Screen: Expressionism in the German Cinema and the Influence of Max Reinhardt.* Berkeley, Calif.: University of California Press, 1969.

———. *Murnau.* Berkeley, Calf.: University of California Press, 1973.

Eyles, Allen. *The House of Horror: The Story of Hammer Films.* London: Lorrimer, 1973.

Flynn, John L. *Cinematic Vampires.* Jefferson, N.C.: McFarland, 1992.

Frank, Alan G. *Horror Movies: Tales of Terror in the Cinema.* London: Octopus, 1974; published as *Monsters and Vampires.* Secaucus, N.J.: Derbibooks, 1975.

Gifford, Denis. *Movie Monsters.* London: Studio Vista, 1969.

———. *A Pictorial History of Horror Movies.* New York: Exeter, 1983.

Glut, Donald F. *The Dracula Book.* Metuchen, N.J.: Scarecrow, 1975.

Halliwell, Leslie. *The Dead That Walk.* New York: Continuum, 1988.

Haworth-Maden, Clare. *The Essential Dracula.* New York: Crescent, 1992.

Hardy, Phil. *The Encyclopedia of Horror Movies.* New York: Harper & Row, 1986.

Huss, Roy, and T. J. Ross, eds. *Focus on the Horror Film.* Englewood, N.J.: Prentice Hall, 1972.

Jones, Stephen. *The Illustrated Vampire Movie Guide.* London: Titan, 1993.

Lennig, Arthur. *The Count: The Life and Films of Bela "Dracula" Lugosi.* New York: Putnam, 1974.

Murphy, Michael J. *The Celluloid Vampires: A History and Filmography, 1897–1979.* Ann Arbor, Mich.: Pierian, 1979.

Nance, Scott. *Bloodsuckers: Vampires at the Movies.* Las Vegas, Nev.: Pioneer, 1992.

Newman, Kim. *Nightmare Movies: A Critical Guide to Contemporary Horror Films.* New York: Harmony, 1988.

Pattison, Barrie. *The Seal of Dracula.* New York: Bounty, 1975; London: Lorrimer, 1975.

Pirie, David. *The Vampire Cinema.* New York: Crescent, 1977; London: Hamlyn, 1977.

———. *Heritage of Horror: The English Gothic Cinema 1946–1972.* London: Fraser, 1973; New York: Equinox, 1973.

Prawer, S. S. *Caligari's Children: The Film as Tale of Terror.* New York: Oxford University Press, 1980.

Reed, Donald. *The Vampire on the Screen.* Inglewood, Calif.: Wagon and Star Publishers, 1965.

Riley, Philip J., ed. *Dracula* (the original 1931 schooting script). Universal Filmscripts Series. Classic Horror Films vol. 13. Abescon, N.J.: Magic-Image, 1990.

Silver, Alain, and James Ursini. *The Vampire Film.* South Brunswick, N.J.: Barnes, 1975; revised edition, N.Y.: Limelight, 1993.

Skal, David. *Hollywood Gothic: The Tangled Web of Dracula from Novel to Stage to Screen.* New York: Norton, 1990.

————. *Dracula: The Ultimate Illustrated Edition of the World Famous Vampire Play.* The original Hamilton Deane play and the Balderston-Deane version. New York: St. Martin's, 1993.

————. *The Monster Show: A Cultural History of Horror.* New York, Norton, 1993.

Slusser, George E., and Eric S. Rabkin, eds. *Shadows of the Magic Lamp: Fantasy and Science Fiction in Film.* Carbondale, Ill.: Southern Illinois University Press, 1985.

Waller, Gregory. *The Living and the Undead: From Stoker's Dracula to Romero's Dawn of the Dead. Essays on the Modern American Horror Film.* Urbana, Ill.: University of Illinois Press, 1986.

Wolf, Leonard. *Horror: A Connoisseur's Guide to Literature and Film.* New York: Facts on File, 1989.

Wright, Gene. *Horror Shows.* New York: Facts on File, 1986.

FICTION

Anthologies

Ambrus, Victor G. *Dracula's Bedtime Storybook: Tales to Keep You Awake at Night.* New York: Oxford University Press, 1981.

Blaisdell, Elinore, ed. *Tales of the Undead, Vampires and Visitants.* London: Crowell, 1947.

Bradbury, Ray. *The October Country.* New York: Ballantine, 1955.

Carter, M. L. *The Curse of the Undead.* Greenwich, Conn.: Fawcett, 1970.

Collins, Charles M., ed. *A Feast of Blood.* New York: Avon, 1967.

Dalby, Richard, ed. *Dracula's Brood.* London: Crucible, 1987.

————. *Vampire Stories.* London: Michael O'Mara Books, 1992.

Datlow, Ellen, ed. *Blood Is Not Enough.* New York: Morrow, 1989; New York: Berkley, 1990.

————. *A Whisper of Blood.* New York: Morrow, 1991; New York: Berkley, 1992.

Dickie, James, ed. *The Undead.* London: Neville Spearman, 1991; London: Pan, 1973; New York: Pocket, 1976.

Elwood, Roger. *Monster Tales.* Chicago: Rand McNally, 1973.

Frayling, Christopher, ed. *The Vampyre: A Bedside Companion.* New York: Scribner, 1978; revised as *Vampyres: Lord Ruthven to Count Dracula.* London: Faber and Faber, 1991.

Garber, Eric, ed. *Embracing the Dark.* Boston: Alyson, 1991.

Gladwell, Adele Olivia, and James Havoc, eds. *Blood and Roses: The Vampire in 19th Century Literature.* London: Creation Press, 1992.

Grant, Charles, ed. *The Dodd, Mead Gallery of Horror.* New York: Dodd, Mead, 1983.

Greenberg, Martin, ed. *Dracula, Prince of Darkness.* New York: DAW, 1992.

———. *A Taste for Blood: Fifteen Great Vampire Novellas.* New York: Dorset, 1992.

Haining, Peter, ed. *The Midnight People.* New York: Popular Library, 1968; London: Frewin, 1968; published as *Vampires at Midnight.* New York: Grosset and Dunlap, 1970; London: Everest, 1975.

———. *The Ghouls.* New York: Stein and Day, 1971; New York: Pocket, 1972 (includes "Dracula's Guest" under the title "Dracula's Daughter").

———. *Gothic Tales of Terror.* Maryland: Penguin, 1973 (includes Polidori's "The Vampyre").

———. *Tales of Unknown Horror.* London: New English Library, 1978.

———. *Vampire.* London: Target, 1985.

Howard, Robert. *Skull-Face and Others.* Sauk City, Wisc.: Arkham House, 1946; Jersey, U.K.: Neville Spearman, 1974.

Jones, Stephen, ed. *The Mammoth Book of Vampires.* New York: Carroll & Graf, 1992.

Lee, Christopher, and Michel Parry, eds. *From the Archives of Evil.* New York: Warner, 1976.

McMahan, Jeffrey N. *Somewhere in the Night.* Boston: Alyson, 1989.

McCammon, Robert R., ed. *Under the Fang.* Baltimore, Md.: Borderlands Press, 1991; New York: Pocket, 1991.

McNally, Raymond T., ed. *A Clutch of Vampires: These Being among the Best from History and Literature.* Greenwich, Conn.: New York Graphic Society, 1973; London: New English Library, 1976.

Moskowitz, Sam, ed. *Horrors Unknown.* New York: Walker & Co., 1971; New York: Berkley, 1976.

Norton, Alden H., ed. *Masters of Horror.* New York: Berkley, 1968 (includes Stoker's "Dracula's Guest").

Parry, Michel, ed. *The Rivals of Dracula.* London: Corgi, 1977; London: Severn House, 1978.

Petrey, Susan, ed. *Gifts of Blood.* Riverdale, N.Y.: Baen, 1991, 1992.

Preiss, Byron, ed. *The Ultimate Dracula.* New York: Dell, 1991.

Ryan, Alan, ed. *Vampires: Two Centuries of Great Vampire Stories.* Garden City, N.Y.: Doubleday, 1987; published as *The Penguin Book of Vampire Stories.* Harmondsworth, U.K.: Penguin, 1988.

Shepard, Leslie, ed. *The Dracula Book of Great Vampire Stories.* Secaucus, N.J.: Citadel, 1977; New York: Jove, 1978.

Stoker, Bram. *Dracula's Guest.* London: Routledge, 1914. Numerous editions.

Tolstoy, Alexis. *Vampires: Stories of the Supernatural.* Harmondsworth, U.K.: Penguin, 1946; New York: Hawthorn, 1969.

Underwood, Peter, ed. *The Vampire's Bedside Companion.* London: Leslie Frewin, 1975.

Varma, Devendra P., ed. *Voices from the Vaults: Authentic Tales of Vampires and Ghosts.* Toronto: Key Porter, 1987; Toronto: McClelland-Bantam, 1988.

Volta, Ornella, and Valeria Riva, eds.; foreword by Roger Vadim. *The Vampire: An Anthology.* London: Neville Spearman, 1963; London: Pan, 1965.

Weinberg, Robert, Stefan Dziemianowicz, and Martin H. Greenberg, eds. *Weird Vampire Tales.* New York: Gramercy, 1992.

Yolen, Jane, and Martin H. Greenberg, eds. *Vampires.* New York: HarperCollins, 1991.

Youngson, Jeanne, ed. *A Child's Garden of Vampires.* Chicago: Adams, 1980.

———, ed. *The Count Dracula Fan Club of Vampire Stories.* Chicago: Adams, 1980.

———, ed. *The Count Dracula Book of Classic Vampire Tales.* Chicago: Adams, 1981.

Short stories

Aickman, Robert. "Pages from a Young Girl's Journal." *The Magazine of Fantasy & Science Fiction* (February 1973); reprinted in *Cold Hand in Mine: Strange Stories.* New York: Scribner's, 1975.

Allan, Peter. "Domdaniel," in the Underwood and Varma anthologies.

Allen, Woody. "Count Dracula." In *Getting Even*. New York: Random House, 1971.

Apuleius, Lucius. "The Vampire." In *Wolf's Complete Book of Terror*, edited by Leonard Wolf. New York: Clarkson N. Potter, 1979.

Beaumont, Charles. "Blood Brother." *Playboy* (April, 1961); reprinted in *The Playboy Book of Science Fiction and Fantasy*. Chicago, Ill.: Playboy Press, 1966.

Benson, E. F. "And No Bird Sings." In the Haining anthology *The Midnight People*.

———. "Mrs. Amworth." In the Volta and Riva and the Shepard anthologies.

———. "The Room in the Tower." In *The Room in the Tower and Other Stories*. London: Mills and Boon, 1912. Also in the Dickie, Shepard, Ryan, and Collins anthologies.

Bischoff, D., and C. Lampton. "Feeding Time." In *The Fifty Meter Monsters, and Other Horrors*, edited by Roger Elwood. New York: Pocket, 1976.

Bixby, Jerome, and Joe E. Dean. "Share Alike." *Beyond* (July 1953); reprinted in *Hunger for Horror*, edited by Roger Adams et al. New York: DAW, 1988.

Blackwood, Algernon. "The Transfer." In the Ryan anthology.

Bloch, Robert. "The Bat Is My Brother." *Weird Tales* (November 1944); reprinted in the Parry anthology.

———. "The Bogey Man Will Get You." *Weird Tales* (March 1946); reprinted in the Carter anthology.

———. "The Cloak." *Unknown* (May 1939); reprinted in the Volta and Riva and the Varma anthologies.

———. "Hungarian Rhapsody." *Fantastic* (June 1958); reprinted in *Pleasant Dreams*. New York: Jove, 1979; and reprinted in Haining, *Vampire*.

——— [Wilson Kane]. "The Living Dead." *Ellery Queen Mystery Magazine* (April 1967); reprinted in Haining, *The Midnight People*, and Ryan and McNally anthologies.

———. "The Yugoslaves." *Night Cry* (winter 1985); reprinted in *Fear and Trembling*. New York: Tor, 1989.

Bradbury, Ray. "Homecoming." *Mademoiselle* (October 1946); reprinted in *Dying of Fright: Masterpieces of the Macabre*, edited by Les Daniels. New York: Scribner, 1976, and in the Bradbury anthology.

————. "The Man Upstairs." *Harper's* (March 1947); reprinted in the Bradbury and the Volta and Riva anthologies.

————. "Pillar of Fire." *Planet Stories* (summer 1948); reprinted in Haining, *The Midnight People.*

————. "Skeleton." *Weird Tales* (September 1945); reprinted in the Bradbury anthology.

Braddon, M. E. "Good Lady Ducayne." *The Strand Magazine* (February 1896); reprinted in the Shepard anthology.

Brown, Fredric. "Blood." *The Magazine of Fantasy & Science Fiction* (February 1955); reprinted in the Carter anthology.

Bryant, Edward. "Good Kids." In the Datlow anthology.

Calvino, Italo. "The Tale of the Vampires' Kingdom." In *The Castle of Crossed Destinies.* New York: Harcourt, 1977.

Campbell, Ramsey. "Conversion" (1976); reprinted in the Parry anthology.

————. "The Sunshine Club." In the Grant anthology; reprinted in the Ryan anthology.

Carr, Terry. "Sleeping Beauty." *New Worlds of Fantasy*, no. 3; reprinted New York: Ace, 1971.

Casper, Susan. "Under Her Skin." *Amazing* (March 1987).

————. "A Child of Darkness." In the Datlow anthology.

Copper, Basil. "Dr. Porthos." In Haining, *The Midnight People.*

Cowles, Frederick. "The Vampire of Kaldenstein." *The Night Wind Howls.* London: Muller, 1938; reprinted in the Parry anthology.

Crawford, F. Marion. "For the Blood Is the Life." *Collier's* (December 16, 1905); reprinted in the Carter, Dickie, and Shepard anthologies.

DeMaupassant, Guy. "The Horla." In the Shepard and Volta and Riva anthologies.

Derby, Crispin. "To Claim His Own." In the Underwood anthology.

Derleth, August. "Bat's Belfry." *Weird Tales* (May 1926); reprinted in Haining, *The Midnight People.*

Derleth, August [Stephen Grendo]. "The Drifting Snow." *Weird Tales* (February 1939); reprinted in Haining, *The Midnight People,* and in the McNally anthology.

Dick, Philip K. "The Cookie Lady." *Fantasy Fiction* (June 1953); reprinted in *Hunger for Horror,* ed. Robert Adams et al. New York: DAW, 1988.

Drake, David. "Something Had to Be Done." *The Magazine of Fantasy & Science Fiction* (February 1975); reprinted in the Parry anthology.

Durrell, Lawrence. "Carnival." Excerpted from *Balthazar*. New York: Dutton, 1958; reprinted in the Volta and Riva anthology; published as "Vampire in Venice" in the McNally anthology.

Evans, E. Everett. "The Undead Die." *Food for Demons*. San Diego: Shroud, 1971; reprinted in the Parry anthology.

Farber, Sharon. "A Surfeit of Melancholic Humours." *Isaac Asimov's Science Fiction Magazine* (March 1984).

———. "Return of the Dust Vampire." In *Whispers*, V, edited by Stuart Schiff. New York: Doubleday, 1986.

———. "Ice Dreams." *Isaac Asimov's Science Fiction Magazine* (March 1987).

Farley, Ralphe Milne. "Another Dracula?" *Weird Tales* (September–October 1930).

Gautier, Theophile. "The Beautiful Vampire." In the Volta and Riva anthology.

Gogol, Nicolai. "Viy." In the Volta and Riva anthology, and as "Black Sunday" in the Haining anthology.

Hart, James S. "The Traitor." *The Magazine of Fantasy & Science Fiction* (fall 1950); reprinted in Haining, *Vampire*.

Hensley, Joe L. "And Not Quite Human." *Beyond* (September 1951); reprinted in *Rod Serling's Triple W: Witches, Warlocks and Werewolves*, edited by Rod Serling. New York: Bantam, 1963.

Heron, E., and H. Heron. "The Story of Baelbrow." *Pearson's Magazine* (April 1898); reprinted in the Parry anthology.

Hoffman, E. T. A. "Aurelia." In the Frayling anthology.

Horler, Sydney. "The Believer: Ten Minutes of Horror." *The Vampire*. London: Hutchinson, 1935; reprinted in Haining, *The Midnight People*.

Howard, Richard. "Dies Irae." In the Underwood anthology.

Howard, Robert Ervin. "Hills of the Dead." *Weird Tales* (August 1930); reprinted in the Howard anthology.

———. "Horror from the Mound." In the Howard anthology and in Haining, *Vampire*.

Jacobi, Carl. "Revelations in Black." *Weird Tales* (April 1933); reprinted in *Revelations in Black*. Sauk City, Wis.: Arkham House, 1947. Also in the Collins and the Dickie anthologies.

Jacobs, Harvey. "L'Chaim." In the Datlow anthology.

James, M. R. "Count Magnus." In *Ghost Stories from an Antiquary*. London: Edward Arnold, 1904; reprinted in the Parry and Varma anthologies.

Johnstone, David A. "Mr. Alucard." In *Over the Edge*, edited by August Derleth. Sauk City, Wis.: Arkham House, 1964.

Kilworth, Garry. "The Silver Collar." In the Datlow anthology.

King, Stephen. "One for the Road." *Maine Magazine* (March/April 1977); reprinted in *Night Shift*. New York: Doubleday, 1978.

———. "Popsy." In *Masques II*, edited by J. N. Williamson. Baltimore: Maclay, 1987.

Kinkopf, Vladimir [Raymond T. McNally]. "Nellie's Grave." *Voices from the Vault: Authentic Tales of Vampires and Ghosts*, edited by Devendra P. Varma. Toronto: Key Porter, 1987; Toronto: McClelland-Bantam, 1988.

Knight, Damon. "Eripmav." *The Magazine of Fantasy & Science Fiction* (June 1958); reprinted in *100 Great Science Fiction Short Short Stories*, edited by Isaac Asimov et al. New York: Doubleday, 1978.

Kornbluth, C. M. "The Mindworm." *Worlds Beyond* (December 1950); reprinted in *Mind to Mind: Nine Stories of Science Fiction*, edited by Robert Silverberg. Nashville, Tenn.: Thomas Nelson, 1971; reprinted in the Ryan anthology.

Kuttner, Henry. "I, the Vampire." *Weird Tales* (February 1937); reprinted in the Lee and Parry anthologies.

Lee, Tanith. "Red as Blood." *The Magazine of Fantasy & Science Fiction*, (July 1979); reprinted in *The Year's Best Fantasy Stories*, edited by Lin Carter. New York: DAW, 1980.

LeFanu, Sheridan. "Carmilla." In *The Dark Blue*. London: n.p., 1871; reprinted in *In a Glass Darkly*. London: Bentley, 1872; in *Carmilla and the Haunted Baronet*. New York: Warner, 1970; and in the McNally anthology; excerpts in the Shepard and the Volta and Riva anthologies.

Leiber, Fritz. "The Girl with the Hungry Eyes." In *The Girl with the Hungry Eyes and Other Stories*, edited by Donald Wollheim. New York: Avon, 1949; reprinted in Haining, *The Midnight People*, and in the Ryan anthology.

———. "Ship of Shadows." *The Magazine of Fantasy & Science Fiction* (July 1969); reprinted in *The Hugo Winners*, vol. 3: *The Best from Fantasy and Science Fiction*, edited by Isaac Asimov. New York: Doubleday, 1977.

Malzberg, Barry N. "Trial of the Blood." In *The Best of Barry N. Malzberg*. New York: Pocket, 1976; as K. M. O'Donnell in *Nighttouch*, edited by G. Goldberg et al. New York: St. Martin's, 1978.

Matheson, Richard. "Drink My Red Blood." *Imagination* (April 1951);

reprinted in the McNally anthology; as "Blood Son" in the Collins anthology; and as "Drink My Blood" in Haining, *The Midnight People*.

———. "No Such Thing as a Vampire." *Playboy* (October 1959); reprinted in *No Such Thing as a Vampire*, edited by Frederick Pickersgill. London: Corgi, 1964; reprinted in Haining, *Vampire*.

McClusky, Thorp. "Loot of the Vampire." In *Loot of the Vampire*. Oak Lawn, Ill.: Robert Weinberg, 1975.

Miller, P. Schuyler. "Over the River." *Unknown* (April 1941); reprinted in Haining, *The Midnight People*, and in the Ryan anthology.

Moore, C. L. "Shambleau." *Weird Tales* (November 1933); reprinted in the Ryan anthology.

Morrow, Sonora. "Hard Times." *Ellery Queen's Mystery Magazine* (December 1974).

Neruda, Jan. "The Vampire." In *Czechoslovak Stories*, edited by Sara Hrbkova. London: Duffield, 1920; reprinted in *Selected Czech Tales*, edited by Marie Busch and Otto Pick. Cambridge: U.K., 1928; and in the Shepard anthology.

Norris, Frank. "Grettir at Thorhall-stead." In the Moskowitz anthology.

O'Keefe, M. Timothy. "Blood Money." In *Alfred Hitchcock's Witch's Brew*, edited by Alfred Hitchcock. New York: Random House, 1977.

Polidori, John. "The Vampyre." *New Monthly Magazine* (April 1819); reprinted in *Three Gothic Novels*, edited by E. F. Bleier. New York: Dover, 1966; and in the Carter, Frayling, and McNally anthologies.

Porges, Arthur. "The Arrogant Vampire." *Fantastic Stories of the Imagination* (May 1961).

Purtill, Richard R. "Something in the Blood." *The Magazine of Fantasy & Science Fiction* (August 1986).

Quinn, Seabury. "Body and Soul." *Weird Tales* (September 1928); reprinted in the Moskowitz anthology.

Ray, Jean. "The Guardian of the Cemetery." *Weird Tales* (December 1934); reprinted in the Perry anthology.

Ritchie, Jack. "Kid Cardula." In *Alfred Hitchcock's Tales to Take Your Breath Away*, edited by Alfred Hitchcock. New York: Dial, 1977.

Robinson, Spider. "Pyotr's Story." *Analog* (12 October 1981); reprinted in *Callhan's Secret*. New York: Berkley, 1986.

Roditi, E. "The Vampires of Istanbul: A Study in Modern Communications' Methods." In *The Delights of Turkey*. New York: New Directions, 1977.

Rowan, Victory. "Four Wooden Stakes." *Weird Tales* (February 1925); reprinted in the Shepard anthology.

Russell, Ray. "The Exploits of Argo." *Rogue* (April 1961); reprinted in *100 Great Science Fiction Short Short Stories,* edited by Isaac Asimov et al. New York: Doubleday, 1978.

Rutter, Owen. "The Vampires of Tempassuk." *Monsters, Monsters, Monsters,* edited by Helen Hoke. New York: Franklin Watts, 1975.

Ryan, Alan. "Following the Way." *Shadows 5,* edited by Charles L. Grant. New York: Doubleday, 1982; and in the Ryan anthology.

———. "I Shall Not Leave England Now." *Shadows 7,* edited by Charles L. Grant. New York: Doubleday, 1984.

———. "Kiss the Vampire Goodbye." *Alfred Hitchcock's Mystery Magazine* (June 1985); reprinted in *Quadrophobia.* New York: Doubleday, 1986.

Scott-Moncrieff, D. "Schloss Wappenburg." In *Not for the Squeamish.* London: Background, 1948; reprinted in the Collins anthology.

Smith, Clark Ashton. "The Death of Ilalotha." *Weird Tales* (September 1937); reprinted in the Dickie anthology.

———. "The End of the Story." *Weird Tales* (May 1930); reprinted in the Dickie anthology.

———. "A Rendezvous in Averoigne." *Weird Tales* (April/May 1931); reprinted in the Collins of Blood and the Ryan anthologies.

Smith, Evelyn E. "Softly While You're Sleeping." *The Magazine of Fantasy & Science Fiction* (April 1961); reprinted in the Carter anthology.

Starkie, Walter. "The Old Man's Story." In *Raggle Taggle.* London: John Murray, 1933; reprinted in the Dickie anthology.

Stenbock, Count Eric Stanislaus. "The True Story of a Vampire." *Studies of Death.* London: Nutt, 1894; reprinted in the Dickie anthology; reprinted as "The Sad Story of a Vampire" in the Shepard anthology.

Stoker, Bram. "Dracula's Guest." In the Stoker, Dickie, McNally, Collins, and Shepard anthologies.

Straum, Niel. "Vanishing Breed." In the Carter anthology.

Tieck, Johann Ludwig. "Wake Not the Dead." In the Collins, Frayling, and Haining anthologies.

Tolstoy, Alexis. "The Family of a Vourdalak." In the Tolstoy and Frayling anthologies.

———. "The Vampire." In the Tolstoy anthology.

Tubb, E. C. "Fresh Guy." *Science Fantasy* (June 1958); reprinted in the Volta and Riva anthology.

Turner, James. "Mirror Without Image." In the Underwood anthology.

Utley, Steven. "Night Life." In the Parry anthology.

Van Vogt, A. E. "Asylum." *Astounding Science Fiction* (May 1942); reprinted in *Away and Beyond.* New York: Pellegrini & Cudahy, 1952; New York: Jove/HBJ Books, 1977.

Wellman, Manly Wade. "The Devil Is Not Mocked." *Unknown Worlds* (June 1943); reprinted in *Zacherley's Vulture Stew*, edited by John Zacherley. New York: Ballantine, 1960; reprinted in *Worst Things Waiting.* Chapel Hill, N.C.: Carcosa, 1973.

————. "The Horror Undying." *Weird Tales* (May 1936); reprinted in the Parry anthology.

————. "The Last Grave of Lil Warren." *Weird Tales* (May 1951); reprinted in *The Supernatural Solution,* edited by Michel Parry. New York: Taplinger, 1976.

————. "The Vampire of Shiloh." Excerpted from "Coven," *Weird Tales* (July 1942); reprinted in Haining, *The Dracula Scrapbook.*

————. "When It Was Moonlight." *Unknown* (February 1940); reprinted in the Dickie anthology and in Haining, *The Midnight People.*

Williamson, Chet. ". . . To Feel Another's Woe." In the Datlow anthology.

Williamson, Jack. "Darker Than You Think." *Unknown* (December 1940); reprinted as a novel, Reading, Pa.: Fantasy Press, 1940.

Woolrich, Cornell. "Vampire's Honeymoon." *Horror Stories* (August 1939); reprinted in *Vampire's Honeymoon.* New York: Carroll & Graf, 1985.

Worrell, Everil. "The Canal." *Weird Tales* (December 1927); reprinted in the Dickie anthology.

Wyndham, John. "Close Behind Him." *Fantastic* (January/February 1953); reprinted in *Nightfrights: Occult Stories for All Ages,* edited by Peter Haining. New York: Taplinger, 1972.

Novels in a series

(The publishers noted in the initial entries below remain the same for the subsequent volumes in the series unless otherwise specified. When two publishers are cited, the first refers to the hardcover edition; the second, to the paperback.)

Ambrus, Victor G. *What Time Is It, Dracula?* New York: Crown, 1991; *Count, Dracula* (1992).

Bergstrom, Elaine. *Shattered Glass.* New York: Jove, 1989; *Blood Alone* (1990); *Blood Rites* (1991); *Daughter of the Night* (1992).

Bloom, Hanya. Vic the Vampire Series. *Vampire Cousins.* New York: Harper Paperbacks, 1990; *Friendly Fangs* (1991).

Ciencin, Scott. *The Vampire Odyssey.* New York: Zebra, 1992; *The Wildlings* (1992); *Parliament of Blood* (1992).

Collins, Nancy. The Sonya Blue Series. *Sunglasses after Dark.* New York: Onyx, 1989; *In the Blood* (1992).

Cooney, Caroline. *The Cheerleader.* New York: Scholastic, 1991; *The Return of the Vampire* (1992); *The Vampire's Promise* (1993).

Courtney, Vincent. *Vampire Beat.* New York: Pinnacle, 1991; *Harvest of Blood* (1992).

Daniels, Les. The Don Sebastian Series. *The Black Castle.* New York: Scribner's, 1978, Berkley, 1983; *The Silver Skull* (1979; Ace Fantasy, 1979); *Citizen Vampire* (1981, 1983); *Yellow Fog.* West Kingston, R.I.: Grant, 1986, New York: Tor, 1988; *No Blood Spilled.* New York: Tor, 1991.

Dee, Ron. *Blood Lust.* New York: Dell, 1990; *Nightlife* (1991); *Dusk* (1991); *Shade.* New York: Zebra, 1994.

Elrod, P. N. Vampire Files. *Bloodlist.* New York: Ace, 1990; *Lifeblood* (1990); *Bloodcircle* (1990); *Art in the Blood* (1991); *Fire in the Blood* (1991); *Blood on the Water* (1992).

Garton, Ray. *Live Girls.* New York: Pocket, 1987; *Lot Lizards.* Shingletown, Calif.: Zeising Books, 1991.

Goulart, Ron. The Vampirella Series. *Bloodstalk.* London: Sphere 1975, New York: Warner, 1975; *On Alien Wings* (1975, 1975); *Deadwalk* (1976, 1976); *Blood Wedding* (1976, 1976); *Deathgame* (1976, 1976); *Snakegod* (1976, 1976).

Herter, Lori. *Obsession.* New York: Berkley, 1991; *Possession* (1992); *Confession* (1993).

Howe, Deborah and James. *Bunnicula, A Rabbit Tale of Mystery.* New York: Atheneum, 1979.

Howe, James. *The Celery Stalks at Midnight.* New York: Atheneum, 1983.

Huff, Tanya. *Blood Price.* New York: Daw, 1991; *Blood Trail* (1992); *Blood Lines* (1993); *Blood Pact* (1993).

Killough, Lee. *Blood Hunt.* New York: Tor, 1987; *Bloodlinks* (1988).

Lichtenberg, Jacqueline. *Those of My Blood.* New York: St. Martin's, 1988; *Dreamspy* (1989).

Lory, Robert. The Dracula Horror Series. *Dracula Returns!* New York: Pinnacle, 1973; *The Hand of Dracula* (1973); *Dracula's Brothers* (1973); *Dracula's Gold* (1973); *The Drums of Dracula* (1974); *The*

Witching of Dracula (1974); *Dracula's Lost World* (1975); *Dracula's Disciple* (1975); *Challenge to Dracula* (1975).

Lumley, Brian. Necroscope Series. *Necroscope.* London: Grafton, 1986, New York: Tor 1988. *Wamphyri!* London: Grafton, 1988, New York: Tor, 1989 (as *Vamphyri!*); *The Source* (1989, 1989); *Deadspeak.* London: Grafton, 1990, New York: Tor, 1990; *Deadspawn* (1991, 1991).
———. Vampire World. *Blood Brothers.* U.K.: Roc, 1992, New York: Tor, 1992; *The Last Aerie.* New York: Tor, 1993.

Pierce, Meredith Ann. The Darkangel Trilogy. *The Darkangel.* Boston: Little, Brown, 1982; *A Gathering of Gargoyles* (1984); *The Pearl of the Soul of the World* (1990).

Ptacek, Kathryn. *Blood Autumn.* New York: Tor, 1985; *In Silence Sealed* (1988).

Rice, Anne. The Vampire Chronicles. *Interview with the Vampire.* New York: Knopf, 1976, New York: Ballantine, 1977; *The Vampire Lestat* (1985, 1991); *Queen of the Damned* (1988, 1989); *The Tale of the Body Thief* (1992).

Ross, Marilyn [Dan Ross]. The Dark Shadows Series. *Barnabas Collins.* New York: Paperback Library, 1968; *The Secret of Barnabas Collins* (1969); *The Demon of Barnabas Collins* (1969); *The Foe of Barnabas Collins* (1969); *The Phantom and Barnabas Collins* (1969); *Barnabas Collins versus the Warlock* (1969); *The Peril of Barnabas Collins* (1969); *Barnabas Collins and the Mysterious Ghost* (1969); *Barnabas Collins and Quentin's Demon* (1969); *Barnabas Collins and the Gypsy Witch* (1969); *Barnabas, Quentin and the Mummy's Curse* (1970); *Barnabas, Quentin and the Avenging Ghost* (1970); *Barnabas, Quentin and the Nightmare Assassin* (1970); *Barnabas, Quentin and the Crystal Coffin* (1970); *Barnabas, Quentin and the Witch's Curse* (1970); *Barnabas, Quentin and the Haunted Cave* (1970); *Barnabas, Quentin and the Frightened Bride* (1970); *Barnabas, Quentin and the Scorpio Curse* (1970); *Barnabas, Quentin and the Serpent* (1970); *Barnabas, Quentin and the Magic Potion* (1970); *Barnabas, Quentin and the Body Snatchers* (1971); *Barnabas, Quentin and Dr. Jekyll's Son* (1971); *Barnabas, Quentin and the Grave Robbers* (1971); *Barnabas, Quentin and the Sea Ghost* (1971); *Barnabas, Quentin and the Mad Magician* (1971); *Barnabas, Quentin and the Hidden Tomb* (1971); *Barnabas, Quentin and the Vampire Beauty* (1972).

Saberhagen, Fred. The Dracula Tapes. New York: Warner, 1975, New York: Ace, 1980; *The Holmes-Dracula File.* New York: Ace, 1978; *An*

Old Friend of the Family. New York: Tor, 1979, New York: Ace, 1987; *Thorn*. New York: Ace, 1980; *Dominion*. New York: Tor, 1982; *A Matter of Taste*. New York: St. Martin's Press, 1990, New York: Tor, 1992; *A Question of Time*. New York: Tor, 1992; *Seance for a Vampire* (1994).

Smith, Lisa J., The Vampire Diaries. *The Awakening*. New York: Harper Paperbacks, 1991; *The Struggle* (1991); *The Fury* (1991); *Dark Reunion* (1992).

Sommer-Bodenburg, Angela. *My Friend the Vampire*. New York: Dial Books for Young Readers, 1984, New York: Pocket, 1986; *The Vampire Moves In* (1985, Simon and Schuster, 1986); *The Vampire Takes a Trip* (1985, Pocket, 1987); *Vampire on the Farm* (1989, 1990).

Somtow, S. P. [Somtow Sucharitkul]. *Vampire Junction*. Norfolk, Va.: Donning, 1984, New York: Berkley, 1985; *Valentine*. New York: Tor, 1992.

Tremayne, Peter. *Dracula Unborn*. Folkestone, U.K.: Bailey Brothers and Swinfen, 1977, London: Corgi, 1977; as *Bloodright: Memoirs of Mircea — Son to Dracula*, New York: Walker, 1979, New York: Dell, 1980; *The Revenge of Dracula*. Folkestone: Bailey Brothers and Swinfen, 1978, New York: Walker, 1979; *Dracula, My Love*. Folkestone: Bailey Brothers and Swinfen, 1980, New York: Dell, 1983.

Waddell, Martin. *Little Dracula's First Bite*. London: Walker, 1986, New York: Puffin, 1986; *Little Dracula's Christmas* (1986, 1986); *Little Dracula at the Seashore*. London: Walker, 1987, Cambridge, Mass.: Candlewick, 1992; *Little Dracula Goes to School* (1987, 1992).

Whalen, Patrick. *Monastery*. New York: Pocket, 1988; *Night Thirst* (1991).

Williamson, J. N. *Death-Coach*. New York: Zebra, 1981; *Death-School* (1982); *Death-Doctor* (1982); *Death-Angel* (1987).

Wilson, Paul. *The Keep*. New York: Morrow, 1981, New York: Berkley, 1982; *Reborn*. Arlington Heights, Ill.: Dark Harvest, 1990, New York: Berkley, 1990; *Reprisal*. Arlington Heights, Ill.: Dark Harvest, 1991, New York: Jove, 1992.

Wright, T. Lucien. *The Hunt*. New York: Pinnacle, 1991; *Blood Brothers* (1992); *Thirst of the Vampire* (1992).

Yarbro, Chelsea Quinn. The Saint-Germain Series. *Hotel Transylvania*. New York: St. Martin's Press, 1977, New York: Signet, 1979; *The Palace* (1978, 1979); *Blood Games* (1979, 1980); *Path of the Eclipse* (1981, 1982); *Tempting Fate* (1982, 1982); *Out of the House of Life*, New York: Tor, 1991; *Darker Jewels* (1993); *Better in the Dark* (1993).

————. The Atta Oliva Clemens Series. *A Flame in Byzantium*. New York: Tor, 1987; *Crusader's Torch* (1988); *A Candle for D'Artagnan* (1989).

Individual vampire novels

Acres, Mark. *Dark Divide*. New York: Ace, 1991.

Aldiss, Brian. *Dracula Unbound*. New York: HarperCollins, 1991.

Alexander, Jan. *Blood Moon*. New York: Lancer, 1970.

Alexander, Karl. *The Curse of the Vampire*. New York: Pinnacle, 1972.

Anderson, Mary. *The Leipzig Vampire*. New York: Dell, 1987.

Ascher, Eugene. *There Were No Asper Ladies*. London: Mitre, 1946; also published as *To Kill a Corpse*. London: World Distributors, 1965.

Baker, Scott. *Dhampire*. New York: Pocket, 1982.

Beath, Warren Newton. *Bloodletter*. New York: Tor, 1994.

Behm, Marc. *The Ice Maiden*. London: Zomba, 1983.

Bischoff, David. *Vampires of Nightworld*. New York: Ballantine/Del Rey, 1981.

Blackburn, John. *Our Lady of Pain*. London: Jonathan Cape, 1974.

Brett, Stephen. *The Vampire Chase*. New York: Manor, 1979.

Briery, Traci. *The Vampire Journals*. New York: Zebra, 1993.

Brite, Poppy Z. *Lost Souls*. New York: Delacorte, 1992; New York: Dell, 1993.

Brust, Steven. *Agyar*. New York: Tor, 1993.

Byers, Richard Lee. *The Vampire's Apprentice*. New York: Zebra, 1992.

Caine, Geoffrey. *The Curse of the Vampire*. Indiana: Diamond, 1991.

Charnas, Suzy McKee. *The Vampire Tapestry*. New York: Simon and Schuster, 1980; New York: Pocket, 1981; New York: Tor, 1986.

Coffman, Virginia. *The Vampyre of Moura*. New York: Ace, 1970.

Combs, David. *The Intrusion*. New York: Avon, 1981.

Cook, Glen. *Sweet Silver Blues*. New York: Signet, 1987.

Cooke, John Peyton. *Out for Blood*. New York: Avon, 1991.

Cooper, Louise. *Blood Summer*. London: New English Library, 1976.

Corby, Michael, and Michael Geare. *Dracula's Diary*. Beaufort, 1982.

Crider, Bill. *A Vampire Named Fred*. Lufkin, Tex.: Maggie, 1990.

Cusick, Richie Tankersley. *Buffy the Vampire Slayer: A Novelization*. New York: Pocket, 1992.

Daniels, Philip. *The Dracula Murders*. London: Lorevan, 1983.

Darke, David. *Blind Hunger*. New York: Pinnacle, 1993.

Davis, Jay, and Don Davis. *Bring on the Night*. New York: Tor, 1993.

Dear, Ian. *Village of Blood.* London: New English Library, 1975.

Dillard, J. M. *Bloodthirst.* (Star Trek no. 37.) New York: Pocket, 1987.

Dobbin, Muriel. *A Taste for Power.* New York: Richard Marek, 1980.

Drake, Asa [C. Dean Andersson]. *Crimson Kisses.* New York: Avon, 1981.

Dreadstone, Carl [Ramsey Campbell]. *Dracula's Daughter.* New York: Berkley, 1977.

Duigon, Lee. *Lifeblood.* New York: Pinnacle, 1988.

Eccarius, J. G. *The Last Days of Christ the Vampire.* San Diego, Calif.: III Publishing, 1992.

Eliot, Marc. *How Dear the Dawn.* New York: Ballantine, 1987.

Engstrom, Elizabeth. *Black Ambrosia.* New York: Tor, 1988.

Estleman, Loren D. *Sherlock Holmes vs. Dracula, or The Adventure of the Sanguinary Count.* New York: Doubleday, 1978; Harmondsworth, U.K.; Penguin, 1979.

Eulo, Ken. *The House of Cain.* New York: Tor, 1988.

Ewers, Hans-Heinz. *Vampire.* New York: John Day, 1934; published as *Vampire's Prey.* London: Jarrolds, 1937.

Farrar, Stewart. *The Dance of Blood.* London: Arrow, 1977.

Farrington, Geoffrey. *The Revenants.* London: Daedulus, 1993.

Fenn, Lionel. *The Mark of the Moderately Vicious Vampire.* New York: Ace, 1992.

Ford, John M. *The Dragon Waiting.* New York: Timescape, 1983; New York: Avon, 1985.

Fortune, Dion. *The Demon Lover.* London: Noel Douglas, 1927; London: Wandham, 1976; New York: Weiser, 1980.

Foster, Prudence. *Blood Legacy.* New York: Pocket, 1989.

Frederick, Otto. *Count Dracula's Canadian Affair.* New York: Pageant, 1960.

Freed, L. A. *Blood Thirst.* New York: Pinnacle, 1989.

Friedman, C. S. *The Madness Season.* New York: DAW, 1990.

Garden, Nancy. *Mystery of the Night Raiders.* (Monster Hunters: Case 1.) New York: Pocket, 1991.

———. *Prisoner of Vampires.* New York: Farrar, Straus & Giroux, 1984.

———. *My Sister, the Vampire.* New York: Knopf, 1992.

Gardine, Michael. *Lamia.* New York: Dell, 1981.

Gardner, Craig Shaw. *The Lost Boys.* New York: Berkley, 1987.

Giles, Raymond. *Night of the Vampire.* New York: Avon, 1969; London: New English Library, 1970.

Gottlieb, Sherry. *Love Bite.* White Rock, B.C.: Transylvania Press, 1994.

Glut, Donald F. *Frankenstein Meets Dracula*. London: New English Library, 1977.

Golden, Christie. *The Vampire of the Mists*. (Ravenloft no. 1.) Lake Geneva, Wisc.: TSR, 1991.

Gomez, Jewelle. *The Gilda Stories: A Novel*. Ithaca, N.Y.: Firebrand, 1991.

Gresham, Stephen. *Bloodwings*. New York: Zebra, 1990.

Griffith, Kathryn Meyer. *Vampire Blood*. New York: Zebra, 1991.

————. *The Last Vampire*. New York: Zebra, 1992.

Hall, Angus. *The Scars of Dracula*. New York: Beagle, 1971; London: Sphere, 1971.

Hambly, Barbara. *Those Who Hunt the Night*. New York: Ballantine, 1988.

Harris, Jesse. *The Vampire's Kiss*. (The Power no. 7.) New York: Knopf, 1992.

Harvey, Jayne. *Great-Uncle Dracula and the Dirty Rat*. New York: Random House, 1993.

Hawke, Simon. *The Dracula Caper*. (Timewars no. 8.) New York: Ace, 1988.

Henrick, Richard. *St. John the Pursuer: Vampire in Moscow*. Lake Geneva, Wisc.: TSR, 1988.

Hill, William. *Dawn of the Vampire*. New York: Pinnacle, 1991.

Hodgman, Ann. *My Babysitter Is a Vampire*. New York: Pocket, 1991.

Hoffman, Mary. *Dracula's Daughter*. New York: Barron's, 1989.

Horler, Sidney. *The Vampire*. London: Hutchinson, 1935; New York: Bookfinger, 1974.

Hughes, William. *Lust for a Vampire*. New York: Beagle, 1971; London: Sphere, 1971.

Hurwood, Bernhardt J. *By Blood Alone*. New York: Charter, 1979.

Jennings, Jan. *Vampyr*. New York: Pinnacle, 1981.

Jensen, Ruby Jean. *Vampire Child*. New York: Zebra, 1990.

Johnson, Ken. *Hounds of Dracula: A Novel*. New York: Signet, 1977; published as *Dracula's Dog*. London: Everest, 1977.

Kimberly, Gail. *Dracula Began*. New York: Pyramid, 1976.

King, Stephen. *Salem's Lot*. New York: Doubleday, 1975; New York: Signet, 1976.

Klause, Annette Curtis. *The Silver Kiss*. New York: Delacorte, 1990.

Knight, Mallory T. [Bernhardt J. Hurwood]. *Dracutwig*. New York: Award, 1969.

Lackey, Mercedes. *Children of the Night.* New York: Tor, 1990.

Larson, Glen A., and Michael Sloan. *The Hardy Boys and Nancy Drew Meet Dracula.* New York: Grossett & Dunlap, 1978.

Lee, Tanith. *Sabella, or the Blood Stone.* New York: DAW, 1980.

———. *Dark Dance.* New York: Dell, 1992.

Levy, Elizabeth. *Dracula Is a Pain in the Neck.* New York: Harper & Row, 1983.

Linzner, Gordon. *The Spy Who Drank Blood.* New York: Space and Times, 1984.

Longstreet, Roxanne. *The Undead.* New York: Zebra, 1993.

Love at First Bite. Los Angeles: Fotonovel, 1979.

Lovell, Mark. *An Enquiry into the Existence of Vampires.* New York: Doubleday, 1974; published as *Vampire in the Shadows.* London: Hale, 1976.

Lupoff, Richard A. *Sandworld.* New York: Berkley, 1976.

Madison, J. J. *The Thing.* New York: Belmont Tower, 1974.

Martin, Ann M. *Ma and Pa Dracula.* New York: Scholastic, 1989.

Martin, George R. R. *Fevre Dream.* New York: Poseidon, 1982; New York: Pocket, 1983.

Martindale, T. Chris. *Nightblood.* New York: Warner, 1990.

Matheson, Richard. *I Am Legend.* New York: Fawcett, 1954; New York: Walker, 1970; New York: Berkley, 1971.

McCammon, Robert R. *They Thirst.* New York: Avon, 1981.

McCuniff Mara, and Tracy Briery. *The Vampire Memoirs.* New York: Zebra, 1991.

McDaniel, David. *The Vampire Affair.* (The Man from U.N.C.L.E. no. 6.) New York: Ace, 1966.

McKean, Thomas. *Vampire Vacation.* New York: Avon, 1986.

McMahan, Jeffrey. *Vampires Anonymous.* Boston: Alyson, 1991.

Monahan, Brent. *The Book of Common Dread: A Novel of the Infernal.* New York: St. Martin's, 1993.

Monette, Paul. *Nosferatu: The Vampyre.* New York: Avon, 1979.

Moriarty, Timothy. *Vampire Nights.* New York: Pinnacle, 1989.

Myles, Douglas. *Prince Dracula Son of the Devil.* New York: McGraw-Hill, 1988.

Myers, Robert J. *The Virgin and the Vampire.* New York: Pocket, 1977.

Neiderman, Andrew. *Bloodchild.* New York: Berkley, 1990.

Newman, Kim. *Anno Dracula.* London: Simon and Schuster, 1992; New York: Carroll & Graf, 1993.

Olson, Paul F. *Night Prophets.* New York: New American Library, 1989.

Owen, Dean [Dudley Dean McGaughley]. *The Brides of Dracula.* New York: Monarch, 1960.

Otfinoski, Steven. *Village of Vampires.* Chicago: Children's Press, 1979.

Parry, Michael. *Countess Dracula.* New York: Beagle, 1971; London: Sphere, 1971.

Pinkwater, Daniel Manus. *Wempires.* New York: Maxwell Macmillan International, 1991.

Platt, Kin. *Dracula, Go Home!* New York: Franklin Watts, 1979; New York: Dell, 1981.

Popescu, Petru. *In Hot Blood.* New York: Fawcett, 1989.

Powers, Tim. *The Stress of Her Regard.* Lynbrook, N.Y.: Charnel House, 1989; New York: Ace, 1989.

Randolphe, Arabella [Jack Younger]. *The Vampire Tapes.* New York: Berkley, 1977.

Raven, Simon. *Doctors Wear Scarlet.* London: Anthony Blond, 1960; New York: Simon and Schuster, 1961.

Reed, Rick R. *Obsessed.* New York: Dell, 1991.

Rechy, John. *The Vampires.* New York: Grove, 1971.

Reeves-Stevens, Garfield. *Bloodshift.* Toronto: Virgo, 1981; New York: Popular Library, 1990.

Rice, Jeff. *The Night Stalker.* New York: Pocket, 1973.

Robbins, David. *Vampire Strike.* New York: Leisure, 1989.

Romero, George, and Susan Sparrow. *Martin.* New York: Day Books, 1977.

———. *Dawn of the Dead.* New York: St. Martin's, 1978.

Romkey, Michael. *I, Vampire.* New York: Fawcett, 1990.

Ronson, Mark. *Bloodthirst.* London: Hamlyn, 1980.

Ross, Clarissa. *The Secret of the Pale Lover.* New York: Lancer, 1969.

Rudorff, Raymond. *The Dracula Archives.* New York: Arbor House, 1972; New York: Pocket, 1973.

Saberhagen, Fred, and James V. Hart. *Bram Stoker's Dracula.* New York: Signet, 1992. (Novelization of the Coppola movie script.)

Sackett, Jeffrey. *Blood of the Impaler.* New York: Bantam, 1989.

Samuels, Victor [Victor Banis]. *The Vampire Women.* New York: Popular Library, 1973.

Savage, Adrian. *Unholy Communion.* New York: Pocket, 1988.

Savory, Gerald. *Count Dracula.* London: Corgi, 1977.

Saxon, Peter. *The Torturer.* New York: Paperback Library, 1967.

————. *The Disorientated Man*. London: Mayflower, 1966; also published as *Scream and Scream Again*. New York: Paperback Library, 1966.

————. *The Darkest Night*. New York: Paperback Library, 1967.

————. *Brother Blood*. New York: Belmont, 1970.

————. *The Vampires of Finistere*. U.K.: Howard Baker, 1970.

————. *Vampire's Moon*. New York: Belmont, 1970.

Scarborough, Elizabeth. *The Goldcamp Vampire*. New York: Bantam, 1987.

Scott, Jody. *I, Vampire*. New York: Ace, 1984.

Scram, Arthur N. *The Werewolf vs. the Vampire Woman*. Beverly Hills, Calif.: Guild-Hartford, 1972.

Selby, Curt [Doris Piserchia]. *Blood County*. New York: DAW, 1981.

Seymour, Miranda. *The Vampire of Verdonia*. London: Andre Deutsch, 1988.

Shepard, Lucius. *The Golden*. Shingletown, Calif.: Mark V. Ziesing, 1993.

Sherman, Jory. *Vegas Vampire*. (Chill no. 4.) Los Angeles: Pinnacle, 1980; also published as *Vampire*. London: New English Library, 1980.

Shirley, John. *Dracula in Love*. New York: Zebra, 1979.

Siciliano, Sam. *Blood Farm*. New York: Pageant, 1988.

————. *Blood Feud*. New York: Pinnacle, 1993.

Simmons, Dan. *Carrion Comfort*. Arlington Heights, Ill.: Dark Harvest, 1989; New York: Warner, 1990.

————. *Children of the Night*. New York: Putnam, 1992; New York: Warner, 1993.

Skipp, John, and Craig Spector. *Fright Night*. New York: Tor, 1985.

————. *The Light at the End*. New York: Bantam, 1986.

Smith, Martin Cruz. *Nightwing*. New York: Norton, 1977; New York: Jove, 1977.

Smith, Robert Arthur. *Vampire Notes*. New York: Fawcett, 1990.

Spinner, Stephanie. *Dracula*. (Step-up Classic Chillers Series.) New York: Random House, 1982, 1988.

Stableford, Brian. *The Empire of Fear*. London: Simon and Schuster, 1988; New York: Carroll & Graff, 1991.

Steakley, John. *Vampire$*. New York: Roc, 1990.

Stevenson, Drew. *The Case of the Visiting Vampire*. New York: Dodd, Mead, 1986; New York: Pocket, 1986.

Stevenson, Florence. *Moonlight Variations.* New York: Jove, 1981.

———. *Household.* New York: Leisure, 1989.

Stewart, Desmond. *The Vampire of Mons.* New York: Harper & Row, 1976; London: Hamilton, 1976.

Stine, R. L. *Goodnight Kiss.* (Fear Street Super Chiller.) New York: Archway/Pocket, 1992.

Stockbridge, Grant. *Death Reign of the Vampire King.* New York: Pocket, 1935.

Stoker, Bram. *Dracula.* Westminster, U.K.: Constable, 1897. First edition. Reprinted 1899, 1904, and 1920 (9th edition). Other important editions include: New York: Doubleday & McClure, 1899. First American edition. Westminster, U.K.: Constable, 1901. Abridged by Stoker; reprinted by White Rock, B.C.: Transylvania Press, 1994. London: Rider, 1912. Corrected edition. New York: Limited Editions Club, 1965. Annotated editions include: *The Annotated Dracula* (1975), edited by Leonard Wolf. London: Penguin, 1993 (reissue). *The Essential Dracula,* New York: Mayflower, 1979, edited by Raymond McNally and Radu Florescu. This is the first edition to restore the opening chapter, "Dracula's Guest."

Storm, Constantine. *Burying the Shadow.* London: Headline, 1992.

Straub, Peter. *Ghost Story.* New York: Coward, McCann & Geoghegan, 1978; New York: Pocket, 1980.

Strieber, Whitley. *The Hunger.* New York: Morrow, 1981; New York: Pocket, 1982; New York: Avon, 1988.

Sturgeon, Theodore. *Some of Your Blood.* New York: Ballantine, 1967.

Talbot, Michael. *The Delicate Dependency: A Novel of the Vampire Life.* New York: Avon, 1982.

Tedford, William. *Liquid Diet.* New York: Diamond, 1992.

Tilton, Lois. *Vampire Winter.* New York: Pinnacle, 1990.

———. *Darkness on the Ice.* New York: Pinnacle, 1993.

Tonkin, Peter. *The Journal of Edwin Underhill.* London: Hodder & Stoughton, 1981.

Valdemi, Maria. *The Demon Lover.* New York: Tor, 1981.

Varney the Vampire, or the Feast of Blood. James Malcolm Rymer (long attributed to Thomas Peckett Prest). London: E. Lloyd, 1840; New York: Arno Press, 1970.

Veley, Charles. *Night Whispers.* New York: Doubleday, 1980; New York: Ballantine, 1981.

Viereck, George Sylvester. *The House of the Vampire.* New York: Moffat, Yard & Co., 1907.

Wahl, Jan. *Dracula's Cat.* Englewood Cliffs, N.J.: Prentice Hall, 1978.

Wallace, Patricia. *Monday's Child.* New York: Zebra, 1989.

Warrington, Freda. *A Taste of Blood Wine.* London: Pan, 1992.

Weathersby, Lee. *Kiss of the Vampire.* New York: Zebra, 1992.

Wilde, Kelley. *Mastery.* New York: Dell, 1991.

Williams, Sidney. *Night Brothers.* New York: Pinnacle, 1989.

Williams, Tad. *Child of an Ancient City.* New York: Dragonflight Books, 1992.

Wilson, Colin. *The Space Vampires.* New York: Random House, 1976; London: Hart-Davis and MacGivvon, 1976; New York: Pocket, 1977; also published as *Lifeforce.* New York: Warner, 1976.

Winston, Daoma. *The Vampire Curse.* New York: Paperback Library, 1971.

FILMOGRAPHY ON DRACULA,
VAMPIRES, AND THE UNDEAD
· · · · · · · · · · · · · · · ·

Most of the early, and by now obscure, silent films about vampires are mostly about "vamps" — female flirts who entice or captivate men. The earliest full-length vampire movie to survive is F. W. Murnau's classic silent film *Nosferatu* (1922), which was based on Stoker's novel *Dracula* (1897).

SILENT FILMS 1896–1928

1896. *Le Manoir du Diable*. Robert-Houdin film, Pathe/Star, France; director, Georges Méliès. American title: *The Haunted Castle*. English title: *The Devil's Castle*. A two-minute trick short: in one scene a huge bat flying about in a medieval castle suddenly transforms into Mephistopheles (the result of stop-start photography). A cavalier arrives with a crucifix and, once confronted with it, the devil throws up his hands and disappears in a cloud of smoke.

1909–22. This period included the following films, which are listed here out of historical interest. *Vampire of the Coast*, 1909, USA. *The Vampire's Trail*, 1910, USA. *Vampyre*, 1912 Swedish short. *Vampe di Gelosia* (The Vamp's Jealousy), 1912 Italian short. *The Vampire*, 1912 Messter short. *Danse Vampiresque*, 1912 Danish short. *The Vampire*, 1913, USA, Kalem film; director, Robert Vignola. *In the Grip of the Vampire*, 1913, USA. *Vampires of the Night*, 1914, USA, Greene's Feature Photo Plays. *The Vampire's Trail*, 1914, USA; director, Robert Vignola. *Vampires of Warsaw*, 1914, USA. *The Vampire's Tower*, 1914, USA, Ambrosia film. *Saved from the Vampire*, 1914, USA. *Les Vampires*,

1915, French serial; director, Louis Feuillade. *The Vampire's Clutch,* 1915, France, Knight film. *Was She a Vampire?* 1915, USA, Universal film. *Kiss of the Vampire,* 1915, USA. *Mr. Vampire,* 1916, USA. *A Night of Horror,* 1916, Germany; director, Arthur Robison. *A Vampire Out of Work,* 1916, USA, Vitagraph film. *Ceneri e Vampe,* 1916, Italy. *A Village Vampire,* 1916, USA. *The Beloved Vampire,* 1917, USA. *Magia,* 1917, Hungary; director, Alexander Korda, starring Mihaly Varkonyi. The hero, while looking into Baron Merlin's magic mirror, discovers that his host is an ancient magician kept alive by drinking the blood of a young man every thousandth full moon. *The Vampire,* 1920, USA, Metro film. *Drakula,* 1920, Hungary; director, Karoly Lajthay; technically the first film based on the Stoker novel, it is now lost.

1922. *Nosferatu, eine Symphonie des Grauens.* Prana Films, Germany; director, Friedrich Wilhelm Murnau; screenplay, Henrick Galeen. Released on March 5, 1922, in Germany; in 1929 in the U.S. as *Nosferatu, the Vampire.* Count Orlok, played by Max Schreck, is the vampire. The script was an adaptation of Stoker's novel, but since Murnau had not secured the proper permission, he changed the setting from the Balkans to the Baltic area, and he changed the names of the main characters. This is the first surviving Dracula film. Visually it still ranks as one of the greatest horror films of all time. Murnau filmed it in an outdoor, realistic setting. Despite some technical gimmicks that cause modern audiences to laugh, such as the speeded up sequences of Dracula's carriage and his loading of coffins, the film remains a masterpiece.

1927. *London after Midnight.* Metro-Goldwyn Mayer, USA. Producer/director, Tod Browning; screenplay, Tod Browning and Waldemar Young, from a novel by Tod Browning entitled *The Hypnotist.* Released in England as *The Hypnotist.* Lon Chaney, "the man with a thousand faces," appears as Inspector Edmund Burke, alias Mooney, who pretends to be a vampire.

1928. *The Vampire.* United Pictures, USA. Released in France as *Vampire a du Mode.* A seductive female temptress is portrayed here, not a vampire.

Talkies 1931–1992

1931. *Dracula*. Universal Studios, USA; producer, Carl Laemmle Jr.; director, Tod Browning; screenplay, Garret Fort, from the play by Hamilton Deane and John F. Balderston; additional dialogue by Dudley Murphy. Dracula is played by Bela Lugosi, who originated the role on Broadway. This is the first real vampire talkie. It remains one of the most popular films of all time, though most critics do not hold it in high regard. The photography is unimaginative, the music contains snatches from Tschaikovsky's "Swan Lake," but Bela Lugosi's authentic Hungarian accent and presence reach out to make his Dracula a part of contemporary American folklore.

1931. *Dracula*. Universal Studios, USA; co-producer, Carl Laemmle, Jr.; director, George Melford. Spanish-language version of the Browning-Lugosi film cited above; superior in mood to the American version, includes the use of the fluid or inquisitive camera. (Available in fully restored 1990 video version.)

1932. *Vampyr*. Les Films Carl Dreyer, France; director/producer, Carl Dreyer; screenplay, Carl Dreyer and Christian Jul, freely adapted from "Carmilla" by Sheridan Le Fanu. Released in America as both *The Vampire* and *Castle of Doom*; in England as *The Strange Adventures of David Gray*. This film is an example of what a real horror film should be. The dreadful is sensed rather than seen. Blood-drinking is suggested rather than portrayed. The entire film has a distant, grainy quality reminiscent of a Seurat painting. This effect was actually an accident during filming — when a piece of gauze fell over the lens and Dreyer turned it into an asset. The story line is confusing, but the mood of the film remains unique; no successors have ever duplicated, much less equaled it.

1933. *The Vampire Bat*. Majestic, USA; producer, Phil Goldstone; director, Frank Trayer; screenplay, Edward Lowe. Lionel Atwill plays a mad doctor who tries to cover up his weird experiments by fomenting a vampire scare among the inhabitants of a far-off Balkan village.

1935. *The Mark of the Vampire*. Metro-Goldwyn Mayer, USA; producer, E. J. Mannix; director, Tod Browning; screenplay, Guy Endore and Bernard Schubert, from the story by Tod Browning. This is an elaborate remake of *London after Midnight* (see above). Bela Lugosi plays Count Mora (Dracula) in the film; his female vampire is played by

Caroll Borland. Lionel Barrymore, an occultist, insists that a vampire is behind the murders in a gloomy castle, but in the end the supposed vampires turn out to be local actors. The real killer was a man who drained the blood of his victim by more scientific means. This film was re-released in 1972.

1935. *Condemned to Live.* Chesterfield-Invincible, USA; producer, Maurey M. Cohen; director, Frank Strayer; screenplay, Karen de Wolfe. In Africa, a woman bitten by a vampire bat gives birth to a baby who becomes vampirelike. As an adult, he is unaware that he becomes a vampire at full moon.

1936. *Dracula's Daughter.* Universal, USA; producer, Carl Laemmle, Jr.; director, Lambert Hillyer; screenplay, Garret Fort, adapted from Bram Stoker's story "Dracula's Guest" and a story by Oliver Jeffries. Gloria Holden plays Dracula's daughter, Countess Marya Zaleska. Dracula's daughter tries to conquer her inherited blood lust, but without success.

1940. *The Devil Bat.* Producer Releasing Corp., USA; producer, Jack Gallagher; director, Jean Yarbrough; screenplay, John Thomas Neville, from George Bricker's story "The Flying Serpent." Bela Lugosi plays Dr. Paul Carruthers, a mad scientist who raises huge vampire bats to become his agents of revenge.

1941. *Spooks Run Wild.* Banner Production-Monogram, USA; producer, Sam Katzman; director, Phil Rosen; screenplay, Carl Foreman and Charles R. Marian. Bela Lugosi played Nardo, a stage magician suspected of being a vampirelike monster.

1943. *Le Vampire.* France; director, Jean Painleve. Documentary filmed on location in the Gran Chaco, South America. Includes scenes of the actual vampire bat stalking its victim and drinking blood.

1943. *Son of Dracula.* Universal, USA; producer, Ford Beebe; director, Robert Siodmak; screenplay, Curt Siodmak, suggested by Stoker's *Dracula.* Lon Chaney, Jr. plays Count Alucard (Dracula spelled backwards). The count emigrates from Europe to the United States in search of fresh blood.

1943. *Dead Men Walk.* (Other titles: *The Vampire* and *Creatures of the Devil.*) Producers Releasing Corp., USA; producer, Sigmund Neufield; director, Sam Newfield; screenplay, Frank Myton. George Zucco plays the vampire, Dr. Lloyd Clayton.

1943. *Return of the Vampire.* Columbia, USA; producer, Sam White; director, Lew Landers; screenplay, Griffin Jay, based on an idea by

Kurt Neumann; additional dialogue, Randall Faye. Bela Lugosi plays Armand Tesla, who appears in England during World War II, seeking revenge against those who first tried to kill him.

1944. *House of Frankenstein.* Universal, USA; producer, Paul Malvern; director, Eric C. Kenton; screenplay, Edward T. Lowe, based on an original story by Curt Siodmak. John Carradine appears in his first role as Count Dracula, alias Baron Latos.

1945. *The House of Dracula.* Universal, USA; producer, Paul Malvern; director, Erle C. Kenton; screenplay, Edward T. Lowe. John Carradine again appears as Baron Latos.

1945. *Isle of the Dead.* RKO Radio Pictures, USA; producer, Val Lewton; director, Mark Robson; screenplay, Ardel Wray and Joseph Mischel. Boris Karloff plays a Greek general who comes back to the island where his wife is entombed. He accuses a young girl of being a vampire (*vrykolaka*).

1945. *The Vampire's Ghost.* Republic Pictures, USA; associate producer, Rudy Abel; director, Lesley Selander; screenplay, Leigh Brackett and John K. Butler, after a story by Leigh Brackett. English actor John Abbott as a vampire posing as a nightclub owner in a small African village.

1946. *Devil Bat's Daughter.* Producers Releasing Corp., USA; producer, Frank Wisbar; director, Frank Wisbar; screenplay, Griffin Jay, based on an idea by Leo T. McCarthy, Frank Wisbar, and Ernst Jaeger. A murderous doctor tries to blame his crimes on the daughter of the "Devil Bat."

1946. *Dr. Terror's House of Horrors.* U.S. Independent. Reissue of parts of four earlier horror films, including sections from Dreyer's *Vampyr.*

1946. *Valley of the Zombies.* Republic, USA; associate producers, Dorrell McGowan and Stuart McGowan; director, Philip Ford; screenplay, Dorrell McGowan and Stuart McGowan, based on a story by Royal K. Cole and Sherman T. Lowe. Ian Keith portrays a resurrected madman dependent upon constant blood transfusions to stay alive.

1948. *Abbott and Costello Meet Frankenstein.* Universal, USA; producer, Robert Arthur; director, Charles Barton; screenplay, Robert Lees, Frederic Rinaldo, and John Grant. Released in England as *Abbott and Costello Meet the Ghosts.* Bela Lugosi plays Dracula. A lighthearted satire on Dracula, Frankenstein, and the Wolf Man; Dracula ends up as a bat in the claws of the Wolf Man.

1951. *The Thing from Another World.* RKO Radio Pictures, USA; producer, Howard Hawks; director, Christian Nyby; screenplay, Charles Lederer, based on the novel *Who Goes There?* by John W. Campbell, Jr. One of the first films to link the classical vampire with science fiction. A figure from outer space crash-lands on Earth, survives on blood, and needs it to germinate his seeds. Considered to be a warning against possible communist invasion, the final message is "Keep watching the skies! Keep watching the skies!"

1952. *Old Mother Riley Meets the Vampire.* Renown, UK; director, J. Gilling; screenplay, Val Valentine. Released in America as both *Vampire over London* and *My Son, the Vampire.* Bela Lugosi played Van Housen, the vampire, in this British comedy.

1953. *Drakula Istanbulda.* Demirag, Turkey; producer, Turgut Demirag; director, Mehmet Muktar; screenplay, Unit Deniz, after the novels *Dracula* by Bram Stoker and *The Impaling Voivode* by Riza Seyfi. Rare first film to fuse Stoker's *Dracula* with Vlad the Impaler although the references are slight. A balding Atif Kaptan plays the vampire Dracula, and the main part of the story is set in Istanbul.

1956. *Plan Nine from Outer Space.* Distribution Corporation of America, USA; producer/director, Edward D. Wood, Jr.; screenplay, Edward D. Wood, Jr. Second title: *Grave Robbers from Outer Space.* This was Lugosi's last film and a strong contender for the worst movie ever made; it is so bad that it now has a major cult following.

1957. *The Vampire.* Gramercy Pictures Productions, United Artists, UK and USA; producers, Arthur Gardner and Jules V. Levy; director, Paul Landres; screenplay, Pat Fiedler. American title: *Mark of the Vampire.* Scientist John Beal accidentally takes pills derived from vampire bats, which turn him into a vampire at night.

1957. *Blood of Dracula.* Carmel/American International Pictures, USA; producer, Herman Cohen; director, Herbert L. Strock; screenplay, Ralph Thornton. Released in England as *Blood Is My Heritage*; in Canada as *Blood of the Demon.* Set in a girls' school, teenager Sandra Harrison turns into a vampire after her evil teacher hypnotizes her.

1957. *Not of This Earth.* Allied Artists, USA; producer/director, Roger Corman; screenplay, Charles Griffith and Mark Hanna. Science fiction blended with vampirism again. An alien from a dying planet lands on earth to see if human blood can revivify his kind.

1957. *I Vampiri.* Titanus-Athena, Italy; director, Riccardo Freda; screenplay, Piero Regnoli, Rik Sjostrom, and Riccardo Freda. Released in America under the titles *The Vampire of Notre Dame, The Devil's Commandment,* and *Lust of the Vampires.* Not a real vampire film at all, despite the title.

1958. *The Return of Dracula.* Gramercy United Artists Release, USA; producers, Arthur Gardner and Jules V. Levy; director, Paul Landres; screenplay, Pat Fiedler. Released in England as *The Fantastic Disappearing Man,* and on American TV as *The Curse of Dracula.* Francis Lederer plays the Hungarian visitor Bellac, the vampire, come to California to prey on the locals. In the end he falls into a mineshaft and is impaled on a wooden stake.

1958. *The Horror of Dracula.* Hammer Films, UK; producer, Anthony Hinds; executive producer, Michael Carreras; director, Terence Fisher; screenplay, Jimmy Sangster, adapted from *Dracula* by Stoker. Dracula is played by Christopher Lee. This is a fine work which ranks with the earlier classic films *Nosferatu* and the 1931 *Dracula.*

1958. *Blood of the Vampire.* Tampean Productions, UK; producers, Robert S. Baker and Monty Berman; director, Henry Cass; screenplay, Jimmy Sangster. Sir Donald Wolfit plays Dr. Callistratus, a doctor revived from the dead but with a blood deficiency; he carries on research among the helpless victims in his prison hospital in order to try to stay alive.

1959. *Curse of the Undead.* Universal, USA; producer, Joseph Gershenzon; director, Edward Dein; screenplay, Michael Pate and Mildred Dein. Also called *The Unearthly.* One of the first films to mix the vampire legend with the traditional American folklore of the Western. Villainous Michael Pate portrays a hired gunslinger named Drake Robey who is also a vampire. Preacher Dan dispatches him with a bullet containing part of a crucifix.

1959. *El Vampiro.* Cinemagrafica ABSA-Mexico; producer, Abel Salazar; director, Fernando Mendez; screenplay, Heinrich Rodriguez and Ramon Obon.

1959. *Tempi Duri Per I Vampiri.* Maxima, Italy; presented by Joseph E. Levine; producer, Mario Cecchi Gori; director, Pio Angeletti; screenplay, Mario Cecchi Gori and others. Released in America as *Uncle Was a Vampire.* Christopher Lee as Uncle Rinaldo, alias Baron Rodrigo, the vampire, in an Italian comedy. The vampire uncle bites his cousin who is working as a porter in a resort hotel, but a kiss from his girlfriend cures the cousin of vampirism.

1960. *The Brides of Dracula.* Hammer Films, Great Britain; producer,

Anthony Hinds; executive producer, Michael Carreras; director, Terence Fisher; screenplay, Jimmy Sangster, Peter Bryan, and Edward Percy. David Peel is the vampire-baron, Baron Meinster, and Peter Cushing is again the Van Helsing character. A naive schoolteacher releases young Baron Meinster from his mother's chains. He then proceeds to turn his mother (Martita Hunt) into a vampire and preys on girls in a nearby school.

1960. *L'Ultima Preda del Vampiro.* Nord Film, Italy; producer, Tiziana Longo; director, Piero Regnoli. Released in America as *The Playgirls and the Vampire.* A sexploitation film.

1960. *Et Mourir de plaisir.* EGE Films-France-Italy; producer, Raymond Eger; director, Roger Vadim; screenplay, Roger Vadim, Claude Brule, and Claude Martin, based on a story by Roger Vadim and also Sheridan Le Fanu's "Carmilla." Released in America as *Blood and Roses.* Vampiress Carmilla (Annette Stroyberg Vadim) enters the body of a young girl and through her carries out her vampiric practices.

1961. *Maschera del Demonio.* Jolly-Galatea, Italy; director, Mario Bava; screenplay, Ennio de Concini and Mario Serandrei, based on the story "Viy" by Gogol. Released in America as *Black Sunday;* in England as *Revenge of the Vampire.* English actress Barbara Steele plays both the heroine Katia and the evil Princess Asa Vajda, the vampire-witch. An excellent film that launched Barbara Steele's career as everyone's ideal of a horror flick scream queen.

1961. *Il Vampiro dell'Opera.* N. I. F. Rome, Italy; director, Renato Polselli. A vampire haunts an old opera house.

1961. *L'Amante del Vampiri.* C. E. F. Consorzio-Italo-Films, Italy; producer, Bruno Bolognesi; director, Renato Polselli; screenplay, Renato Polselli, Giuseppi Pellegrini, and Ernesto Castaldi. Released in America as *The Vampire and the Ballerina.* An imitation of the 1960 film *L'Ultima Preda del Vampiro.* A vampire and his servant prey on showgirls.

1961. *Ercole al Centro della Terra.* Omnia SPA Cinematografica, Italy; producer, Achille Piazzi; director, Mario Bava; screenplay, Alessandro Continenza, M. Bava, Duccio Tessari, and Franco Prosperi. Released in America as *Hercules in the Haunted World* and also *Hercules versus the Vampires.* Christopher Lee played Lyco, chief of the vampiric demons, in this muscleman epic.

1961. *El Vampiro Sangriento.* Azteca-Mexico; producer, Rafael Perez

Grovas; director, Miguel Morayta; screenplay, Miguel Morayta. Released in America as *The Bloody Vampire*. Count Frankenhausen is a vampire, and in the end he remains uncaught.

1961. *Ataud del Vampiro*. Cinemagrafica ABSA-Mexico; producer, Abel Salazar; director, Fernando Mendez; screenplay, Ramon Obon, after a story by Raul Zentino. Released in America as *The Vampire's Coffin*. A mad doctor resuscitates a vampire in this sequel to *El Vampiro Sangriento*.

1961. *El Mundo de la Vampiro*. Cinemagrafica ABSA Mexico; producer, Abel Salazar; director, Fernando Mendez; screenplay, Ramon Obon, based on an idea by Paul Zentino. Released in America as *World of the Vampire*. Vampire on the trail of revenge ends up on a stake.

1962. *Maciste contre il Vampiro*. Ambrosiana Cinematografica, Italy; producer, Paolo Moff; directors, Giacomo Gentilomo and Sergio Corbucci; screenplay, Sergio Corbucci and Ducc Tessari. Released in America as *Goliath and the Vampire*. Muscleman vampire versus superhero.

1962. *La Strage dei Vampiri*. Italy; producer, Dino Sant'Ambrogio; director, Robert Mauri; screenplay, Robert Mauri. Released in America as *Curse of the Blood Ghouls*. Italian Gothic.

1962. *La Invasion de los Vampiros*. Mexico; producer, Rafael Perez Grovas; director, Miguel Morayta; screenplay, Miguel Morayta. Released in America as *The Invasion of the Vampires*. The vampire Count Frankenhausen continues on in this sequel to *El Vampiro Sangriento*.

1962. *House on Bare Mountain*. Olympic International, USA; producers, Bob Cresse, David Andrew, and Wesdon Bishop; director, R. L. Frost; screenplay, Denver Scott. Sexploitation with all three classic horrors — Dracula, the Frankenstein monster, and the Wolf Man.

1962. *La Maldicion de los Karnsteins*. Hispaner Films, NEC Cinematografica, Spain-Italy; director, Thomas Miller (alias Camillo Mastrocinque); screenplay, Julian Berry after "Carmilla" by Le Fanu. Christopher Lee plays Count Ludwig Karnstein. Released in England as *Crypt of Horror*; in America as *Terror in the Crypt*. The third film version of Le Fanu's tale, to which it adheres rather closely.

1963. *I Tre Volti della Paura*. Emmerpi-Galatea-Lyre, Italy; director, Mario Bava; screenplay, Marcello Fondato, Alberto Bevilacqua, and Mario Bava. Released in America as *Black Sabbath*. Three stories in one film, one of which is based on Alexis Tolstoy's "The Wurdalak," about the Urfe family of vampires. Boris Karloff, the narrator, also plays Gorca, the head of the vampire household.

1963. *Kiss of the Vampire.* Hammer Films, UK; producer, Anthony Hinds; director, Don Sharp; screenplay, John Elder (alias Anthony Hinds). American TV title: *Kiss of Evil.* A well-made film about a couple honeymooning in Bavaria, where they become involved in a vampire cult.

1964. *The Last Man on Earth.* Produzioni La Regine and American International, Italy/USA; director, Sidney Salkow (and Ubaldo Ragona); producer, Robert L. Lippert; screenplay, William Leicester, based on the Richard Matheson classic novel *I Am Legend.* Vincent Price portrays scientist Robert Morgan, the last surviving human after an atomiclike plague, pitted against a group of mutant vampires and zombies who are bent on killing him.

1964. *Dr. Terror's House of Horrors.* Amicus, England; producers, Milton Subotsky and Max Rosenberg; director, Freddie Francis; screenplay, Milton Subotsky. Death, in the guise of Dr. Schreck, played by Peter Cushing, predicts the death of five passengers on a train. The last segment is about a doctor (Donald Sutherland) who is convinced by another doctor (Max Adrian) to kill his French bride (Jennifer Jayne) because she is purportedly a vampire. But in the end, with a fine twist, the other doctor turns out to be the real vampire.

1965. *Dracula — Prince of Darkness* or *Blood for Dracula.* Hammer Films, UK; producer, Anthony Nelson Keys; director, Terence Fisher; screenplay, John Sansom (alias Jim Sangster), from an idea by John Elder (alias Anthony Hinds) based on the characters in Bram Stoker's *Dracula.* In this sequel to *Horror of Dracula* (1958), Christopher Lee again plays Dracula, who is revived by blood from a victim flowing into his ashes, and in the end is destroyed by falling into running water.

1965. *Terrore nello Spazio.* Castilla, Italy; producer, Fulvio Lucisano; director, Mario Bava; screenplay, Ib Melchior and Louis M. Heywood. Released in America as *Planet of Blood;* for TV as *Planet of Terror* and *Planet of the Vampires.* Beings from another planet try to take over the bodies of humans who have crash-landed on their strange planet.

1965. *Devils of Darkness.* Planet Films, UK; producer, Tom Blakeley; director, Lance Comfort; screenplay, Lyn Fairhurst. Count Sinistre, a vampire, tries to ravish modern-day victims from Brittany.

1965. *La Sorella di Satana.* Italy/Yugoslavia; directors, Michael Reeyes and Charles Griffiths. Released in America as *The She-Beast.* A vampiress appears in modern-day Communist Transylvania.

1966. *Billy the Kid vs. Dracula.* Circle/Embassy, USA; producer, Carroll Case; director, William Beaudine; screenplay, Karl Hittleman. Dracula, played by John Carradine, preys on a western town until he is killed by the outlaw Billy the Kid, played by Chuck Courtney.

1966. *Queen of Blood.* American International Pictures. Directed by Curtis Harrington. A mission to Mars inadvertently brings back a vampiress who feeds on the crew.

1966. *Blood Bath.* American International, USA; producer, Jack Hill; directors, Jack Hill and Stephanie Rothman; screenplay, J. Hill and S. Rothman. American TV title: *Track of the Vampire.* Set in Venice, California, William Campbell plays artist Antonio Sordi, who paints his victims and then kills them in vats of boiling wax. In the end they come back to life and kill him.

1966. *Dr. Terror's Gallery of Horrors.* American General, USA. The first two segments are about vampires: in the first one, "King Vampire," a nineteenth-century London vampire turns out to be the secretary of the police inspector in charge of a murder case; the second story, "Count Alucard," retells the initial chapters of Stoker's novel, but Harker is attacked by a female vampire instead of by Dracula. Harker then turns into a werewolf in order to destroy Count Alucard, the vampire king.

1966–71. *Dark Shadows.* USA, ABC TV serial. Producer, Robert Costello; director, Dan Curtis. A long-running horror soap shown on late-afternoon TV. The 175-year-old, black-caped vampire named Barnabas Collins, played by Jonathan Frid, became a popular folk hero to housewives and teenagers. The basic story line involves young Victoria Winters (Alexandra Moltke), who comes to be governess to ten-year-old David Collins at Collinwood Manor, an old Gothic castle in Maine, where she encounters the vampire. The series spawned two movies: *House of Dark Shadows* (1970) and *Night of Dark Shadows* (1971).

1967. *Le Bal des Vampires.* Cadre-MGM, France, UK; producer, Gene Gutowski; director, Roman Polanski; screenplay, Gerard Brack and Roman Polanski. Released in America as *The Fearless Vampire Killers or: Pardon Me, but Your Teeth Are in My Neck.* A well-filmed satirical approach to vampires. Polanski cleverly uses the occult symbols. Vampire hunter Professor Ambrosius (Jack MacGowan) travels with his assistant Alfred (Roman Polanski) to Transylvania in search of the vampire Count Von Krolock (Ferdy Mayne). He also encounters a Jewish vampire and a homosexual vampire. Very funny.

1967. *A Taste of Blood.* Creative Film Enterprises, Inc., USA; producer/director, Herschell Gordon Lewis; screenplay, Donald Standford, with characters based on those in Stoker's *Dracula.* An American unknowingly drinks the blood of his ancestor, Count Dracula, and becomes a vampire, killing the descendants of those who executed the count.

1968. *Dracula Has Risen from the Grave.* Hammer Films, UK; producer, Aida Young; director, Freddie Francis; screenplay, John Elder. Christopher Lee's third appearance as Dracula, in a dull film with a garbled story line. Dracula is revived by the blood of a pusillanimous priest and in the end is impaled on a large wooden cross.

1968. *Le Viol du Vampire.* ABC made-for-TV movie; producer, Sam Selsky; director, Jean Rollin; screenplay, J. Rollin. Sexploitation film.

1969. *The Blood of Dracula's Castle.* Paragon Pictures/Crown International, USA; producers, Al Adamson and Rex Carlton; director, Al Adamson; screenplay, Rex Carlton.

1969. *Malenka la Vampire.* Victory Films SA (Madrid) and Cobra Film (Rome), Spain/Italy; director, Armando de Osorio.

1969. *The Blood Beast Terror.* Tigon, UK; producer, Arnold Miller; director, Vernon Sewell; screenplay, Peter Bryan.

1970. *Jonathan, Vampire Sterben Nicht.* Beta Films, Germany; director/screenplay, Hans W. Geissendorfer. An erotic film, freely adapted from Stoker's novel with the vampire leader as a kind of fascist dictator.

1970. *Taste the Blood of Dracula.* Hammer-Warner Pathe, UK; producer, Aida Young; director, Peter Sasdy; screenplay, John Elder (alias Anthony Hinds), based on characters in Stoker's *Dracula.* Christopher Lee plays Dracula in this fourth of the Hammer series of Dracula movies. A salesman acquires Dracula's cape and ring and sells them to a depraved disciple of the count and his followers. The followers then kill the disciple, who in turn comes back to life as Dracula himself, seeking vengeance on the descendants of those who killed him. The vampire is finally destroyed in a church by the son and daughter of two of his victims.

1970. *Count Dracula.* Fenix/Corona/Filmar/Towers of London, Italy/Spain/Germany; producer, Harry Alan Towers; director, Jesus

Franco. Based on Stoker's *Dracula,* featuring Christopher Lee wearing a mustache like Stoker's vampire. A note at the outset of the film proclaims, "for the first time we retell Bram Stoker's *Dracula* exactly as he wrote it." Proud but empty words! Arthur Holmwood, Lucy's fiancé, does not even appear in the movie; Dr. Seward, head of the insane asylum, has been reduced to an employee of Van Helsing; but it is one of the few films that adheres somewhat to the novel. Unfortunately it is not a good movie; cheaply made, the screenplay is clumsy, and the camera work pedestrian.

1970. *Count Yorga, the Vampire.* Erica Films-American International Pictures, USA; producer, Michael MacReady; director/screenplay, Bob Kelljan. Released in America as *Loves of Count Yorga.* Robert Quarry played the count, a vampire from Eastern Europe who appears in a California setting in search of fresh blood. A success among college audiences.

1970. *Blood of Frankenstein.* USA; Zandor Vorkov played Count Dracula.

1970. *Lust for a Vampire.* Hammer Films, UK; producers, Harry Fine and Michael Style; director, Jimmy Sangster; screenplay, Tudor Gates. Yutte Stensgaard played a character reminiscent of Le Fanu's Carmilla.

1970. *The Vampire Lovers.* Hammer Films, UK; producers, Harry Fine and Michael Style; director, Roy Ward Baker; screenplay, Tudor Gates. This is the fourth film version of Le Fanu's "Carmilla." Ingrid Pitt plays Carmilla, a vampire who lives through three generations and raises havoc among the village inhabitants. Some of the faint lesbian suggestions in Le Fanu's novelette come through in this film.

1970. *Countess Dracula.* Hammer Films, UK; producer, Alexander Paal; director, Peter Sasdy; screenplay, Jeremy Paul. Set in central Europe, Ingrid Pitt has the lead as a sadist who bathes in the blood of her victims, loosely based on the legends surrounding the Blood Countess, Elizabeth Bathory (1560–1614). Unfortunately the countess changes from old to young too fast to be believable, and the acting is atrocious, as some speak English with heavy Hungarian accents and others do not.

1970. *Scars of Dracula.* Hammer Films, UK; producer, Aida Young; director, Roy Ward Baker; screenplay, John Elder. Christopher Lee plays Dracula. An obviously fake rubber bat drips blood onto Dracula's remains, which brings him back to life. In the end the vampire is impaled on a metal stake and electrically fried. This film is particularly good in showing the ways in which the vampire stalks his victim and compels the victim to drink his blood.

1970. *Guess What Happened to Count Dracula?* A Merrick International Picture, USA; producer, Leo Rivers; executive producer, Laurence Merrick. The nadir of horror films. Blatant sexploitation. Made three times on the same set: once with actors wearing clothes under the original title; second with actors without their clothes in *Does Dracula Suck?* and third, as a degenerate romp under the title *Does Dracula Really . . . ?* No taste, no talent, bad filming techniques, and poor acting.

1970. *House of Dark Shadows.* MGM, based on the ABC TV series. Producer/director, Dan Curtis; screenplay, Sam Hall and Gordon Russell; starring Jonathan Frid, Grayson Hall, Kathyrn Leigh Scott, and Joan Bennett. Barnabas Collins is revived when a grave robber opens his sealed coffin. He returns to the New England estate Collinwood, where he claims to be an English relative of the Collins family. In the end he is killed by a crossbow while trying to turn his girlfriend into a vampire.

1970. *Vampyros Lesbos. Die Erbin des Draculas.* West Germany/Spain; director, Franco Manera (Jesus Franco). Filmed in Turkey. Count Dracula's descendant Nadina lures young women to her isolated island, where she seduces and kills them in order to remain young. The story combines elements of the actual history and legend of the Blood Countess, Elizabeth Bathory, Sheridan Le Fanu's "Carmilla" and Stoker's story "Dracula's Guest."

1971. *The Omega Man.* Warner, USA; color remake of Richard Matheson's *I Am Legend.* Director, Boris Sagal; producer, Walter Seltzer; screenplay, John William. Charleton Heston stars. Robert Morgan, the last man left after an atomic holocaust, is pursued and killed by vampirelike mutants and thus himself becomes legend, as vampires had once been to humans.

1971. *The Velvet Vampire.* New World Pictures, USA; directed by Stephanie Rothman. The story of a centuries-old vampiress named Diana Le Fanu (Celeste Yarnall) who sleeps in a coffin with her dead husband. She seduces male and female visitors until a bunch of hippies finish her off with a cross.

1971. *The Return of Count Yorga.* American International, USA; director, Bob Kelljan. Superior sequel to the first Count Yorga film

(1970). At the end of the film the count is destroyed, but one of his pursuers has become a vampire, so the cult lives on.

1972. *Grave of the Vampire (Seed of Terror)*. Entertainment/Pyramid, USA; producer, Daniel Cady; director, John Hayes. A vampire emerges from his grave to break a man's back and rape his girl-friend. She goes insane and has a male vampire baby. The reluctant half-vampire does not want to be one. His father fights brutally with him in the film climax.

1972. *Blacula*. American International, USA; producer, Joseph T. Naar; director, William Crain; screenplay, Joan Torres and Ray-mond Koenig. Count Dracula (Charles McCauley) infects the black African prince Manuwalde (the noted Shakespearean actor William Marshall) while on a visit to Transylvania in 1815 and proclaims, "I curse you with my name! You will become Blacula the vampire!" Manuwalde is revived in contemporary Los Angeles and goes in search of his dead wife. When the detective in pursuit of Manuwalde holds up a crucifix in front of the black vampire prince, he comments, "That will not be necessary." The film grossed more money for American International than any of their previous films, so a sequel was inevitable.

1972. *Dracula's Saga (Le Saga de los Draculas)*. Profilmes, Spain; pro-ducer/director, Leon Klimovsky. The old Count Dracula, living amid a family of vampires, is afraid that his line might die out, so he has his lovely female vampires seek out suitable human mates with predictable results. Narcisco Ibanez Menta portrays the aging count.

1972. *Captain Kronos — Vampire Hunter*. Hammer Films, UK; director/ screenplay, Brian Clemens; producers, Albert Fennel and Brian Clemens. Captain Kronos, a Nordic knight with a mysterious past, meditates and chants in Zen-like manner. The setting is a nine-teenth-century European village where Captain Kronos, accompa-nied by his faithful companion, the hunchback Professor Grost, is called upon to destroy the local vampires. But these vampires hap-pen to be immune to the usual stakes and crosses. So Kronos and Grost forge a sword of silver which does the job.

1972. *The Deathmaster*. RF World Entertainment, USA; producers, Fred Sadoff and Robert Quarry; director, Ray Danton. A vanity vehicle for the actor Robert Quarry who should have known better. He plays a Count Yorga–type vampire masquerading as a California guru. Young hippies flock to him as "the man with all the answers," and he smilingly replies, "If you ask the right questions." Unbelievably dumb, filled with incompetent actors.

1972. *In Search of Dracula.* Aspekt Films, Sweden; director, Calvin Floyd; screenplay, Yvonne Floyd in association with Raymond McNally and Radu Florescu, based on the book *In Search of Dracula.* The first Dracula documentary to connect Count Dracula with Vlad the Impaler, and the first Dracula film shot on location in Transylvania. Christopher Lee stars as both Count Dracula and the fifteenth-century prince Vlad Dracula. The movie tells the story of Count Dracula in Stoker's novel, Vlad's atrocities, vampire folklore, and the image of Dracula and vampires in literature and the movies. Too talky and intellectual to be commercially successful. Later released to theaters as a feature film with added footage largely drawn from old Bela Lugosi movies.

1972. *The Night Stalker.* ABC TV, USA; director, John L. Moxey. Darren McGavin as reporter Carl Kolchak; Barry Atwater is superb as the ominous Eastern European vampire Janos Skorzeny. Well done, with high Nielsen ratings — 75 million viewers made history by tuning in, thus making it the most-watched TV movie at that time.

1972. *Dracula, A.D. 1972.* Hammer Films, UK; producer, Josephine Douglas; executive producer, Michael Carreras; director, Alan Gibson; screenplay, Don Houghton. Christopher Lee stars again as Dracula, and Peter Cushing as Van Helsing. Young people in the film assume center stage, especially the actor Christopher Neame who was being groomed to replace Lee but never did. The story presents a sequel to events in 1872 when Dracula and Van Helsing clashed and Dracula was destroyed and his ashes buried. A teenager, Johnny Alucard, holds a black magic ritual in the church housing Dracula's ashes. Dracula revives and starts to spread his vampire cult. But one of the girls visiting the church at the time turns out to be Jessica Van Helsing, who informs her grandfather, a descendant of the famous vampire killer, Abraham Van Helsing. With help from the police, Jessica's grandfather destroys Dracula. Badly made film with inane dialogue, especially the few words given to Lee. The best part of all this was a promo-short shown at the original opening called *Horror Ritual* in which Barry Atwater (superb as the vampire in *The Night Stalker*) appears as the count declaring, "Dracula is back because you have called him!" The promo is an amusing kind of spoof.

1973. *Scream, Blacula, Scream.* American International, USA; producer, Joseph Naar; director, Bob Kelljan; screenplay, Joan Torres, Raymond Koenig, and Maurice Jules from a story by Torres. William Marshall again stars as the black prince of darkness, Manuwalde. Voodoo magic brings Manuwalde back to life and he begins recruiting disciples, one played by Pam Grier. In the end, voodoo magic destroys Blacula.

1973. *Crypt of the Living Dead.* Atalas Films/Coast Industries, Turkey/USA; producer, Lou Shaw; director, Ray Danton; screenplay, Lou Shaw based on a story by Lois Gibson. Story line is that a professor is murdered on Vampire Island while excavating the tomb of Hannah, wife of Louis VII, who had been buried alive in 1269. The professor's son comes to investigate and discovers that the 700-year-old corpse is in perfect condition, the unmistakable sign of the vampire. Shortly thereafter the undead Hannah attacks humans.

1973. *Dracula (or Bram Stoker's Dracula).* Universal Studios, USA/UK; producer/director, Dan Curtis; screenplay, Richard Matheson from the novel by Bram Stoker. In this production, originally made for American television, Jack Palance appears in the title role, replete with fangs and cape but looking more like Attila the Hun than Dracula. There is an attempt at a foreign atmosphere by having some German spoken at the outset. The movie also included a reference to Dracula being Vlad the Impaler. The best scene is where Dracula, upon finding that his long-lost love has been destroyed, groans like a wild animal as he smashes the funeral urns. In the final scene Dracula is killed by a huge lance as the sun is coming up. A disappointment; a cut and truncated version was put on the big screen, but it rightfully failed.

1973. *Lady Dracula (Lemora, the Lady Dracula).* Media Cinema, USA; producer, Robert Fern; director, Richard Blackburn; screenplay, Richard Blackburn and Robert Fern. Set during the 1920s in Georgia, a vampiress (Leslie Gilb) lures a thirteen-year-old church choir singer (Cheryl Smith) to her home in the forest. The sensual vampiress successfully gathers around herself a bunch of devoted little children. The Catholic Film Board gave it a condemned rating.

1973. *Blood for Dracula (Andy Warhol's Dracula).* CC Champion/Yanne-Rassam/Bryanston, Italy/France; producer, Andy Warhol; writer/director, Paul Morrisey. Joe Dallesandro stars as the gardener, Udo Kier as Count Dracula, and Vittorio de Sica as the nobleman.

. . .

Dracula, dying from a lack of virgin blood in old Transylvania, travels to Italy, but the local Italian gardener tends to be always one virgin ahead of him. In the finale the gardener pursues Dracula and hacks off the count's arms and legs, but the dismembered count miraculously just keeps on going.

1974. *The Legend of the Seven Golden Vampires.* Hammer/Shaw Bros., Hong Kong/UK; producer/screenplay, Don Houghton; director, Roy Ward Baker. Hammer teamed with Hong Kong movie mogul Run Run Shaw, noted for successful Kung Fu martial arts films to produce this movie. The story opens in the forests of Transylvania where a Chinese monk, Kah, has gone on a pilgrimage to Castle Dracula. Dracula (John Forbes-Robertson) is revived and proceeds to destroy Kah in order to inhabit the monk's body. The movie then shifts to Imperial China around 1904, where at the University of Chunking, Professor Lawrence Van Helsing, anthropologist and occult expert (aptly played by veteran Peter Cushing), is lecturing about the legend of the seven golden vampires. In the audience is Hsi Ching, whose grandfather was killed by vampires. He persuades Van Helsing to go to his native village, the heartland of vampires. There the vampires rise up and even Hsi Ching becomes infected, but he impales himself once he realizes that he has the vampire disease. In the end, Van Helsing's martial arts companions successfully battle the vampires, and the final confrontation takes place between Dracula and Van Helsing in the vampires' temple.

1974. *Immoral Tales (Contes Immoraux).* France; producer, Anatole Dauman; director/writer, Walerian Borowczyk. This film includes a sequence based loosely on the life and legend of the notorious Hungarian countess Elizabeth Bathory, whose story inspired, in part, Stoker's *Dracula.* Bathory is played by Paloma Picasso.

1974. *Old Dracula (Vampira).* Columbia/World Film Services, UK; producer Jack Wiener; director, Clive Donner; screenplay, Jeremy Lloyd. One of the worst Dracula films ever made. David Niven playing old Dracula is beyond belief. Replete with large fangs, Niven plays the owner of a horror castle into which tours and Playboy bunnies are booked. Old Dracula examines the guests in their sleep in his quest for a rare blood type needed to revive his dead wife. Old Dracula succeeds in resurrecting his wife, but she has been transformed from Caucasian to black, apparently due to the blood used in the transfusion. Young vampire hunters pursue old Dracula, but upon confronting him at the airport as he waits to depart for Transylvania on a 747, they are confounded to see that he, too, has become black, since he has ingested the same blood he gave to his wife.

1975. *Vampyres (Daughters of Dracula)*. Essay Films, UK; producer Brian Smedley-Ashton; director, Joseph (Jose) Larroz; screenplay, D. Daubeney. Softcore sex tale about two women who are not true vampires but bisexual ghosts who pose as hitchhikers in order to lure unsuspecting motorists to their crypt with promises of lurid sex. Predictably, the motorists are bled in some fairly gory scenes. As one critic put it, "the blood flows like Mogen David at a bar mitzvah."

1975. *Mary, Mary, Bloody Mary*. Translor/Proa, USA/Mexico; producers, Robert Yamin and Henri Bollinger; director, Juan Moctezuma; screenplay, Malcolm Marmorstein, based on a story by Don Rice and Don Henderson. Cover-girl Christina Ferrare portrays a bisexual vampiress named Mary who is an artist by day. Her father, played by aging John Carradine, arrives to try to destroy his vampiric daughter because he erroneously thinks she wants to die.

1975. *Deafula*. Signscope, USA; producer, Gary R. Hollstrom; writer/director, two-time Emmy winner Peter Wechsberg. One of the first full-length movies made for the deaf. All dialogue is signed with a voice-over translation. Deaf director/writer Wechsberg, playing the lead, plays a young theology student in modern Portland, Oregon, who was infected by Dracula before his birth. He grows fangs and begins to don a black cape to transform into Deafula. In the end Deafula is cornered by the police in a church where, overwhelmed by religious symbols, he expires.

1975. *The Rocky Horror Picture Show*. Twentieth Century-Fox, UK; executive producer, Lou Adler. A rock musical with vampires and other monsters in drag. A straight couple accidentally ends up in a castle where a bunch of deviants are holding a convention. There they encounter a Transylvanian transsexual with Dracula characteristics. A cult film, usually shown at midnight in select theaters, it is often an occasion for audience participation, many of whom know the lines in the film so well that they react to them by throwing rice, squirting squirt guns, and dancing.

1976. *Dracula and Son (Dracula, Père et Fils)*. Quarter Films, France; producer, Jean-Marie Poiré; director, Edouard Molinaro; screenplay,

Eduard Molinaro, Jean-Marie Poiré, and Alain Godard. Grey-haired Christopher Lee stars in the title role in this comedy shot in France and based loosely on the novel *Paris Vampire* by Claude Kootz. The Communist government drives Dracula and his son from their Transylvania castle. The count ends up in London, where he becomes a horror film star. But his son, portrayed by Bernard Menez, goes off to Paris to become a maladjusted immigrant laborer. Father and son chance to meet, and the elder Dracula tries to straighten out his son. The dubbing into English is defective.

1977. *Doctor Dracula*. Independent International, USA; directors, Al Adamson and Paul Aratow. The central character is really Count Dracula, who successfully opposes the plans of the secret Society of the Bleeding Rose, but he in turn is blown to pieces. A very poor movie.

1977. *Martin*. Libra Films, USA; producer, Richard Rubenstein; writer/director, George Romero. John Amplas is the psychopath Martin, a living vampire who is fixated on blood. The setting is the depressing steel town of Braddock, Pennsylvania, where both young and old are trapped in a dismal, dying situation. Bored Martin injects his female victims with a knockout drug, then opens their veins and drinks their blood. An old man named Cudo uses European methods, such as crucifixes, garlic, and mirrors, to try to deal with the vampire, but to no avail. In the end, Martin has a "normal" heterosexual encounter with an older woman, played by Elayne Nadeau; this, however, brings about his final destruction.

1977. *Rabid (Rage)*. New World, Canada; producer, John Dunning; director, David Cronenberg. Porn actress Marilyn Chambers, subjected to an untried surgical technique, unwittingly develops a syringelike, phallus-shaped organ in her armpit through which she drinks blood from her sleeping lovers. Like a rabid animal, Chambers spreads a disease that causes her victims to foam at the mouth and violently attack other humans. The epidemic spreads until most of the city of Montreal goes rabid. The film has the usual weird Cronenberg touches, such as a pointless car crash.

1978. *Dracula's Dog (Zoltan, Hound of Dracula)*. Crown International, USA; producers, Albert Band and Frank Ray Perilli; director, Albert Band; screenplay, Frank Ray Perilli. An aptly titled movie in more ways than one, with stars Jose Ferrer, Reggie Nalder, and Michael Pataki. A vampiric dog is revived in a contemporary American setting, where he and his human buddy go about seeking a descendant of Dracula to be their master. But the descendant is intent on covering up his heritage. The beast is killed in the end, but one of its puppies is depicted baying ominously at the moon.

1978. *The Satanic Rites of Dracula (Count Dracula and His Vampire Bride)*. Hammer/Warner, UK. Made in 1973, but not released in the U.S. until 1978. Set in the future, Count Dracula, played again by Christopher Lee, is developing the deadliest bacillus known to man — a new strain of the Black Death. A black magic ritual shows a young girl being sacrificed, and Scotland Yard determines that prominent Englishmen are involved in the cult. A cellar full of female vampires is uncovered. Professor Van Helsing, played again by Peter Cushing, comes to the rescue. But, before the good professor can seek and destroy Dracula, he is wrestled to the ground. Dracula plans to sacrifice Van Helsing's granddaughter in the black magic ritual. Van Helsing waylays Dracula, and the customary chase scene ensues. Knowing that a hawthorne tree can deter vampires, Van Helsing stands behind one and taunts Dracula. Dracula leaps at Van Helsing, only to become caught in the thorny branches. Van Helsing grabs a picket from a nearby fence and plunges it into Dracula's chest.

1978. *Count Dracula*. BBC/WNET TV, UK/USA; producer, Morris Barry; director, Philip Saville; screenplay, Gerald Savory. A relatively faithful rendition of Stoker's novel with Louis Jourdan starring as the count and Frank Finley as Van Helsing. One minor deviation from the novel occurs when Quincey Morris rather than Arthur Holmwood strikes the hammer blows to stake Lucy the vampire. When Dracula wards off his female vampires from Harker with the words "This man belongs to me!" the presentation does dare to show the count tossing a small bag containing a crying baby to sate his vampire brides. The production is of high quality, but Louis Jourdan is too old for the role — stiff, cold, aloof, and not scary. The special electronic effects of negative images and reverse mattes of Jourdan's face unfortunately jar the viewer and disrupt the story.

1979. *Count Dracula: The True Story;* Canada; TV documentary. Producer/director, Yurek Filjakowski. Partly filmed in Romania, the movie traces some of the local customs about the dead, as well as some links to the historical Dracula. It is based on information from *In Search of Dracula*.

1979. *Dawn of the Dead.* United Films Distributors, USA; producers, Richard Rubenstein and Dario Argento; director/writer, George Romero. Designed as a continuation of successful *Night of the Living Dead,* two National Guardsmen are ordered to kill the growing number of flesh-eating undead still hanging around. Fran, who works at a local TV station, and her boyfriend, copter pilot Stephen, along with the two National Guardsmen, fly over Pennsylvania and land in a shopping mall under attack by the undead. Good but gross.

1979. *Vampire.* MTM, ABC TV. Producer, George Hoblit; director, E. W. Swackhammer; screenplay, Steve Bochco and Michael Kozoll. Richard Lynch stars as the 800-year-old vampire terrorizing contemporary San Francisco — he even frequents a disco. Jason Miller is the anti-vampiric hero; E. G. Marshall the Van Helsing–like wise old man, and Jessica Walter portrays a victim.

1979. *The Curse of Dracula.* From the NBC TV series *Cliffhangers*; producer, Richard Milton; developed by Kenneth Johnson. Dracula, played with a thick, indeterminate but certainly not Transylvanian accent by Michael Nouri, is posing as a San Francisco professor who teaches evening courses in Eastern European history at South Bay College. His main antagonist is Kurt Van Helsing, grandson of Abraham. Kurt tries to thwart Dracula by destroying his coffins, because the count is after Van Helsing's helper, portrayed by Carol Baker. Dracula has already succeeded in killing Mary's mother before the movie begins. The film portrays a guilt-ridden Dracula who does not enjoy his vampiric existence and yearns to sit in the sun. This shift in the traditional story line yields no dramatic fruit, as Nouri is boring in the main role.

1979. *Nocturna, Granddaughter of Dracula.* Compass International, USA; producer, Vernon Becker; director/screenplay, Harry Tampa. Aging horror actor John Carradine dons the fangs and cape once more as Count Dracula in the New York disco scene. Nai Bonet portrays the vampiress, Nocturna, Dracula's granddaughter. She runs off to New York with a young English musician (Tony Hamilton), and her vampire grandfather follows in hot pursuit. Yvonne De Carlo makes a cameo appearance as Jugulia, who saves the young folks from the count's grandfatherly wrath.

1979. *Nosferatu, the Vampire (Nosferatu: Phantom der Nacht).* Twentieth Century-Fox, France/Germany; producer/director/screenplay,

Werner Herzog, based on Murnau's classic silent film *Nosferatu eine Symphonie des Grauens*. Shot in Delft, Schiedam, and Oostvorne in the Netherlands; Pernstein, Nedvedice, Telc, and the Tatra Mountains in the former Czechoslovakia; Partnach-Klamm in Germany; and Guanajuato in Mexico. Klaus Kinski as the vampire delivers a startling performance, and he's a chillingly dead ringer for Max Schreck in the 1922 movie, replete with huge pointed ears, prominent teeth, and four-inch-long fingernails. But unlike Murnau's vampire count, Kinski conveys a suffering vampire. Isabelle Adjani is Lucy Harker, and Bruno Ganz is her husband, Jonathan. The story takes place one hundred years ago in Wismar, Germany. Lucy awakens from a nightmare; her husband, Jonathan tries to calm her down. Harker is then sent off by his weird boss, Renfield, to Transylvania in order to negotiate a deal with a certain count, who wishes to buy an abandoned house near Harker's own. Lucy feels an ominous sense of dread, which she communicates to her sister, Mina.

Jonathan arrives in Transylvania at the count's castle and meets the fear-inspiring owner. The count is fascinated with Harker's medallion of his wife and signs the contract at once. At midnight he enters Jonathan's bedroom to attack him. Next day Jonathan discovers Dracula resting in his coffin; finally the count leaves for Germany with his army of rats. His phantom boat arrives in Wismar, and he moves into his house there.

Jonathan returns home to find the plague sweeping the city. The vampire begs Lucy to love him. At first she rejects him, but later gives in to save her fellow humans. At cockcrow the vampire attempts to flee but instead dissolves in the sunlight. In the end, Jonathan Harker has become the new vampire, and he rides off to spread his cult throughout the civilization of his day.

1979. *Dracula*. Universal Studios, UK/USA; producer, Walter Mirisch; director, John Badham; writer, W. D. Richter, based on the Hamilton Deane–John Balderston play; music, John Williams. The most lavish Dracula film to that date; shot in Tintagel, Cornwall, England, the Benedictine monastery of St. Michael in the west of England, and the town of Mevagissey. The film stars Frank Langella as Dracula and Sir Laurence Olivier as Van Helsing. Langella had starred in the Broadway revival of the Deane-Balderston play, which was played for laughs, but the main reasons for its success were the wonderfully moody black-and-white sets by Edward Gorey. Unfortunately, the movie did not use the Gorey sets, and Langella played the role as a serious, romantic, Byronesque lover with great sex appeal. Not scary, but it ranks among the best for the erotic element alone.

1979. *Bram Stoker's Dracula.* Thames TV, UK (part of the TV series *Tales of Mystery and Imagination*). A stylized dramatization with late nineteenth-century costumes and settings; plodding remake, easily forgettable.

1979. *Love at First Bite.* Mel Simon/American International, USA; producers, Joel Freedman and George Hamilton; director, Stan Dragosti; screenplay, Robert Kaufman, based on the story by Robert Kaufman and Mark Gindes. George Hamilton plays the count in this very successful spoof; Arte Johnson excels as the fly-eater, Renfield; Susan St. James is the love interest; and Richard Benjamin plays her boyfriend, a Freudian psychiatrist.

1979. *Thirst.* F. G. Film Productions/New South Wales Film Corp., Australia; producer, Anthony I. Ginnane; director, Rod Hardy; screenplay, John Pinkney, based on his "instant terror" stories. Beautiful businesswoman Kate Davis (Chantal Contouri) is captured by the Hyma Brotherhood, a secret organization housed in a remote rural area. Dr. Fraser (David Hemmings), the leader of the Brotherhood, and his followers feel that they have become superior humans by drinking blood. Dr. Fraser wants Davis to join his group, since he believes that she is a descendant of their founder, the notorious Hungarian Blood Countess Elizabeth Bathory. A spooky production.

1979. *Mama Dracula.* Valisa Films/Radio Television Belge Française, Belgium; producer/director, Boris Szulzinger; screenplay, Boris Szulzinger, Pierre Sterckx, and Marc-Henri Wajnberg. Louise Fletcher plays the lead in this abortive comedy based loosely on the Blood Countess Elizabeth Bathory. She kills young girls and bathes in their blood. Maria Schneider is her principal victim.

1979. *Salem's Lot.* CBS-TV, USA; director, Tobe Hooper; script, Paul Monash, based on the novel of the same name by Stephen King. Three-hour TV adaptation with Reggie Nalder as vampire Kurt Barlow, pursued by Ben Mears (David Soul) and Mark Petrie (Lance Kerwin); the vampire looks like a green Nosferatu. Unbelievable and hence not scary, but James Mason is great as Straker, the vampire's minion.

1980. *Dracula's Last Rites (Last Rites)*. New Empire/Canon, USA; producer, Kelly Van Horn; director, Dominic Paris; screenplay, Dominic Paris and Ben Donnelly. Filmed in upstate New York. The local mortician (named Lucard — three guesses what that spells backwards), the sheriff, and the doctor are all vampires who suck the blood of accident victims. Then they drive stakes into their hearts, presumably to prevent them from rising from the dead as vampires and competing for the limited local blood supply. For some unexplained reason, Lucard is fixated on sinking his teeth into members of a family named Fonda. Gerald Fielding and Patricia Lee Hammond star, accompanied by the formerly fine character actor Victor Jorge.

1982. *Vincent Price's Dracula*. M&M Film Productions/Atlantis, UK; director, John Muller; screenplay, Kate and Seaton Longsdale. Hour-long documentary in which Vincent Price talks about both Dracula and Vlad the Impaler along with film clips from Romanian films and segments from the 1979 documentary *Count Dracula: The True Story*.

1983. *The Keep*. Paramount/Capitol, USA; producers, Gene Kirkwood and Howard Koch; director/screenplay, Michael Mann, based on the novel by F. Paul Wilson. Set in Romania during the Nazi occupation of World War II. Scott Glenn stars as the stranger Glaeken Trismegestus, Robert Prosky as Father Fonescu, and Ian McKellen as Dr. Cuza, the historian. The castle is haunted by a mysterious evil force that grabs up every Nazi and spits out their entrails. It turns out that the evil is Moribus, a vampire.

1983. *The Hunger*. MGM/UA, USA; producer, Richard A. Shephard; director, Tony Scott; screenplay, Ivan Davis and Michael Thomas, based on the novel by Whitley Strieber. A slick yuppie vampire extravaganza. Catherine Deneuve, looking as cold as ever in a tight leather getup with dark glasses, portrays Miriam. She and her lover, John (played by anemic rock star David Bowie), live on Manhattan's East Side. They pick up a young couple in what appears to be a sexual encounter, but is really just a pretext to drink their blood. For some unexplained reason, Miriam is able to keep her lovers alive for only a relatively short time. John begins aging very rapidly and blood from the seemingly bountiful pickups does not arrest the aging process. In desperation, John seeks help from young gerontologist Sarah Roberts (Susan Sarandon), but he ages two hundred years while sitting patiently in the doctor's waiting room. When Sarah visits John's home, Miriam seduces her. Shriveled John "dies" and takes his place in one of the boxes in the attic where Miriam stores the remains of all her former lovers. In the end, Sarah proves to be stronger than Miriam: Miriam's decaying lovers destroy her, and Sarah takes on younger companions. One reviewer aptly characterized Deneuve as "the last of a dying breed who live forever." Director Tony Scott, brother of Ridley, had done mostly commercials, and it shows.

1983. *Dracula Blows His Cool.* We shall mercifully pass this one over in silence.

1983. *The Evil Dead.* Renaissance/New Line Cinema, USA; producer, Robert G. Tapert; director/screenplay, Sam Raimi. Vacationing college students seek shelter in a remote cabin in the forest, where they discover a book, and a tape explaining that the book is the ancient Sumerian *Book of the Dead.* The incantations are read and translated by the tape, and the demons are inadvertently released. The evil undead eventually take over most of the teenagers, who are turned into monsters, until only Ash is left. A wonderful black comedy made with derring-do and successful verve.

1985. *Day of the Dead.* Laurel, USA; producer, Richard Rubenstein; director, George Romero; screenplay, Tom Savini and George Romero. The setting is a vast underground storage facility in Florida transformed into an emergency laboratory and living quarters. The undead have taken over most of the earth. A few remaining scientists debate what to do, while the undead gather above. The humans struggle in vain to survive, but to do so they must adapt to the undead lifestyle rather than the traditional other way around. A fine effort by Romero.

1985. *Transylvania 6-5000.* New World, USA/Yugoslavia; producers, Mace Neufeld and Thomas Brodek; director/screenplay, Rudy DeLuca. The plot centers on Jack Harrison (Jeff Goldblum) and Gil Turner (Ed Begley, Jr.), two reporters from a newspaper dispatched to Romania to get a line on Frankenstein. A local mayor called Lepescu (Jeffrey Jones) wants to turn his area into a Dracula amusement park for foreign tourists. Mad scientist Dr. Malavaqua (Joseph Bologna) thwarts the mayor's grand plans by supporting the local Romanian bloodsuckers, including nymphomaniac vampiress Odette (Geena Davis) and other assorted weirdos.

1985. *Fright Night.* Vistar/Columbia, USA; producer, Herb Jaffe; director/screenplay, Tom Holland. Teenager Charley Brewster (William Ragsdale), interested largely in his acne, his car, and the potential seduction of his girlfriend, spends his spare time watching "Fright Night Theater" on TV, a series of horror movies hosted by a former horror star played by Roddy McDowall. Charley suspects that his new neighbor, played by Christopher Sarandon, has murdered young women and is a vampire. Of course, no one believes the adolescent, but eventually he manages to enlist the help of McDowall, who at first merely humors the boy but soon realizes that he's right. The two then form a team to destroy the vampire. The final special effects are superb.

1985. *Dracula Exotica.* With Jamie Gillis and Samantha Fox. No need to comment.

1985. *Once Bitten.* Samuel Goldwyn, USA; producers, Dimitri Villard, Robert Wald, Frank Hildebrand, and Howard Storm; director, Howard Storm; screenplay, David Hines, Jeffrey Hause, and Jonathan Roberts, based on a story by Dimitri Villard. The countess (Lauren Hutton), living in Los Angeles during the 1980s, needs a triple treatment of virgin blood each Halloween in order to stay young looking. But, as everyone knows, virgin blood is hard to find in L.A., even among teenagers. Mark Kendall (Jim Carrey) portrays a high school student romancing his reluctant girlfriend. By chance, Mark meets the countess in a funky Hollywood bar and she introduces him to some novel, kinky, oral sex. Once bitten, he is hooked, and so is she. Stupid.

1985. *Return of the Living Dead.* Hemdale-Fox Films Ltd./Orion; producer, Tom Fox and Graham Henderson; director, Dan O'Bannon; screenplay, Dan O'Bannon, based on a story by Rudy Ricci, John Russo, and Russell Streiner. Metal cylinders containing contaminated materials from a disastrous army experiment near Philadelphia during the late sixties accidently fall off a truck, break open, and release a fatal nerve gas spore which reanimates the dead in a local graveyard where some punks are having a party. A one-joke idea stretched into a movie like a Procrustean bed.

1986. *Vamp.* Baker/New World, USA; producer, Donald Borchers; director/screenplay, Richard Wenk, based on a story by Donald Borchers and Richard Wenk. College friends Keith (Chris Makepeace) and A.J. (Robert Rusler) want to pledge a fraternity, but get fed up with the sophomoric demands. In the midst of a silly ritual the boys promise to do anything to make the upcoming frat party a success. Their frat brothers want a stripper. The two lads are mightily impressed by the very sexy dancing of a stripper played by the statuesque Grace Jones. When young A.J. goes backstage to talk things over with her, she promptly seduces him; she is a 2,000-year-old vampiress. A foolish, kinky story line.

1987. *The Understudy: Graveyard Shift II* (not to be confused with Ralph Singleton's 1990 movie based on Stephen King's *Graveyard Shift*). Cinema Ventures/Lightshow, Canada; producer, Michael Bockner; director/screenplay, Gerard Ciccoritti. A 350-year-old vampire named Stephen Tsepes is a clever, laid-back cab driver in New York City. He meets Michelle, a video director estranged from her husband, Cliff Stoker. Michelle wants to have only a one-night stand with Tsepes, but he turns her into a vampire like himself. She learns to enjoy her vampiric existence, but her husband does not, and he plots to get his wife back by hiring a vampire killer to destroy Tsepes. The film effectively blends the erotic and the gory and contains witty commentary on the bizarre New York dating scene.

1987. *The Lost Boys*. Warner Bros., USA; produced by Harvey Bernhard; director, Joel Schumacher; screenplay, Janice Fischer, James Jeremias, and Jeffrey Boam, based on a story by Janice Fischer and James Jeremias. A recently divorced woman and her two teenaged sons move to the northern California town of Santa Cruz in order to be near her father. The boys are attracted to an old amusement park, and Michael (Jason Patric) falls for a lovely girl (Jami Gertz) who introduces him to a punky band of bikers led by ominous David (Kiefer Sutherland). They are vampires, and Michael becomes one of them. There is a surprising Hitchcockian twist at the end involving Max (Edward Herrmann). Very well done; the teenagers like being evil and do not want to grow up into responsible adults.

1987. *Near Dark*. F/M Entertainment, USA; producers, Steven-Charles Jaffe and Eric Red; director, Kathryn Bigelow; screenplay, Eric Red and Kathryn Bigelow. A group of outlaw vampires travel the U.S. southwest in a Winnebago. Local boy Caleb (Adrian Pasdar) meets attractive vampire Mae (Jenny Wright); she bites him, and he begins to become an undead. Jesse (Lance Henriksen), leader of the vampire "family," wants Caleb to prove himself by making his first kill, but Mae shields her lover because he's not quite ready. When the vampires go for Caleb's sister and father, he balks. Most of the vampires, on the run from the law and exposed to the desert sunlight, explode one by one. A blood transfusion brings Caleb back to his normal pre-vampiric state, and cures Mae as well. A wondrous movie that emphasizes the "family" loyalty of the vampires as they roam the American West like alien criminal cowboys. An impressive solo debut for director Kathryn Bigelow; the movie became a cult favorite of contemporary viewers.

1987. *Evil Dead 2: Dead by Dawn.* Renaissance/Rosebud Cinema. Producer, Robert Tapert; director, Sam Raimi; screenplay, Sam Raimi and Scott Spiegel. More a remake of *Evil Dead* than a sequel. Ash, played by Bruce Campell, the only survivor from the horrors of the first *Evil Dead* film, goes to an isolated cabin in the forest with his girlfriend. There Ash again finds the dangerous tape recorder, it translates the Sumerian *Book of the Dead,* and the dead are summoned to life yet again. The director Sam Raimi utilizes many of the fantasy camera techniques developed by Melies, such as stop-start photography, hand-held shots, rear-screen projections, and miniatures; a remarkable technical *tour de force.* Suitable for those viewers who are not interested in a serious story line but have a sense of humor.

1987. *Return of the Living Dead, Part II.* Greenfox/Lorimar; producer, Ken Wiederhorn; director/screenplay, Eugene Cashman. Although the 1985 movie actually ended with the nuclear annihilation of the whole cast, many of them are inexplicably back in this film. The movie opens with those mysterious cannisters seeping their noxious waste into the local cemetery and reviving the dead, who seek human brains to eat, rather than just blood. Director Wiederhorn does not have the writing skill of the first director-writer, Dan O'Bannon.

1988. *Dance of the Damned.* Concorde/Virgin Vision, USA; director, (Roger Corman protégée) Katt Shea Ruben; producer, Roger Corman. A suicidal female stripper (Starr Andreef) meets a vampire (Cyril O'Reilly) who offers her $1,000 to spend the night with him describing all the human pleasures he can no longer enjoy. He offers to allow her to join in his otherworldly existence, but she refuses.

1988. *Not of This Earth.* Concorde, USA; director/screenplay, Jim

Wynorski, based on a story by Charles B. Griffith and Mark Hanna; producers, Jim Wynorski, Roger Corman, and Murray Miller. A remake of the 1957 movie of the same name. Porn queen Traci Lords plays nurse to a vampire from outer space who is transporting human blood to his dying planet.

1988. *Fright Night, Part II.* Columbia, USA; producers, Herb Jaffe and Mort Engeberg; director/screenplay, Tommy Lee Wallace, based on the characters created by Tom Holland. A big-budget sequel to one of the most successful vampire movies of the 1980s, *Fright Night.* Charlie Brewster, again played by William Ragsdale, meets Regine Dandridge (Julie Carmen) who turns out to be a seductive vampiress. Peter Vincent (again portrayed by veteran actor Roddy McDowall), the over-the-hill actor and vampire expert, aids Charlie in coping with the vampiress and her minions.

1988. *Return to Salem's Lot.* Larco/Warner Bros., USA; producer, Paul Kurta; director, Larry Cohen; screenplay, Larry Cohen and James Dixon. A quirky comedy. Joe Weber (Michael Moriarty), an anthropologist, travels to Maine with his teenage son, Jeremy (Ricky Addison Reed), in order to renovate an old house left to him by his aunt. The town is teeming with vampires who have become rich Republicans. These modern-day vampires still drink human blood once in a while but have basically shifted to drinking cattle blood, since, as their old leader Judge Axel (Andrew Duggan) explains, drinking human blood has become too dangerous due to the presence of alcohol, drugs, and AIDS. These wealthy vampires convince the anthropologist to write their own history, but he begins to worry that his son is getting hooked on the vampire way of life. The film thus tries to use the vampire theme as a satirical commentary on current political and social ills in contemporary America.

1988. *My Best Friend Is a Vampire.* Kings Road Entertainment, USA; director, Jimmy Huston; producer, Dennis Murphy. Jeremy (Robert Sean Leonard) is bitten by Nora (Cecilia Peck), a vampire, shortly before Professor McCarthy (David Warner) destroys her. Jeremy does not realize what has happened to him, but once informed he adjusts to his new lifestyle. Unfortunately, McCarthy is after Jeremy's best friend, Ralph, because McCarthy believes Ralph to be the vampire. Jeremy, with the help of girlfriend Darla, stops McCarthy cold for a happy ending.

1988. *Waxwork.* Vestron, USA; director, Anthony Hickox. Teens tour

David Warner's wax museum and come upon a rejuvenated Count Dracula who has come to life and is ready to attack. A comedy that fails to be funny.

1988. *Vampire in Venice*. Scena/Reteitalia/Vestron, UK/USA; director, Augusto Caminito. Veteran German character actor Klaus Kinski returns to reprieve his Nosferatu role from 1979. He goes to Venice in search of both love and death during Carnival. Christopher Plummer plays the Van Helsing character out to get the vampire. A poorly written, confusing tale.

1988. *Dracula's Widow*. DeLaurentis Entertainment, USA; producer, Stephen Traxler; director, Christopher Coppola; screenplay, Kathryn Ann Thomas and Christopher Coppola. This first major film by Francis Ford Coppola's nephew is basically a reworking of the Stoker story line: Dracula's widow, Vanessa (Sylvia Kristel), is accidentally sent from Castle Bran in Romania to a Hollywood wax museum. Once there, she plans to use the museum owner, Raymond Everett (Lenny Von Dohlen), to help her return to Romania to locate her lost husband. When he informs the countess that Count Dracula is dead, having been dispatched by Dr. Van Helsing years before, she begins killing wantonly. The police, including Lannon (Josef Sommer) are baffled by the murders, but Van Helsing's grandson turns up and unravels it all. There is, unfortunately, not enough of a story line to justify the film.

1988. *Vampire's Kiss*. Hemdale Films/Tri-Star Pictures, USA; director, Robert Bierman; producers, Barbara Zitwer and Barry Shils; screenplay, Joe Minion. In this comedy, a New York literary agent named Peter Lowe, played by Nicholas Cage, is convinced that he has been bitten by a vampire (Jennifer Beals) and that he must satisfy a craving for blood. An office sexual harassment incident is inexplicably forced in as a subplot.

1988. *Sundown: The Vampire in Retreat*. Vestron, USA (released in the U.S. in 1991); director, Anthony Hickox; producer, Jefferson Richard; screenplay, Anthony Hickox and John Burgess. Starring David Carradine as Count Mardulak (actually Count Dracula). A family travels to the desert town of Purgatory to try to solve a production problem at a plant designed to produce artificial blood. The place is populated by vampires divided into two warring factions: one group, led by Mardulak, wishes to live in peace with humans; the other wants to revert to the old ways and hunt humans for blood. The good, peace-loving vampires defeat the evil, aggressive ones, and we learn, to no one's surprise, that Mardulak is really Count Dracula.

1988. *To Die For.* Skouras/Academy/Trimark, USA; director, Deran Sarafian; producers, Barin Kumar and Greg Sims. At a shipboard party Vlad Tepish encounters Kate, escorted by Martin, and she immediately falls in love with Vlad. That same night, Simon, one of Martin's friends, is killed by Tom, Vlad's archenemy. Vlad buys a Gothic mansion from Kate, who is a real estate agent, and he hires her roommate Celia as his secretary. Though Vlad appears to be in love with Kate, he seduces Celia, who becomes very possessive. Vlad seduces Kate next. Tom murders Celia, who returns as a vampire only to be betrayed by Martin. Tom also tries to kill Kate, but Vlad defends her, kills Tom, and exposes himself to the daylight to save Kate from becoming a vampire. Vlad is depicted as a reincarnation of Vlad the Impaler, Dracula.

1989. *Daughter of Darkness.* King Phoenix Entertainment/Accent, USA/Hungary (made for TV); director, Stuart Gordon. A young American (Mia Sara) journeys to Ceausescu's Romania to try to locate her lost father. She discovers that he is Anton Crainic (Anthony Perkins), a 200-year-old vampire, who protects his daughter from the cursed undead in their old family.

1990. *Nightlife.* Mexico/USA (made for TV); director/writer, Daniel Taplitz; screenplay, Anne Beatts. Set in Mexico, a one-time mummy named Angelique (Maryam D'Abo) finds she can get blood without killing. Her archenemy, vampire Vlad (Ben Cross) is staked in the end. An effective combination of horror and comedy.

1990. *Dark Shadows.* Dan Curtis Production, MGM-UA (pilot made for short-lived revival of popular series), USA; director, Dan Curtis. Ben Cross plays the vampire Barnabas Collins and the horror scream-queen Barbara Steele is Doctor Julia Hoffman, a medical researcher who claims that she may be able to cure the vampire of his blood addiction.

1990. *Def by Temptation.* Bonded Enterprises/Orpheus Pictures/Troma, USA; director, James Bond III. This horror comedy was billed as "the black rap chiller thriller of the decade." A young black preacher (James Bond III) comes to New York and is tempted by an attractive vampiress (Cynthia Bond).

1990. *Red-Blooded American Girl.* Paramount Pictures, Canada; director, David Blyth; producer, Nicolas Stiliadis; screenplay, Allan Moyle. A mad scientist, played by Christopher Plummer, who is engaged in a major genetics experiment, unwittingly transforms his volunteer subject Paula (Heather Thomas) into a vampire. She seeks out male victims. A young pharmaceutical genius, Owen Urban (Andrew Stevens) is brought in on the case and he falls deeply in love with Paula.

1991. *Children of the Night.* Fangoria Films, USA; director, Tony Randel. Set in a small Midwestern town, the head vampire (David Sawyer) lives in a secret underground crypt protected by water. Karen Black and Maya McLaughlin portray mother and daughter vampires, while Peter DeLuise plays the visiting teacher sent to free the town from the vampires' control.

1991. *Subspecies.* Full Moon/Paramount, Romania/USA; director, Ted Nicolaou; producer, Ion Ionescu. A low budget flick whose redeeming traits are that it was filmed on location in Romania and that it succeeds in creating a contemporary Gothic atmosphere. Vladislav, king of the Vampires, is destroyed by his demonic, half-breed son, Radu, who covets the Transylvanian blood stone.

1991. *Forever Knight.* CBS-TV series "Crime Time after Prime Time." Nick Knight (Geraint Wyn Davies) is a Toronto police detective who is also a vampire. He lives by night, catches assorted criminals, but is always tempted to bite them on the neck.

1991. *I, Desire.* ABC TV, USA. Barbara Stock portrays the thirsty vampire supported by actors David Naughton, Dorian Harewood, Brad Dourif, and Marilyn Jones in a poor effort.

1991. *To Die For 2: Son of Darkness.* Arrowhead/Trimark, USA; director, David Price; producer, Richard Weinman. Count Vlad Tepish, who has been revived by some blood that fell on his burned remains, appears along with Tom and Celia in a remote Northern California town, where he becomes known as Dr. Max Schreck. Eventually he opens a hospital in L.A., where he dispenses blood plasma to vampires Tom and Celia. Celia encounters young Danny, who runs a bed-and-breakfast with his sister; she seduces him and turns Danny into a vampire. Meanwhile, Nina brings her adopted baby to the local hospital where Schreck examines him. The good doctor helps. Strange murders occur, but Tom is doing the killing, not Vlad. Tom chains the vampire Jane to a tree and sunlight kills her. Tom destroys Danny. Celia drives a stake into Tom. Martin destroys Schreck and poor Nina is left with her crying vampire baby who is starving to death. Not a happy ending, but good photography.

1991. *Waxwork II: Lost in Time.* Electric Pictures, USA; director, Anthony Hickox. Sarah (Monika Schnarre) is framed for a murder that her severed hand (from the first film) actually committed. To try to prove her innocence, Mark (Zach Galligan) takes her into the past to wage war with evil from horror films and fiction. While there, they meet Nosferatu and some other familiar monsters.

1991. *The Reflecting Skin.* Fugitive/Virgin/Live, UK/Canada; director/screenplay, Philip Ridley; producers, Dominic Anciano and Ray Burds. Jeremy Cooper plays the lead, a young boy named Seth Dove through whose eyes one sees the film's action. Seth's father tells the boy about vampires who suck the blood of the living to stay young. Seth thinks that the reclusive, mysterious, English lady next door is a vampire. She is actually mourning the death of her husband who hanged himself. His father, accused of pederasty, pours gasoline on himself, lights it and burns to death in front of Seth. Seth's brother, returning from the army, is attracted to the supposed vampire and they have an affair. Seth warns his brother that she's a vampire but to no avail. In the end, she is killed by some mysterious men. An effective, strange movie.

1992. *Un Vampire au Paradis.* Auramax/Canal Plus/MC-4, France; director/screenplay, Abdelkrim Bahoul. An escaped lunatic (Farid Chopel) thinks he is a vampire. He flies around Paris and bites people, while hoping to be killed himself. A young French girl (Laure Marsac) suddenly starts acting strangely and spouting Arabic, so her parents send for an African exorcist.

1992. *Buffy the Vampire Slayer.* Twentieth Century-Fox/Sandollar/Kuzui, USA; producers, Kaz Kuzui and Howard Rosenman; director, Fran Rubel Kuzui; screenplay, Joss Whedon. Three valley girls, led by the high school cheerleader Buffy (Kristy Swanson), go on a shopping spree. A raunchy old vampire hunter named Merrick (Donald Sutherland) miraculously materializes out of nowhere and informs Buffy that she is the only genuine vampire killer in the immediate area. The town bad boy (Luke Perry) joins her in trying to rid a Los Angeles suburb of Romanian vampires. Rutger Hauer plays the vampire king Lothos, and Paul Reubens plays his sidekick Amilyn. Neither funny nor scary.

1992. *To Sleep with a Vampire.* Concorde Pictures, USA; producer, Mike Elllott; executive producer, Roger Corman; director, Adam Friedman; screenplay, Carolyn Gail, based on the Katt Shea Ruben movie

Dance of the Damned. A sad vampire (Scott Valentine) wanders into a strip joint, where he meets an exotic dancer named Nina (Charlie Spradling) who is thinking about committing suicide. Instead he convinces her to come to his apartment where they begin a kinky sexual relationship. He forces her to exchange bodies with him so he can experience sunlight.

1992. *Innocent Blood.* Warner Bros., USA; producer, Lee Rich; director, John Landis; screenplay, Michael Wolk and John Landis. A black comedy about a lovely but lonely reluctant vampiress named Marie (Anne Parillaud), recently jilted, who is driven to seek out truly bad people to victimize. She reads about crime wars in Pittsburgh and decides to go there to put the bite on Sal "The Shark" Macelli (Robert Loggia). After accidently turning Sal into an even more dangerous vampire than herself, Marie almost succeeds in killing him, but he shoots at her, and she is forced to flee. Finally Marie is able to get a policeman to help her destroy the vampire.

1992. *My Grandpa Is a Vampire* (also called *Moonrise* or *Grampire*). Tucker/Moonrise, New Zealand; director, David Blyth. Vernon T. Cooger, a misfit 300-year-old vampire played by eighty-one-year-old Al Lewis, is the town's practical joker who seems to be always getting into trouble. The townspeople plan to put an end to his bothersome existence. However, his devoted grandson and his friend (Justin Gocke and Milan Borich) attempt to save him from the mob that is intent on driving a stake through his heart.

1992. *Tale of a Vampire.* State Screen Productions, UK/Japan; director/screenplay, Shimako Sato, inspired by Edgar Allan Poe's poem "Annabel Lee." The vampire Alex (Julian Sands) is searching for his eighteenth-century lover in contemporary London. He is confronted by a dark, faceless antagonist (Kenneth Cranham) who has been infected with immortality by his wife after her liaison with the vampire Alex! Enough said.

1992. *Bram Stoker's Dracula.* Columbia Pictures/American Zoetrope/Osiris Films, USA; director/producer, Francis Ford Coppola; screenplay, Jim Hart and Francis Ford Coppola. Gary Oldman is Prince Vlad Dracula; Winona Ryder is Mina, who falls deeply in love with him. Oscar-winner Anthony Hopkins is Van Helsing. A dazzling visual tour de force; ranks deservedly among the best Dracula-vampire movies ever made. Won Oscars in 1993 for sound, costumes, and make-up.

1992. *Dracula: Fact or Fiction?* World Vision Home Video, USA; director/producer, Steve Michelson. A documentary about the legends and realities of Dracula and his vampire kin, featuring interviews with Dr. Donald Reed, president of the Count Dracula Society in L.A., Jeanne Youngson, president of the Dracula Society in New York City, and Dr. Raymond McNally. Accompanied by footage from *In Search of Dracula* and a Romanian feature film about Vlad the Impaler.

TRAVEL GUIDE

. . . .

A DRACULA TOUR OF ENGLAND, IRELAND, AND SCOTLAND

Places to see in LONDON.

The Dracula mansion at 138 Piccadilly. This was Dracula's main London lair in the novel, with a back courtyard from which he could escape if necessary, as he does in the story. It now stands next door to the Hard Rock Café, accessible via the Green Park underground stop.

Highgate Cemetery. The probable burial place of Lucy, Dracula's first female victim in England. Closest underground stop is Archway. A marvelous Victorian setting with restricted access and a variable schedule; call for hours of access, tour schedule, and prices.

The London Zoo in Regent's Park. Where Dracula got help from a captive wolf.

The Lyceum Theatre, Wellington Street. Here Bram Stoker was general manager for the actor Henry Irving for almost twenty-seven years. It was converted from a theater into a dance hall, and is now in very dilapidated condition and closed to the public. At the rear of the building was the Beef Steak Room, where Stoker and Irving spent many nights entertaining guests.

Stoker's residences. All in the Chelsea section near the embankment of the Thames River, the Chelsea Pensioners' Hospital, and King's Row, they can be reached via the Sloane Square underground stop. They are: 27 Cheyne Walk, Stoker's first London address; 17 St. Leonard's Terrace, where Stoker lived while writing *Dracula* during the early 1890s; 18 St. Leonard's Terrace, where Stoker moved in 1895 and was living when *Dracula* was published, as evidenced by a plaque on the outside wall; and 26 St. George's Square, where Stoker died in 1912.

Hampstead. A London suburb, a half hour from central London by underground. Visit Jack Straw's Castle, an inn, and the Spaniards, a pub, both mentioned in the novel, and Hampstead Heath, where Lucy Westenra attacked children.

To the north.

At WHITBY, North Yorkshire, visit Tate Pier. Dracula first landed here aboard the Russian schooner *Demeter,* along with fifty boxes containing his native earth. He leaped ashore in wolf form to mount the stone steps of the East Cliff up to St. Mary's churchyard and the ruins of Whitby Abbey.

Stop at the Whitby Tourist Information Center just north of the train station and get a Dracula map, which includes both a map of the town and a tour plan. Whitby is located on the headlands bisected by a harbor formed by the mouth of the Esk River; on one side is the East Cliff and on the other, the West Cliff; both of which are important in the novel. From the Bram Stoker Memorial Seat, a wood and iron bench in Victorian style located at the south end of Spion Kop or the West Cliff above Pier Road, one can see most of the Dracula sights.

The East Crescent. Mina Murray and Lucy Westenra spent summers in a guest house here, which is visible by looking down from the Stoker Seat. Walk along the East Terrace, just behind the Stoker Seat, as it intersects with North Terrace to the open sea; there one can see the spot where Mina looked out toward the East Cliff and saw Lucy seated at their favorite bench in St. Mary's churchyard with a dark, menacing figure bending over her.

To trace Mina's path on the night she followed sleepwalking Lucy to her encounter with Dracula, go along the East Terrace just behind the Stoker Seat, cross the harbor bridge, and go north onto Church Street; at the bottom of Tate Hill and Henrietta Street climb the 199 steps up to the churchyard, just as frantic Mina did in her vain effort to try to reach her friend before it was too late.

In St. Mary's churchyard, notice the blackened tombstones which rise from the ground like leprous fingers and read the many inscriptions that Stoker faithfully transcribed into his novel. Looming ominously above St. Mary's are the ruins of Whitby Abbey; the original convent was founded by the abbess Hilda and sacked by the Danes ten years later. Legend has it that Hilda herself sometimes appears there as a ghostly figure dressed all in white.

Near the Esk Bridge, at 9 Marine Parade, is a shop called The Dracula Experience where one can see ten scenes from the novel in old-fashioned, life-size, wax museum–style dioramas. Souvenirs are available in the shop.

CRUDEN BAY, Scotland. Here Stoker began and completed his serious writing of *Dracula*. Stay at the Kilmarnock Inn, where Stoker first resided when he came to Cruden Bay for summer holidays. Walk to the Stoker cottage nearby at Whinnyfold, where he later resided; the cottage has not changed much since Stoker's day, aside from a new window and front entrance. Look across the bay to the ruins of Slains Castle, which Stoker certainly saw daily from his cottage and which may have inspired his descriptions of Castle Dracula.

IRELAND.

Take a taxi from the Dublin airport or a short bus trip from central Dublin to the suburb of Clontarf, the birthplace of Bram Stoker. There, at no. 15 The Crescent in a prim terraced house, Count Dracula's creator was born. His wife-to-be, Florence Balcombe, was born at no. 1 The Crescent. Walk to the Clontarf graveyard and Protestant church ruins on Castle Avenue. Stoker was baptized in the now ruined church in December 1847. He attended services at St. John the Baptist Church on Seafield Road after 1866.

DUBLIN. Trinity College in the heart of Dublin, where Stoker studied from 1864 to 1870.

30 Kildare Street, within walking distance of Trinity College, where Stoker lived when he was made auditor of the Historical Society in 1872. A plaque on the outside wall commemorates it as a Stoker residence.

16 Harcourt Street. A Stoker letter of 1874 designates this as his home at that time.

Every year since 1991 Mr. Dennis McIntyre (director) has organized a Bram Stoker International Summer School in Clontarf. Contact: The Bram Stoker Society, 43 Castle Court, Killiney Hill Road, Co. Killiney, Dublin, Ireland.

A DRACULA TOUR OF ROMANIA

The historical Dracula places.

BUCHAREST. Visit the old fortress walls built by Dracula in the Lipscani section of the old city. The nearby Museum of the History of the City of Bucharest has a copy of the Dracula decree ordering the reinforcement of the city walls, as well as some weapons from his day.

Rent a car or take a bus to the SNAGOV MONASTERY located on an island on a lake fifteen miles north of Bucharest to visit Dracula's tomb. During the regular tourist season there are motorboats that take one across from the mainland to the island monastery; otherwise one can rent a rowboat to get there during the off-season. A monk or a nun is usually available to conduct a tour.

To get to DRACULA'S PALACE at TIRGOVISTE one must rent a car in Bucharest. Proceed north from the city to Pitesti Highway and take the cutoff at Gaesti, Route 72, to reach Tirgoviste; the ruins of Dracula's main palace are here. Visitors can mount the restored main palace tower, from which one can see where Dracula once planted his impaled victims.

To reach CASTLE DRACULA, return to Pitesti Highway and take Route 7C to Dracula's ecclesiastical capital of Curtea de Arges, the site of his coronation and the burial place of many of Romania's early rulers. Proceed north about 20 km to visit Castle Dracula, which one can spot from the road. There is now a hydroelectric plant located at the foot of the castle. Carefully climb some 1,300 steps to the ruined castle. According to legend, Dracula's wife committed suicide by throwing herself from one of the castle towers.

TRANSYLVANIA. From Pitesti take Route ES74 to BRASOV. Visit the remains of St. Bartholomew's church (1260), which Dracula had burned, on the outskirts of the city, and Timpa Hill where Dracula impaled hundreds of local merchants and then dined amid his victims.

From Brasov take Route 60 and drive in your rental car to SIGHISOARA in the northwest part of Romania along the main Transylvanian highway. Here you will find Dracula's birthplace. In the center of the city is the Dracula homestead, marked by a plaque indicating that Vlad Dracul, Dracula's father, resided there from 1431 to 1436. The building has been converted into a restaurant. Walk through the old town to get a feeling for the place where young Dracula played and studied. The town has retained its lovely fifteenth-century architecture and atmosphere.

Southwest of Brasov, along the main mountain road, catch a glimpse of the ruins of CASTLE KONIGSTEIN (King's Rock) perched on top of an eerie ledge with a sheer drop to the valley below. This is where Dracula was ambushed and arrested as a traitor in 1462 on orders from the Hungarian king Matthias Corvinus.

West of Brasov, follow Route E68 to SIBIU. Visit the Evangelical Church, which was once Catholic and where Mihnea the Bad, son of Dracula, was assassinated and buried. One can see Mihnea's crypt stone in the rear of the church, near the tomb of Valentin Franck von Frankenstein, a Transylvanian nobleman.

Going west from Sibiu on Route E68/81, turn south to reach HUNDEDOARA on 68B. See the well-preserved castle of John Hunyadi, where young Dracula was trained to be a crusader-knight for Christendom. Visit the nearby Castle of Radu Gorj in the Jiu valley near Petrosani, the subject of Jules Verne's novel *The Carpathian Castle* and a likely inspiration for Stoker.

Northern Romanian places in Stoker's novel.

Drive on the central highway to KLAUSENBURG (today called Cluj), the largest city in Transylvania, where Jonathan Harker spent the night at the Hotel Royale (no longer in existence) and dined on paprika chicken on his way to meet Dracula.

In BISTRITZ (modern Bistrita) Harker stayed at the Golden Krone Hotel, ate "robber steak" — bits of bacon, onion, and beef seasoned with pepper and roasted like shishkebab — and drank local Golden Mediasch wine.

Just east of Bistrita, drive through the fabulously picturesque BORGO PASS (Borgo Prund), which Stoker described so well. Here is where Harker first met Dracula. A new Dracula Castle Hotel was built by the Romanian tourist agency in bastard Gothic style at the Tihuta Pass. But the only authentic castles in the area are the ruins of Castle Rodna and Bethlen Castle, with its strange dragon insignia set in stone.